Forging Stalin's Army

Forging Stalin's Army

Marshal Tukhachevsky and the Politics of Military Innovation

Sally W. Stoecker

Foreword by David Glantz

Westview Press
A Member of the Perseus Books Group

Published in 1998 in the United States of America by Westview Press, 5500 Central Avenue, Boulder, Colorado 80301-2877, and in the United Kingdom by Westview Press, 12 Hid's Copse Road, Cumnor Hill, Oxford OX2 9JJ

A CIP catalog record for this book is available from the Library of Congress.
ISBN 0-8133-3410-1 (hardcover)
ISBN 0-8133-3735-6 (pbk.)

The paper used in this publication meets the requirements of the American National Standard for Permanence of Paper for Printed Library Materials Z39.48-1984.

10 9 8 7 6 5 4 3 2 1

To Fred and Carolyn

Contents

Tables and Figures

Tables

Figures

Foreword

Like his famous World War II counterpart, marshal of the Soviet Union G. K. Zhukov, the figure of Mikhail Tukhachevsky stands like a colossus in the pages of Soviet military history. While even those who know little about the history of the Red Army and the Soviet state have likely heard of these two prominent figures, their experiences and accomplishments also dominate the historical memory of those most knowledgeable in the field. In fact, both Zhukov and Tukhachevsky have become virtual cult figures in the Russian Federation, adding light and a measure of glamour to what otherwise seems to have been a depressing and failed historical epoch.

Zhukov's rise to fame is understandable. Painted as the victor of the Soviet's "Great Patriotic War" by former Soviet and present Russian historians, Zhukov's reputation grew on the basis of his own memoirs and the magnificent feats that Soviet historiography ascribed to him. Only now are we learning that Zhukov, too, as all famous men, was human and shared basic human flaws.

In Tukhachevsky's case, fame was more fleeting. Well known in the West in the 1920s and 1930s, after his summary execution in 1937, this premier victim of Stalin's purges became a nonperson in the Soviet Union and but a faint memory in the West. His rehabilitation as a preeminent historical figure began in the 1960s, after the death of his nemesis Stalin, and culminated in the 1980s when Tukhachevsky emerged as a new star in an otherwise bleak Soviet era. As in the case of Zhukov, Tukhachevsky's recent notoriety is based upon a curious mixture of a limited selection of his own writings, the often politically correct accounts of Soviet authors, and the laudatory writings of a limited circle of Western historians. Given the frail and often suspect historical basis for the fame of both figures and the recently improved access to Soviet archives, history demands that both men's reputations be reassessed. This volume begins that critical process.

Sally W. Stoecker provides a comprehensive and fresh view of the development of the pre–World War II Red Army based on "state-of-the-art" Soviet archival materials. She examines in detail the causes, nature, and consequences of military innovation by quite naturally concentrating on the period from 1928 through 1933, when much of that innovation took place. Her critique and qualification of the "totalitarian" model of political development, once dominant in Western understanding of Stalin's Soviet Union, are refreshing and capture the complexities of interwar Soviet military development, which many military historians have overlooked. While questioning Soviet adherence to the "totalitarian" model in the late 1920s and early 1930s, she also vividly demonstrates how the return to that model by Stalin in the terrible late 1930s had disastrous consequences for the Soviet military and state.

Sally's fresh interpretive approach exploits copious amounts of fresh archival materials to define and explain the critical process of military innovation, thereby updating John Erickson's now classic view of the Red Army's prewar experiences, *The Soviet High Command*. This book also adds vital archival detail to such forgotten or misunderstood events as the 1929 Sino-Soviet conflict in the Far East, which provided context for the Tukhachevsky reforms. Of particular value is Sally's extensive use of (and quotes from) Tukhachevsky's long secret and unavailable seminal five-volume study, *Future War*, which, until recently, historians have known existed but have not seen. Furthermore, she details the nature and scope of foreign assistance to the Soviet Union and cross-fertilization of ideas between Germany and the Soviet Union during the interwar period. While doing so, she lays to rest some of the most flagrant misinterpretations and misunderstandings dominant in Western historiography.

This book thus epitomizes the fresh scholarship we can expect to continue in the realm of Soviet military affairs. Sally has pioneered the path that other scholars can exploit and build upon as they search for the real Mikhail Nikolaevich Tukhachevsky.

David M. Glantz
Carlisle, PA

Acknowledgments

The idea for this study can be traced to the advice and works of three individuals: Edward L. Warner III, Bruce Parrott, and Kimberly Zisk. Ted Warner, with whom I had the pleasure of working at RAND during the Cold War, often made reference to the interwar period as one needing more study. When it came time to decide on a thesis topic, the Red Army of the 1920s seemed a natural choice. Bruce Parrott, my dissertation adviser at Johns Hopkins University (SAIS), urged me to confine my study of the Red Army to the First Five Year Plan period. Although at first it seemed too limiting to devote an entire dissertation to just five years, I soon grew to appreciate just how full and interesting those years were when looked at from various angles: economic, strategic, political, and technological. I collected an enormous amount of information in the military archives in Germany and in Russia between 1990 and 1993—thanks to support from the Fulbright Commission, RAND, and the American Council of Teachers of Russian—but I was still lacking a framework in which to incorporate it. Then, in the summer of 1993, while reviewing a new book by Kimberly Marten Zisk on innovation in the Soviet Army in the post-Stalin era, it occurred to me that I too could attempt to explain the process of military innovation in the RKKA using an institutional framework and a discussion of various sources of innovation.

This has been a lengthy but fascinating project in a variety of intellectual and personal ways. First of all, I would like to thank Peter Kracht, formerly of Westview Press, for his support and decision to publish my study. I am extremely grateful to my advisers and reviewers for their incisive comments, which collectively improved this work: Eliot Cohen, Julian Cooper, David Glantz, Jacob Kipp, Amy Knight, Bruce Parrott, and Roger Reese. In particular, David Glantz and Amy Knight offered me encouragement throughout the revision stage and their support was invaluable to the completion of this manuscript. David Bridges, my research assistant at American University, deserves "stormy applause" for researching and writing about the historiography of the "Tukhachevsky affair."

Thanks are also due to colleagues who shared their materials and thoughts with me along the way: Manfred von Boetticher, Jonathan Bone, Willis Brooks, Stephen Brown, R. W. Davies, Bruce Menning, Lennart Samuelson, Gottfried Schramm, David Stone, and Manfred Zeidler.

Several individuals also went all out in helping me turn my thesis into a book. Lori Kranz and Carla Astrab edited and formatted the manuscript; Lesley Rimmel pored over photographs and posters of the Red Army in the Hoover Archive at Stanford; and my brother, James Manson Stoecker, designed the book's dust jacket.

Most important, however, has been the steadfast commitment and good humor of my husband, Fred Biery, and the inspirational smiles of our precious daughter, Carolyn.

Sally W. Stoecker

Soviet leaders review the May Day parade on Red Square one month before Tukhachevsky's execution. Left to Right: J. V. Stalin, K. E. Voroshilov, V. K. Molotov. Second row: L. M. Kaganovich, A. A. Andreev, and G. Dmitrev. May 14, 1937. Acme News Pictures, Inc.
Reprinted with permission of Corbis-Bettman, Inc.

Marshal Mikhail Nikolaevich Tukhachevsky (Courtesy of the Hoover Institution Archives, Stanford University)

People's commissar of military and naval affairs, Kliment Voroshilov, observes maneuvers from the command post of a coastal battery. (Courtesy of Hoover Institution Archives, Stanford University)

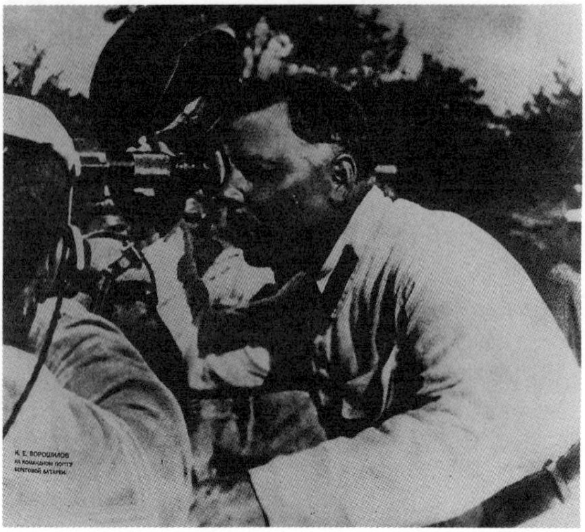

Deputy people's commissar of military and naval affairs, Jan Gamarnik, speaking at a gathering of Red Navy officers and sailors. (Courtesy of Hoover Institution Archives, Stanford University)

"Hands Off!"
(Courtesy of the Poster Collection, Hoover Institution Archives)

"The Defense of the USSR"
(Courtesy of the Poster Collection, Hoover Institution Archives)

The last firing practice at the Kazan tank school is celebrated with champagne by German and Soviet participants. August 1933. (Courtesy of Manfred Zeidler.)

German officers camouflaged as civilians at the Kazan train station prepare to return to Germany via Leningrad. September 1933. (Courtesy of Manfred Zeidler)

1

Introduction: The Context for Innovation in Stalin's Army

The Workers' and Peasants' Red Army (RKKA), established in 1918 and headed up by Lev Trotsky, was handed a blank slate on which to create a new army comprised of new soldiers who would serve the state in a variety of new ways. The days of the bourgeois, professional army were gone and the Workers' and Peasants' Red Army was just that—an army whose composition reflected the society at large and would carry out missions of both a civilian and a war-making nature. So "new" was this organization that even the importance of a military doctrine was in question and the pages of numerous military journals were filled with debates on the structure, missions, and equipping of the new army. Under Stalin, the army's mandate for change and modernization continued with the help of a variety of very competent military leaders, especially the enigmatic reformer and strategic thinker, Mikhail Nikolaevich Tukhachevsky.

This book is about the process of doctrinal, technological, and weapons innovation within the RKKA during the early years of industrialization in the Soviet Union, 1928–1933—a time when the expectations of grand economic achievements leading to an independent and autarkic state, free of so-called capitalist caprices, were high. Among the key sources of innovation during these years were the vision and entrepreneurship of the "brainchild of the Red Army," Marshal Tukhachevsky; the tactical and technical lessons learned from military encounters in the Far East at the turn of the decade; struggles over budgetary allocations by the government and party and the role of the military hierarchy in trying to influence those decisions in their favor; the contributions of foreign experts and the use of foreign military equipment in Russia; the opportunities to study military tactics and strategy abroad; and indigenous research and development projects. Before turning to the individual sources of innovation and the politics surrounding them, I examine the context in which this innovation was occurring in terms of the historiography of the Red Army's early years, the unique interwar environment, and the impact of civilian participation in the Red Army's affairs.

Totalitarianism and the Red Army

The post–World War II era ushered in a wave of political theorizing in the West that compared the Soviet Union under Stalin to Germany under Hitler, characterizing both as totalitarian regimes. Hannah Arendt, one of the earliest philosophers to describe in great detail the similarities between the totalitarianism of Stalin and Hitler, saw these two regimes as quite distinct from other dictatorships or autocracies. In her view, a totalitarian regime lacked hierarchy; there were no intervening institutional levels between the Führer and the masses, thereby making total control of the country possible.

> Totalitarian domination ... aims at abolishing freedom. Technically, this absence of any authority or hierarchy in the totalitarian system is shown by the fact that between the supreme power and the ruled there are no reliable intervening levels, each of which would receive its due share of authority and obedience. The will of the Führer can be embodied everywhere and he himself is not tied to any hierarchy.[1]

Arendt agreed with Isaac Deutscher that "Stalin saw every institution, independent of its actual function, only as a 'transmission belt' connecting the party with the people,"[2] and not as independent organizations equipped with their own legitimate agendas.

Building on Arendt's work, many scholars of the totalitarian school in the 1950s and 1960s focused largely on the fascist and communist leaders' aberrant personalities, which drove them to extreme forms of terror in order to protect their power and implement their programs, but also began to explore how the party, economic, and educational institutions served these leaders.[3] Indeed, the totalitarian model did not allow for external challenges to the leader's decisionmaking because autonomous sources of influence were considered moot.[4] In the mid- to late 1960s and throughout the 1970s, many studies began to challenge the use of the totalitarian model to explain the politics of the post-Stalin era, yet the Stalin regime itself continued to be characterized in totalitarian terms.[5] While the totalitarian model captured some aspects of the Stalinist system, particularly in the late 1930s during the height of the Great Terror, it oversimplified other important aspects. The relationships among and roles of institutions within the state apparatus were rarely examined, and the interplay between technical expertise and ideology was virtually ignored.

Since that time, a few studies have successfully applied organizational, balance-of-power, and various "hybrid" political and social science theories to Stalin's policymaking, thereby challenging the totalitarian image of Soviet society under Stalin. Arch Getty's reconstruction of the "Great Purges," Kendall Bailes's examination of the role of the technical intelligentsia, Eugene Zaleski's scrutiny of the economic organs in the Stalin era, and Sheila Fitzpatrick's discussion of the cultural revolution in Russia between 1928 and 1931 have all admirably illustrated the limitations of applying the totalitarian model to the entire period of Stalin's rule.[6] These studies suggested that policymaking in many societal spheres was not always dominated by Stalin and his henchmen, but was sometimes ad hoc, fragmented, and conducted by local authorities. Indeed, there were occasions when decisions and policies were made without Stalin's participation.[7] As Getty makes clear, "None of these [more recent] works has suggested that Stalin was not the most powerful political actor, but some of them have implied that he was not necessarily the author of every initiative."[8] Getty himself illustrated that the purges in the 1930s were not all part of a single phenomenon carefully orchestrated by Stalin. Rather, in an effort to cleanse its ranks of "undesirable" members, the communist party was marked by confusion and chaos, with local party bosses calling many of the shots.

Despite these more nuanced scholarly portrayals of the Stalin era in technical, economic, and cultural areas, most of the Western scholarship on the Red Army under Stalin has continued to cast its discussion in a totalitarian framework. Several studies have depicted the military as perpetually dominated and controlled by the communist party and Stalin, thereby preventing it from acting as an independent or "traditional" bureaucracy with goals of its own that it sought to advance and did so, in some cases, very successfully. With few exceptions, the earlier scholarship illustrated the military's impotence vis-à-vis the communist party and its *Vozhd*.

In tying the functioning of the state directly to the leader himself, this totalitarian image did not lend itself to nuanced analyses of military affairs during the twenty-six years of Stalin's rule. Instead of distinguishing between what could be called "transitional" and "mature" Stalinism, the scholarship considered the Stalin era in toto and made sweeping generalizations about military acquiescence to the party, in light of the army's emasculation by Stalin in his 1937 arrest and murder of numerous High Command officers.[9] In essence, the scholarship projected features of mature Stalinism—more befitting of the totalitarian model—onto the early Stalin period.[10]

Scholars were so convinced of Stalin's overarching influence in military affairs that some, such as Roman Kolkowicz, went so far as to conclude that the Red Army lacked its own military doctrine until the war broke out, when Stalin drew up his "permanent operating factors" that acted as a doctrine of sorts during World War II.[11] Kolkowicz viewed Stalin's army in a totalitarian context, whereby the Red Army was "hemmed in" by communist party controls that denied the military a distinct identity.[12] He also saw Stalin's domination of the military as unrelenting and "total" and his personal participation in military matters as quite disruptive.

> It was Stalin, the mediocre ideologue and ruthless pragmatist, who finally tackled this central problem of the rulers of any communist society, the question of what should be the status of the military in the one-party totalitarian state. He defined the military's role, its organization, its relations with the party, and its social and political functions ... The Red Army emerged from this process as an adjunct of the ruling Party elite; its officers were denied the full authority necessary to the practice of the military profession; they were kept in a perennial state of uncertainty about their careers, and the military community, which tends toward exclusiveness, was forcibly kept open through an elaborate system of control and indoctrination.[13]

Kolkowicz implied that Stalin's "terror machine" was in operation for the duration of his regime and that only after Stalin's death did the military begin to assert itself. However, it appears that the military was granted substantial autonomy—with the exception of the limited political purge of RKKA party organizations in 1929 and 1933—until roughly 1936.[14]

Mikhail Tsypkin argued, in his thesis on the Soviet military research and development (R&D) system, that Stalin's intervention in military research and development was so pervasive and disruptive that it not only stunted innovation in weapons design, but also prevented the emergence of a military-industrial complex in the Stalin era.[15] Tsypkin's proposition, which seems to apply to Stalin's entire tenure, rests primarily on memoir literature regarding events that occurred in the mid- to late 1930s and not during the earlier, First Five Year Plan period.[16] While the first ten years of Stalin's rule do not seem to fit this model, certainly the latter half of the 1930s more accurately fits the totalitarian model, when terror ran rampant and Stalin became intimately involved in decisionmaking at all levels, including weapons design.

Many other works, while perhaps not referring to the totalitarian model explicitly, appeared to discuss the formation of the Red Army in a quasitotalitarian framework. For example, one of the earliest studies of the Red Army, by Dmitri Fedotoff-White, described how the communist party's stability was enhanced by the permeation of army ranks with political "watchdogs," especially during the tumultuous years of collectivization.[17]

Michael Deane also saw the interests of the party and military as inherently conflictual and necessitating party controls. Deane wrote, with respect to the army's role in the collectivization of agriculture, "It is significant, however, that during these difficult years, there was no organized military opposition against Stalin or his drastic policies. In no small part, the credit for this fact lies in the tight controls which [head of the political directorate of the Red Army, PURKKA][18] Jan Gamarnik maintained through the political administration."[19] Deane, like Kolkowicz, viewed the military as a potential threat to the party that had to be tamed by political control, albeit control that was gradually evolving into a less combative and more cooperative relationship with the commanders.

John Erickson's landmark study of the Red Army during the interwar years is more difficult to classify.[20] Although he made reference to Stalin's "personalized control" and "close supervision" of military policy,[21] his lengthy descriptions of the military-to-military collaboration with the Reichswehr and military-dominated decisionmaking about the motorization and mechanization of the army, both of which took place without Stalin's close supervision or intervention, implicitly challenge the totalitarian model.[22] Without stating so outright, Erickson's work portrayed an activist military with strong spokesmen in Voroshilov and Tukhachevsky, who managed to modernize the Red Army without asking for Stalin's blessing at every turn.

Using collectivization as a focal point, Mark Von Hagen illustrated the ways in which the civilians sought to "harness the discipline and loyalty of soldiers to their ambitious scheme of rural transformation between 1929 and 1930."[23] Although the opponents of collectivization within the High Command lost out in the short run, Von Hagen argues, these "anticollectivization professionals" (i.e., Kliment Voroshilov, Jan Gamarnik, and Vasilii Bliukher) were successful in the long run in persuading Stalin to reduce his reliance on the army for such "civilizing" activities as participation in collectivization that detracted from combat readiness and professionalism. Thus, Von Hagen also implicitly challenged the totalitarian framework in illustrating the army's ability to convince the party and Stalin of their errors. Roger Reese notes in his new study of the Red Army, which examines in part the soldiers' resistance to the collectivization campaign, that the army's success in forcing Stalin to back down was rather ironic.[24] While the communist regime had originally intended that military service mold the peasant into a loyal communist and soldier, the peasant turned the tables and in resisting collectivization used the army to mold the policies of the regime.[25]

In summary, some of the most influential early studies of the Red Army tended to focus on Stalin's domination of the military and the means used to ensure loyalty to the communist party, such as the establishment of pervasive political controls to suppress military-inspired dissent. Some scholars suggested that the military acquiesced to party domination completely, even during the frenzied years of collectivization, and were therefore acting akin to Deutscher's "transmission belts"—merely bowing to and carrying out the wishes of *der Führer*. In their opinion, the military did not attempt to challenge its domination by the party until after Stalin died.

Challenges to the totalitarian model can also be found in the writings of Robert C. Tucker, who described the period of the New Economic Policy as the "Golden Age of Soviet Russia when the state, dictatorial though it was, did not trespass too much on the popular domain, on the way of life of the people."[26] Tucker then contrasted this period of economic and social relaxation with the "full-blown Stalinism" that followed it in 1929, when Stalin officially launched his industrialization and collectivization campaigns and the state resumed its former prominence in the lives of the people and in all economic institutions and enterprises. Not all scholars have agreed on the year when full-blown Stalinism was launched, however. John Armstrong, for example, has argued that Stalin did not secure absolute control of the party until about 1933 and that the Seventeenth Congress of the Communist Party of the Soviet Union (CPSU), held in February 1934, celebrated that accomplishment.[27] Leonard Schapiro claimed that Stalin "fully subjugated" the party only in 1936.[28] Merle Fainsod seemed to date that control as having been clinched in December 1930 following Comrade Rykov's ouster from the Politburo, which signified the successful elimination of the right opposition.[29]

But though the timing of full-blown Stalinism has been disputed, some long-held assumptions about the First Five Year Plan have not been challenged or debated. For example, scholars have frequently viewed the period from 1929 forward as a time when Stalin's main and immediate objective was a large and steady defense buildup and industrialization was synonymous with "massing military power."[30] The tension between military outlays and investment in heavy industry for general economic growth was simply not acknowledged in much of the Western literature.[31] Julian Cooper, however, considerably enhanced our understanding of the nuances in defense budgeting and procedure. He was perhaps the first scholar to recognize that resource allocations to the annual state budgets for military personnel and equipment were distinct from the allocations, such as capital investments, to the defense industries, which fell under the figures for the national economy at large.[32] Cooper also confirmed that wide discrepancies in these allocations could occur, rendering the five year plan not steady in its year-to-year annual increases, but subject to ebbs and flows.

Precisely because the threat of military intervention in the Soviet Union was so remote, fast-paced defense industrialization was not a top priority. It is clear from Soviet documentation that a debate existed between those who promoted peacetime rearmament and those who favored the gradual development of the entire economy without straining that development in order to provide for the specialized needs of a large defense industry. Some military officers went so far as to condemn the creation of defense industries altogether, arguing that the country's needs would be better served by making civilian enterprises convertible to defense production in wartime.[33]

Other military figures promoted large-scale rearmament programs early on when the capacity of the state's industrial production to support specialized industries was extremely doubtful. In fact, as will be shown later, Stalin accused Tukhachevsky of "Red Militarism" because he tried to put defense production ahead of general industrial development when he drew up a "grandiose" rearmament plan in 1930. This tension between short-term and longer-term industrial objectives persisted until the early 1930s, when the invasion of Manchuria by Japan was viewed as threatening to the USSR's security, making rearmament a higher priority for the party and the state. As Robert W.

Davies has shown in a recent study of Soviet defense expenditures during the First Five Year Plan, budget increases in defense production and investment increased sharply in October–December 1931 and again in 1932—even while industrial growth rates were declining as a whole—in light of the threat posed by the subsequent invasion of Manchuria by Japan.[34]

The relationship between defense planning and defense industrialization and production in the interwar years is the topic of a new study based largely on archival documents from the Russian State Economic Archives by the Swedish economic historian Lennart Samuelson. Samuelson suggests that although there were many rough drafts of a defense five year plan, an official version was never adopted. Instead, there were long-term mobilization targets for wartime production (*mobzaiavki*) that were essentially hypothetical until the late 1930s and the Third Five Year Plan—when the defense factories were positioned to begin the mass production of large quantities of weapons and equipment. But regardless of the exact timing of such increases in expenditure and production, most of the recent scholarship shows that the First Five Year Plan was not synonymous with defense and that the defense buildup throughout the 1930s was neither steady nor evenly distributed. The previous tendency to equate the First Five Year Plan with an all-out defense buildup dictated by Stalin and the habit of projecting "mature" Stalinism on the initial years of his leadership were due to a dearth of original sources from the late 1920s and early 1930s. With the opening of formerly inaccessible archives to scholars, this problem is being remedied. Moreover, the early Stalin era traditionally was overshadowed by the more dramatic events surrounding the fatal purge of the military in 1937–1938 and the events leading up to the Wehrmacht's "surprise" invasion of Russia in 1941.

Innovation in the Interwar Years

This study of innovation in the Red Army challenges the conclusions of scholars who analyzed Red Army doctrinal and technical modernization before 1935 in a totalitarian context. Drawing on organizational theory, this work treats the military as an independent institution that was capable of successful innovation during the First Five Year Plan (1928–1933)[35] with the aid of budgetary resources, reform-minded officers, foreign expertise, indigenous R&D programs, and combat experience obtained in the Far East. It is important to underscore that much of the innovation that occurred at this time persisted in the long run, despite Stalin's liquidation of most members of the High Command in the latter half of the 1930s. The Red Army's field manuals and performance in World War II are testimony to the importance and resilience of many operational concepts whose roots lay in this First Five Year Plan period and which evolved in the early 1930s into theories of "decisive and deep operations" that included airborne assaults, independent tank detachments and missions, and new roles for the air force.[36]

But how shall we define "innovation" and how can its "success" be determined? Innovation refers to technological or doctrinal change whose principal aim is to improve the military establishment's ability to carry out its professional mission. Borrowing from Kimberly Zisk's definition of innovation, technological and doctrinal change may represent a "reconceptualization" of current military practices[37]—that is, the change need not be unique in the world, but should be unique to the Soviet Union. According to Zisk, "a policy innovation occurs when a new idea is adopted by an organization or a state and followed by policy action, no matter how long the idea has been present in the world, and no matter how many other states have adopted the policy beforehand."[38] An example of such a "reconceptualization" of military doctrine in the Soviet Union in the 1930s would be the introduction and adaptation of Guilio Douhet's ideas about independent air operations to the Red Air Force. Reconceptualization presupposes a certain receptivity to foreign ideas, which was clearly an important ingredient of successful military innovation in the Soviet Union at this time.

Stephen Rosen examined several cases of operational and technological innovation and attempted to explain why and how they were successful rather than why and how they failed—as so much of the literature had heretofore shown.[39] Rosen defined success in innovation as occurring when ideas and technologies were adopted and put into practice, despite the obstacles that stood before them. In his view, talented military personnel, a lengthy period of time in which to work, and information were the key resources for successful innovation in Great Britain and the United States,[40] whereas money and civilian intervention—commonly viewed as determinants of innovation—were weakly correlated with successful innovation.

A recent study of military innovation in the interwar years by Williamson Murray and Allan Millett provides perhaps the most thorough analysis of the process of innovation in military establishments available.[41] They illustrate that despite numerous restraints on militaries in the interwar years—ranging from meager resources to diplomatic treaties and protocols—"innovation swept forward on a transnational basis."[42] Although the authors deal primarily with innovation occurring in the French, British, U.S., German, and Japanese military establishments, many of the conditions contributing to successful innovation described by them can also be applied to the Red Army. For example, an important ingredient, Murray notes, is the creation of a context or environment conducive to innovation. He illustrates how effectively Reichswehr General Hans von Seeckt "was able to create a culture of innovation by the kind of officer corps he created at the end of World War I ... [a culture that] placed a high value on study and analysis of changes in doctrine, tactics, and technology; in other words he created a climate ideally suited to innovation," in spite of severe budgetary cutbacks. Thus, despite the harsh measures imposed on the Reichswehr by the Treaty of Versailles in 1919, the radical changes in army organization that the conditions of the treaty specified led to the creation of a highly professional General Staff that placed a premium on the careful and rigorous study and debate of the lessons of past wars and the possibilities of future scenarios. The General Staff very successfully circumvented the Treaty of Versailles in training their troops and testing new weapons clandestinely on Soviet soil.

Similarly, a military culture conducive to innovation was also present in the Soviet Union for at least half of the interwar period. From the time of the communist revolution in 1917 until roughly 1930 when Stalin's censors began to take hold, questions surrounding the formation of a new "Red" Army facing new threats and possessing new roles—distinct from their imperial predecessors—were debated sharply in the halls of the military academies, on the pages of the military journals, and in RKKA staff circles. The lessons of past wars, the prospects of new technologies, the nature of war, and its future incarnations were topics debated frequently and openly throughout the 1920s. By 1930, however, Stalin's domestic policies were under way and all manner of publications were required to reflect enthusiasm and support for them. However, as this study will illustrate, even censorship and requirements to adhere to Stalin's "general line" failed to stop key innovators such as Marshal Tukhachevsky, who simply cloaked their revolutionary ideas in Marxist-Leninist robes as a means of helping to ensure that editorial authorities would accept them.

Within this ripe context, then, military innovation was successful because the military culture of the Red Army—before the mid-1930s—permitted an accurate assessment of the external threat, analysis of the proper response to military threats, and preparation for this response.

Tukhachevsky's clear and prescient vision of the contours and military requirements of a future war against hostile Eastern and Western neighbors allied with other powers in a "coalition war" set the parameters in which military innovation could occur.

In explaining *why* technological and doctrinal innovations were successful during this crucial period in Soviet history, one could argue that the military had nowhere to go but up; any form of innovation would have been helpful to the war-torn Red Army. In the aftermath of World War I and the civil war, demobilization whittled the army's ranks down to half a million men; its technical outfitting was substandard; and a special commission of the central committee deemed the RKKA "unfit for military action" (*neboesposobna*) in 1924.[43] One might also use the Red Army's victory over the Wehrmacht in World War II as clear and convincing evidence of successful military innovation, although weapons and operational concepts alone cannot fully explain military victories. The theories developed in the late 1920s and early 1930s, and the weapons that enabled them to be carried out, however, deserve some credit for contributing to the Red Army's victory over the Wehrmacht, which established the USSR as a leading military power in the world for many decades to follow. As Murray reminds us, military cultures try to perform the undoable and to "bring order and linearity to a world governed by chaotic complexity."[44] He goes on to underscore the uncertainty that surrounds innovation and the difficulty of predicting the future.

> To understand innovation in the interwar period one must not lose track of the fact that the interplay among human factors, uncertain knowledge, misreadings of the past, political and strategic parameters placed innovation on a complex playing field in which not only were the players uncertain of the future but they were often more concerned with immediate problems than with long-range changes.[45]

Was the Red Army a Traditional Bureaucracy?

Kimberly Zisk and Stephen Rosen, in their recent works on military innovation, have introduced nuance to some of the "classical" characterizations of bureaucracies put forth by Morton Halperin and others,[46] who describe them as "inert,"[47] striving to secure handsome budgetary resources from the state[48] and maintain control over their use, seeking to protect themselves from encroachment by civilian interlopers, and establishing autonomy.[49] Morris Janowitz had similar things to say about conservative military bureaucracies whose "professionals have a long record of resistance to change and maintained outmoded organizational forms."[50] Murray, in a similar vein, points out that the nature of the job, wherein soldiers' lives are often put at risk, reinforces the need for discipline and distaste of the "untried."

> Military institutions exist in a culture of disciplined obedience in which soldiers, sailors, and airmen must remain steadfast in the face of terrifying conditions, while their psychological instinct for self-preservation urges them to fight. But disciplined organizations rarely place a high value on untried ideas, concepts, and innovations.

But conservatism does not preclude innovation, as Barry Posen has suggested when he writes that militaries are so wedded to the status quo, so "change resistant," that they are incapable of initiating change on their own behalf.[51] In the case of the Red Army in the interwar years, change and innovation were mandated and the army was encouraged, if not required, to break with the past and the imperial "status quo." Therefore, while wartime defeat and civilian intervention are certainly contributing factors to innovation, they do not tell the whole story. Neither the Russian defeat in World War I nor Stalin's and the communist party's intervention in military affairs *fully* explains how the Red Army innovated in doctrinal and weapons development between the world wars in general and during the First Five Year Plan in particular. Rather, a certain set of political, economic, and cultural conditions and technological opportunities was present at this time in Soviet history and in the interwar period generally. These conditions enabled reform-minded military officers or "public entrepreneurs,"[52] like Mikhail Tukhachevsky, to devise, promote, and institute many operational and technical military innovations that would permit the Red Army to become a formidable military power in Europe.

The Lessons of the Great War

The Russian experience in World War I provided important lessons for the nascent Red Army of the 1920s. The most important among them was the overriding significance of industrial production in wartime. According to William Fuller, the Imperial Army was organizationally and tactically better prepared for war in 1914 than ever before, yet it continued to be plagued by "material insufficiency" and was forced to rely on what he called "magic" and "miracle."[53] Thus, one of the fundamental lessons of World War I was essentially the same as that derived from most of Russia's military campaigns of recent history: The army needed a larger and faster industrial war-making capacity, a powerful defense industry. Defeat in World War I undoubtedly gave a strong impetus to the industrialization campaign under Stalin, which in turn supported the RKKA in World War II and ultimately contributed to its victory. Stalin's compelling and oft-cited speech of 1931, in which he defended the accelerated pace of the industrialization campaign—pledging to complete the first plan in four years instead of five—is clear testimony to his determination to prevent Russia from suffering defeat again.

> To delay the pace [of industrialization] means to lag behind. And those who lag get beaten. But we don't want to be beaten. No, we don't want to! The history of old Russia is about her being perpetually beaten for backwardness. Mongolian Huns beat her. Turkish Pashas (*Beki*) beat her. Swedish feudal lords beat her. Polish-Lithuanian landowners beat her. Anglo-French capitalists beat her. Japanese barons beat her. Everyone beat her—because of her backwardness. For military backwardness, for cultural backwardness, for governmental backwardness, for industrial backwardness, for agricultural backwardness. ... We lagged behind the advanced countries by 50–100 years. We must close this gap in ten years. Either we do this or they will bury us.[54]

In addition to underscoring the importance of a war-making capacity and a large arsenal of modern weapons and equipment, the Great War provided lessons in military art. Perhaps the key lesson was to avoid the Germans' mistake of relying on one specific strategy, in this case a fast-paced offensive, to the exclusion of others. So enamored of the offense was German General von Schlieffen that he failed to plan adequately for setbacks and defensive operations. When the war took a course different from that envisioned, and indeed got bogged down in the trenches, the Germans were unable to extricate themselves. Thus, themes of the ever-changing nature of war and the need for a flexible strategy—which included offensive and defensive maneuvers and underscored the importance of strategic reserves—found new expression in the Soviet military literature.[55]

Civilian Participation or Intervention?

Although civilian participation in military affairs appears to have been generally beneficial to many democratic states in the interwar period simply because military innovators needed allies in political and technical realms who would support their ideas and resource requests, the same generalization cannot be made about civilian participation in the Red Army.[56] Indeed, civilian participation was viewed with circumspection and in many cases was feared because it meant more than simply finding allies in legislative positions; it often meant performing unwanted civilian tasks, such as assisting with Stalin's collectivization campaign, attending mind-numbing political indoctrination sessions, or being subject to arbitrary dismissal. However, civilian intervention was not uniformly bad. Some party initiatives, such as the "war scare" of 1927, benefited the army. Sometimes these conflicting tendencies occurred simultaneously.[57] For example, the infamous party-initiated 1927 war scare was an enormous boost to the military, who jumped on the bandwagon and successfully exploited the theme of an impending Western attack for many years. Although the Soviet Peoples Commissar of Military and Naval Affairs Kliment Voroshilov at first claimed in 1927 that war was rather unlikely, he grew enamored of the dramatic effect of the war scare propaganda and used it repeatedly in his subsequent articles and speeches. This gave impetus to the growth and importance of paramilitary groups and other civilian voluntary organizations devoted to training for or contributing resources to the homeland's defense.

But the civilian initiative that was most controversial and disruptive to the military was the recruitment of Red Army units to assist in the collectivization campaign at the turn of the decade.[58] Voroshilov was among the members of the High Command opposed to this initiative, given the large percentage of peasants (75 percent) in the appropriately named Workers' and Peasants' Red Army. During a speech at the Tolmachev Political Academy in Byelorussia, Voroshilov stated in no uncertain terms that the starvation occurring in the countryside was bad for morale and gave rise to "peasant sentiments" (*krest'ianskie nastroeniia*) among Red Army rank-and-file soldiers.[59] This, in turn, affected combat readiness negatively. Formerly classified military orders issued in 1932 to confront widespread desertion in the army also suggest that collectivization, and especially the forced famine in the Ukraine, created serious morale problems for the soldiers.[60]

The First Five Year Plan period witnessed an all-out assault on "bourgeois specialists"—a codeword for engineers who were trained either in the West or at the Soviet Academy of Sciences and failed to join the communist cause[61]—in civilian technical areas between 1928 and 1931. However, the attack on the "military specialists" *(Voenspetsy)* who were former officers of the Imperial Army appeared to be somewhat milder.[62] Some of the civilian experts arrested in 1928 and tried for espionage were actually put to work in *sharagi* (prison design bureaus and factories),[63] so desperate was the Red Army for qualified technical personnel. There is also evidence of dissatisfaction on the part of the Soviet secret police (OGPU) chief Genrikh Yagoda,[64] with the social status of many scientists in the technical committees performing research on weapons design in 1928 leading to their arrest and dismissal.[65]

Two authors have recently referred to large-scale arrests of military specialists in the late 1920s and early 1930s. Tom Nichols writes, "In 1930, the purges of engineers and industrial figures were accompanied by widespread arrests of the 'military specialists' (*Voenspetsy*) including officers of stature such as Svechin."[66] According to another source, the late 1920s and 1930s witnessed the conviction of some 3,000 commanders and "former officers of the Old Army."[67] Yet Svechin was one of very few "military specialists" (along with Andrei Snesarev and Alexander Verkhovksii) to be denounced in 1931 by the Communist Academy for his views on the economic potential of the Soviet state and strategies for future war. Despite his denunciation, alleged arrest, and brief detention,[68] Svechin returned to work and continued to teach at the General Staff Academy throughout the 1930s and was promoted to the rank of division commander in 1935.[69] Only in 1938, at the height of the Great Terror, was he arrested and discharged from the army.[70]

According to Dmitri Fedotoff-White, two official party purges occurred in 1929 and 1933.[71] Voroshilov viewed these purges positively because the percentages of communist party members dismissed from the RKKA were consistently lower than the percentages of communists dismissed from the party at large, thereby allegedly connoting greater party loyalty in the army than in other organizations.[72] However, as Roger Reese has pointed out, it was indeed rather difficult to be expelled from the party and discharged from the military simultaneously. In most cases expulsion from the party did not affect one's military career, unless one was an officer anticipating promotion, in which case party membership was desirable.[73] In 1929, an average of 4 percent of the commanding personnel per military district were expelled, and almost half of them were accused of having contact with "alien elements" such as kulaks.[74] An article in *Red Star* revealed that the chief task of the 1929 purge—which followed on the heels of the Sixteenth Party Conference[75]—was to cleanse the ranks of sympathizers with the "right opportunists," whose ideas deviated from the party's "general line."

> The purge has shown that party organizations in military units are ideologically stable. But many cells underestimate the importance of a decisive battle with conciliation (*primirenchestvo*) towards the right deviation. Some communists do not understand the party's general line [e.g., the Siberian Military District].[76]

Weak internal cohesion within units and specific wrongdoings such as drunkenness and rudeness by soldiers were also identified as problems. Reese also found that despite the regime's rhetoric, few military communists were actually expelled from the party, and even fewer were discharged from the army for political reasons such as association with the "right deviation." In most cases, soldiers were accused of drunkenness and other forms of unseemly behavior. Moreover, fellow communists tended to be lenient toward one another, and soldiers who appealed the charges levied upon them often won and the charges were dropped.[77] Thus, it is questionable just how "effective" these periodic purges were in eliminating ideological troublemakers and ensuring loyalty to the party at this time of domestic upheaval. Nonetheless, distinctions should be made between these party purges, the attack on Svechin and other "old specialists" by fellow military colleagues, and the execution of key High Command officers in 1937–1938 during the Great Terror, or *Yezhovshchina*.[78] Not only were the earlier periodic purges much milder in terms of punishment, but the impact on the military's morale and cohesion was also far less pronounced.[79]

Political or ideological indoctrination of Red Army combat units by political commissars—a more subtle form of civil intervention—though a common feature of the early Stalin era, did not appear to affect the design of weapons systems or the conceptualization of operational combat theories; it did not impede innovation. As this book shows, the ideological factor actually worked to the advantage of one of the Red Army's main innovators, Mikhail Tukhachevsky. Tukhachevsky's predilection for a strategy of destruction based on decisive, offensive combat operations coincided nicely with the Bolshevik "offensive spirit"—based partly on the successful maneuver tactics of the civil war and the "can-do," "storm-any-fortress" mentality that was pervasive during the collectivization and industrialization campaigns. By publicly calling Svechin a "Right Opportunist" and stressing his failure to comprehend Marxist-Leninist theory, Tukhachevsky was able to tackle and eventually officially overturn the more defense-oriented strategies of his former colleague and implement his own.[80]

In sum, civilian intervention in military affairs was a mixed blessing for the Red Army. While there is considerable evidence of tensions between the Supreme Economic Council (VSNKh—in charge of the defense industries until 1932) and the Red Army, there is also evidence of harmony between the military and some bureaus within VSNKh. On one occasion, Tukhachevsky requested that the newly organized civil aviation directorate avoid being placed under the purview of VSNKh, fearing that the economic council would "ruin the matter."[81] Voroshilov and I. A. Khalepskii, chief of the Directorate of Motorization and Mechanization of the RKKA, complained bitterly that VSNKh was to blame for the delays in weapons design and production and for endless reams of red tape. By the same token, at least one of VSNKh's largest bureaus, The Special Technical Bureau for Special Military Inventions (Ostekhbiuro), was supported by the military. Responsible for military inventions, the Ostekhbiuro was actually protected by some members of the military from being burdened by too many petty requests.[82] On balance it appears that in some areas, civilian and military goals overlapped and were mutually beneficial, while in others they were antagonistic. Although there is no evidence that civilian intervention was *the* or even *a* major determinant of military innovation at this time, some features of the civil-military relationship—such as the highly propagandized war scare—were extremely beneficial to the Red Army.

Motives and Opportunities for Innovation During the First Five Year Plan

Before examining the factors and opportunities that facilitated innovation, it is important to provide an overview of the motivations for and conditions underlying innovation. Certainly, the First Five Year Plan environment was conducive to innovation. Stalin's "great transformation" of the Soviet Union from a backward, predominately peasant-based, agricultural society into a modern industrialized state filled the populace with tremendous spirit and hope for a brighter tomorrow. But why did the Red Army seek change? First, Stalin's overall emphasis on technological progress that would eventually permit the USSR to "catch up to and overtake" the capitalist countries presented the Red Army with a perfect opportunity, if not a mandate, to enhance its own technological standing.

Second, Stalin's insistence on "breaking with the past" and shedding all vestiges of the tsarist regime made military innovation in weapons and theories de rigueur. Moreover, a chief tenet of Marxist-Leninist theory was the inevitability of war between the socialist and imperialist camps, which also mandated that the Soviet Union advance technologically in order to prepare for the "inevitable" conflict.

Third, responding to the foreign threat by reworking one's own military doctrine and weapons systems—what Zisk calls "reactive innovation" to foreign military programs—was clearly at work in the Red Army.[83] Tukhachevsky took the lead in publicizing the inadequacy of the Red Army's doctrine and level of technological development, which lagged woefully behind those of its prospective enemies, and developed many schemes for redressing those inadequacies. At least until 1931, the "threat" was not of an actual attack on Soviet soil, but was manifested in the superior technology of European and U.S. armies and the economies capable of mass-producing armaments for them. In planning for future battle contingencies, the military found itself lacking not only in technically advanced weapons, but also large inventories of them.

After the Japanese invasion of Manchuria in 1931, which highlighted the prospect of a two-front war, the need for rapid rearmament became more compelling.[84] It is perhaps ironic that the Soviet Union was able to borrow ideas, designs, and technical expertise from its German capitalist foes in order to improve the combat capabilities that would eventually be employed against them. I use the term "emulative innovation" instead of "reactive innovation" to describe the Soviet practice of drawing on foreign expertise and purchasing foreign equipment and weapons for examination and partial incorporation in its own military programs.

The Russian army's technological backwardness—painfully revealed in the Great War—was an underlying motive of innovation. Virtually all Soviet military writers of this period—many of whom had served in the Imperial Army—agreed that the Great War was far more relevant than the civil war as a model for the study of future military conflicts. Qualities such as combat spirit, ideological fervor, and the ability to improvise, which helped the Bolsheviks prevail over White detachments in the civil war, would not suffice in a war against the advanced armies of industrialized countries. As Voroshilov himself repeatedly said, "a future war will be a war of factories," and if the Red Army is going to fight, it had better choose the "imperialist war" instead of the civil war as its model.[85]

Tukhachevsky also played down the significance of the civil war for military theory in general, pointing out that some of the conditions intrinsic to that war—such as the advantages of boundless terrain on which to maneuver freely and the availability of enemy stockpiles remaining on Soviet soil after World War I—could not be replicated in the future.[86] Like Voroshilov, Tukhachevsky was insistent that only World War I provided insights on issues such as the revision of tactics and strategies, the nature of coalition war, the importance of mobilizing the economy for weapons production in wartime, and the salience of technologically advanced weapons.[87]

How, then, did the Red Army manage to innovate successfully in weapons design, operational theory, and force structure in such a short period of time when it had so many strikes against it? When the theories and guns in its possession were outdated, when it had little experience with combat success against invasion by foreign powers historically, and when the military-industrial cadres were generally ill-equipped to design and produce high-quality weapons?

To answer this question, I explore the various conditions, opportunities, and personalities that, taken together, enabled the Red Army to innovate successfully between 1928 and 1933. They include the relatively unrestricted access to foreign imports and technical expertise, be they officially recognized or conducted underground; the tireless efforts of military leaders who strove to make defense a high priority when many domestic initiatives topped the party's agenda; the extraordinarily innovative contributions to military thought and weapons procurement of Mikhail Tukhachevsky in particular; the opportunities for testing new operational concepts and weapons technologies on the battlefield presented by the conflicts in the Far East; and the impact that the conflicts had on the leadership in making defense a high priority.

In Chapter 2, I challenge the common view that the prime motivation for industrialization in general, and the First Five Year Plan in particular, was the threat of war requiring a defense buildup. I explore how the Red Army tried to make its case for increased funding compelling to party and government authorities in order to underwrite its technical and doctrinal innovation at a time of fierce competition for scarce resources. In addition, debates about military priorities within the communist party and the exploitation of propaganda opportunities by the Red Army, such as the 1927 war scare, are examined in detail.

Chapter 3 focuses on the conflicts in the Far East at the turn of the decade and how they contributed to the innovation of the Red Army in terms of making defense a higher priority within the communist party and providing combat experience for the troops as well as a testing ground for new weapons prototypes and tactical concepts. Party documents, especially those of the Sixteenth and Seventeenth Congresses, are examined for insight into the perceptions of Far East military threats by members of the party and military elite, followed by a review of the conflicts themselves. The 1929 conflict between RKKA troops and Kuomindang forces on the Chinese Eastern Railway, though small in scale, provided an instant testing ground for Soviet tank prototypes and other pieces of equipment then under development and gave the Special Far East Army, or ODVA (Osobaia Dal'nevostochnaia Armiia), a chance to employ some new concepts of operations in the field that theretofore had existed only on paper. In anticipation of Japanese aggression against China and the Soviet Union, the Far East border was continuously reinforced in the aftermath of the 1929, conflict and lines of communication were gradually established there. With the Japanese invasion of northern China in the fall of 1931, the military threat to the Soviet Union's eastern border became even more palpable. With it came an increased concern for military preparedness in the country generally.

The impact of the German-Soviet military collaboration on Soviet military innovation is examined in Chapter 4. Although the clandestine military ties between the Reichswehr and Red Army were established in the early to mid-1920s, the most intensive phase, or *Höhepunkt,* of the officer exchanges and testing of combat equipment occurred during the First Five Year Plan period.[88] While the collaboration suffered from many problems, not the least of which was secrecy and suspicion on both sides, it enabled numerous Red Army officers to participate in high-level General Staff exchanges, have access to German tank prototype blueprints, test aircraft and tanks, and acquire chemical weapons. In their assessments of the collaboration, members of the Soviet High Command consistently hailed these contributions of the clandestine collaboration to the modernization of the Red Army in a variety of ways.

Soviet technological innovation in the area of tank R&D is discussed in Chapter 5. Although Soviet propaganda at this time was replete with antiforeigner and anticapitalist themes, in fact there was a clear recognition among party, military, and economic leaders that it would be virtually impossible to industrialize the country quickly without the expertise of foreign technical specialists and the acquisition of foreign machines and equipment.[89] Soviet Commissar of War Kliment Voroshilov was among the most vociferous of Soviet leaders in his insistence upon what can best be called the "grand paradox" of the First Five Year Plan: the achievement of economic autarky through the extensive importation of machinery and the vigorous recruitment and employment of thousands of foreign technical experts.[90] Given the scarcity of qualified Soviet technicians,[91] there is no question that the "socialist construction" of the First Five Year Plan was facilitated largely by the enlistment of German, Czechoslovak, American, and Hungarian engineers and assorted technical experts who installed and operated imported machinery and even participated in "socialist competition."[92] The military recognized the need to borrow foreign models and prototypes, especially in the area of automobiles, tractors, and tanks, in order to expedite the research, design, and completion of its own prototypes, eventually leading to the mass production of them.[93] Instead of doing all the research from scratch, the Soviet designers acquired blueprints and, where possible, actual models of tanks and other weapons.[94] Drawing on official military documents on tank development, I illustrate how the Soviet designers usually decided to adopt some features of foreign tanks and change others to adapt to their own needs, or preserve indigenous design features that were especially well regarded, such as tank armaments. In so doing, I challenge the conclusions of Anthony Sutton, who downplayed the Soviets' indigenous research and development programs and claimed that the United States basically created the Soviet military-industrial complex through numerous trade concessions.[95]

Finally and most important, Mikhail Tukhachevsky's preeminent role as the RKKA's key visionary and strategic thinker, responsible for a broad range of successful doctrinal and technological innovations, is examined in Chapter 6. Drawing on Eugene Lewis's study of public entrepreneurship, I compare Marshal Tukhachevsky's "operational mode" with that of the "Father of Nuclear Navy," Admiral Hyman Rickover, in order to show the degree to which these men brought unprecedented and long-lasting change, professionalism, and prestige to their respective military establishments.[96] A postscript, describing what ultimately happened to Marshal Tukhachevsky, follows in Chapter 7.

Notes

1. Hannah Arendt, *The Origins of Totalitarianism* (New York: Meridian Books, 1951), p. 405.

2. Ibid., p. 418. Here, referring to Isaac Deutscher, *Stalin: A Political Biography* (London, 1949).

3. C. J. Friedrich and Z. K. Brzezinski, *Totalitarian Dictatorship and Autocracy*, 2d ed. (Cambridge: Harvard University Press, 1965).

4. Ibid., pp. 239–273. Or, if not moot, at least easily pacified or subjugated. See Friedrich's chapter 6, "Islands of Separateness," concerning the church, family, university, and military. See also Aryeh Unger, *The Totalitarian Party: Party and People in Nazi Germany and Soviet Russia* (Cambridge: Cambridge University Press, 1974).

5. Perhaps the most pithy reexamination of the totalitarian model is contained in Carl Friedrich, Michael Curtis, and Benjamin Barber, *Totalitarianism in Perspective: Three Views* (New York: Praeger, 1969). Leonard Schapiro agreed with Friedrich that "totalitarianism is not a final and immutable 'model' of government, but more in the nature of a spectrum, with varying degrees of intensity and totality." See L. Schapiro, *Totalitarianism* (London: Pall Mall Press, 1972), p. 124. For other post-Stalin refutations of the totalitarian model, see G. Skilling and F. Griffiths, eds., *Interest Groups in Soviet Politics* (Princeton: Princeton University Press, 1971); Jerry Hough and Merle Fainsod, *How the Soviet Union Is Governed,* (Cambridge: Harvard University Press, 1979); Edward L. Warner III, *The Military in Contemporary Soviet Politics: An Institutional Analysis* (New York: Praeger, 1977).

6. J. Arch Getty, *Origins of the Great Purges: The Soviet Communist Party Reconsidered, 1933–1938* (Cambridge: Cambridge University Press, 1985); Kendall Bailes, *Technology and Society Under Lenin and Stalin: Origins of the Soviet Technical Intelligentsia, 1917-1941* (Princeton: Princeton University Press, 1978); Eugene Zaleski, *Planning for Economic Growth in the Soviet Union: 1918–1932* (Chapel Hill: University of North Carolina Press, 1971); and Sheila Fitzpatrick, ed., *Cultural Revolution in Russia, 1928–1931* (Bloomington: Indiana University Press, 1978).

7. Getty, *Origins of the Great Purges,* p. 5.

8. Ibid.

9. It should be noted that distinctions between early and "mature" Stalinism were drawn explicitly by T. H. Rigby in his essay "Stalinism and the Mono-organizational Society" and implicitly by Stephen Cohen in "Bolshevism and Stalinism," both contained in *Stalinism: Essays in Historical Interpretation* (New York: Norton, 1977).

10. R. C. Tucker wrote in 1963 that industrialization and collectivization were "the twin policies on the basis of which [Stalin] carried through the process of total state regimentation of society. This was the period of the emergence of full-blown, as distinguished from a merely embryonic, totalitarian state system." Tucker, *The Soviet Political Mind: Studies in Stalinism and Post-Stalin Change* (New York: Praeger, 1963), p. 41.

11. Roman, Kolkowicz, *Soviet Party-Military Relations: Contained Conflict,* Paper No. 3371. (Santa Monica: RAND, May 1966), p. 32. Stalin's "permanently operating factors" — little more than a framwork for discussion of any war — included the importance of a stable rear, high morale, a sufficient number of good weapons, and skilled commanders.

12. See the discussion of party-army relations in totalitarian systems in Friedrich and Brzezinski, *Totalitarian Dictatorship and Autocracy,* 1st ed. (New York: Praeger, 1956), p. 281, cited in Kolkowicz, *Soviet Party-Military Relations,* p. 9.

13. R. Kolkowicz, *The Soviet Army and the Communist Party: Institutions in Conflict,* R-446-PR (Santa Monica: RAND, 1966), pp. 514–515.

14. In 1929 a purge (*chistka*) of the Red Army's party organizations took place during which 6 percent of the communists in the RKKA were expelled. The reasons for their expulsions included antimoral behavior (ties with Nepmen, speculators), bureaucratism, and formalism — "conditions leading to the stagnation (*zastoiu*) of party thought"; lack of camaraderie; alcoholism; and violations of party ethics. See "Chistka povysila klassovuiu boesposobnost' partiinykh organizatsii," *Krasnaia zvezda,* 6 September 1929, p. 3.

15. Mikhail Tsypkin, "Origins of the Soviet Military Research and Development System" (Ph.D. diss., Harvard University, 1985).

16. Ibid.

17. Dmitri Fedotoff-White, *The Growth of the Red Army* (Princeton: Princeton University Press), 1944.

18. PURKKA was the abbreviation for the RKKA's political directorate (*politicheskoe upravlenie*), which operated as an arm of the communist party.

19. Michael J. Deane, *Political Control of the Soviet Armed Forces* (New York: Crane Russak & Co., 1977), p. 38.

20. John Erickson, *The Soviet High Command: A Military-Political History, 1918–1941* (London: St. Martin's Press, 1962).

21. Ibid., p. 329.

22. Ibid., p. 356.

23. Mark Von Hagen, *Soldiers in the Proletarian Dictatorship: The Red Army and the Soviet Socialist State, 1917–1930* (Ithaca: Cornell University Press, 1990), p. 327.

24. Roger Reese, *Stalin's Reluctant Soldiers: A Social History of the Red Army,* 1925–1941 (Lawrence: University of Kansas Press, 1996), p. 98.

25. Ibid.

26. Tucker, *The Soviet Political Mind,* p. 81. See also Stephen Cohen, "Bolshevism and Stalinism," pp. 19–24.

27. John Armstrong, *The Politics of Totalitarianism: The Communist Party of the Soviet Union from 1934 to the Present* (New York: Random House, 1961).

28. Schapiro, *Totalitarianism,* p. 28.

29. Fainsod, *How Russia Is Ruled,* p. 157.

30. Tucker, *The Soviet Political Mind,* p. 82.

31. Merle Fainsod referred to the "Third Revolution" as emphasizing "rapid industrialization and the building of military strength." See Fainsod, *How Russia Is Ruled,* p. 108. It should be noted that in 1982, David Holloway made mention of "the conflict between immediate investment in military production and building up a strong civilian industry to provide a basis for military power." See Ronald Amann and Julian Cooper, eds., *Industrial Innovation in the Soviet Union* (New Haven: Yale University Press, 1982), p. 281.

32. Julian Cooper, "Defence Production and the Soviet Economy," CREES Discussion Paper (University of Birmingham, 1976), p. 31.

33. Konstantin Mekhonoshin, "Metall-baza sotsialisticheskoi industrializatsii," *Izvestiia,* 16 June 1930.

34. R. W. Davies, "Soviet Military Expenditure and the Armaments Industry, 1929–1933: A Reconsideration," *Europe-Asia Studies,* vol. 45, no. 4 (1993), pp. 583–584.

35. These years cover the First Five Year Plan, 1928/1929–1932/1933, as discussed by Zaleski, *Planning.*

36. 1936 Field Regulations of the RKKA (Polevoi Ustav-36), translated in JPRS-UMA-86-031, 12 June 1986. Numerous articles in the *Military Historical Journal* have dissected and continue to dissect the operations and battles of World War II in particular, illustrating the Red Army's employment of deep battle concepts in the second half of the war.

37. Kimberly Marten Zisk, *Engaging the Enemy: Organization Theory and Soviet Military Innovation, 1955–1991* (Princeton: Princeton University Press, 1993), p. 4. James Q. Wilson provides a similar definition of innovation as "not any new program of technology, but only those that involve the performance of new tasks or a significant alteration in the way in which existing tasks are performed." See James Q. Wilson, *Bureaucracy: What Government Agencies Do and Why They Do It* (New York: Basic Books, 1989), p. 222.

38. Zisk, *Engaging the Enemy,* p. 4.

39. Stephen Peter Rosen, *Winning the Next War: Innovation and the Modern Military* (Ithaca: Cornell University Press, 1991), p. 5. Rosen illustrated that almost all the literature on innovation has shown how it failed, rather than succeeded, owing to the perception that bureaucracies are inherently resistant to change.

40. Ibid., p. 252.

41. Williamson Murray and Allan R. Millett, *Military Innovation in the Interwar Period* (Cambridge: Cambridge University Press, 1996).

42. Ibid., p. 335.

43. P. A. Rotmistrov, *Istoriia voennogo iskusstva* (Moscow: Voenizdat, 1963), pp. 457–458. The military reforms of 1924-1928 brought new structural changes to the RKKA, but did little in the way of re-equipping or modernizing the army's combat capabilities.

44. Murray and Millet, *Military Innovation in the Interwar Years,* pp. 303–304.

45. Ibid., p. 304.

46. In addition to Halperin's classic work on American bureaucracies, see Graham Allison, *The Essence of Decision: Explaining the Cuban Missile Crisis* (Boston: Little, Brown), 1971.

47. According to Halperin, "The bureaucratic system is basically inert; it moves only when pushed hard and persistently. The majority of bureaucrats prefer to maintain the status quo, and only a small group is, at any one time, advocating change." Morton Halperin, *Bureaucratic Politics and Foreign Policy* (Washington: Brookings Institution, 1974), p. 99.

48. Ibid., pp. 56–57.

49. Ibid., p. 51.

50. Morris Janowitz, *The Professional Soldier: A Social and Political Portrait* (Glencoe: Free Press, 1960), p. 22.

51. Barry Posen, *The Sources of Military Doctrine: France, Britain, and Germany Between the Wars* (Ithaca: Cornell University Press, 1984), especially chapter 2.

52. Eugene Lewis, *Public Entrepreneurship: Toward a Theory of Bureaucratic Political Power, The Organizational Lives of Hyman Rickover, J. Edgar Hoover, and Robert Moses* (Bloomington: Indiana University Press, 1980).

53. Fuller demonstrated the numerous and multifaceted organizational and doctrinal reforms or "innovations" that took place in the Russian army historically. With each defeat came significant and sometimes radical changes that, unfortunately, tended to be either oriented toward the wrong theater of war geographically or overambitious and/or driven by fear. See William Fuller, *Strategy and Power in Russia 1600-1914* (New York: Free Press, 1992), pp. 450–451.

54. Stalin, "O zadachakh khoziaistvennikov," 4 February 1931, in *Sochineniia,* vol. 13, pp. 38–39.

55. Rotmistrov, *Istoriia voennogo iskusstva,* pp. 351–366.

56. Murray and Millett, *Military Innovation in the Interwar Period,* pp. 360-361.

57. This idea seems to contradict Huntington's belief that "objective civilian control (i.e., civilian efforts to enhance military professionalism and autonomy) is thus directly opposed to subjective civilian control (civilian efforts to lessen military autonomy)," with the implication that the two forms of control could not coexist. See Huntington, *The Soldier and the State,* p. 83.

58. Reese, *Stalin's Reluctant Soldiers,* pp. 84–99, and Von Hagen, *Soldiers,* pp. 308–325.

59. RTsKhIDNI, "Vystuplenie Voroshilova na aktive iacheiki Tolmachevskoi Akademii," 11 March 1929, F. 74, op. 1, d. 154, l. 1–4. It is interesting that Voroshilov would make such comments at this ideologically high-charged party institution. As Kolkowicz and others have described, a group within the Tolmachev Academy denounced efforts to give the military commanders more authority (and enhance military professionalism) than the

political commissars. This movement came to be known the "Tolmachev heresy" and was quashed in 1928. Kolkowicz, *The Soviet Army and the Communist Party,* p. 84.

60. RGVA, F. 33987, op. 2, d. 351, Sekretnyi prikaz 17, 15 March 1932. The Moscow, Leningrad, and Ukrainian military districts had the highest number of deserters, followed by the Northern Caucasus (SKVO), Siberian, Central Asian, and Georgian Districts.

61. Loren Graham, *Science and Philosophy in the Soviet Union* (New York: Knopf, 1972), p. 11. The Communist Academy was created in 1918 as a counterbalance to the "old-specialist rich" National Academy of Science, which did not contain a single communist for many years into the Soviet regime, according to Graham.

62. Erickson, *The Soviet High Command,* p. 315.

63. Translation of Georgii Ozerov's *Tupolevskaia sharaga* by A. Charaguine, *En prison avec Tupolev* (Paris: Editions Albin Michel, 1973), pp. 9–10. See also Sutton, *Western Technology and Soviet Economic Development, 1917-1930* (Stanford: Stanford University Press, 1971), pp. 322–323. R. W. Davies also referred to the arrest and recruitment of two Soviet aircraft designers, Polikarpov and Grigorovich, who were put to work in OGPU-supervised design bureaus. See *The Soviet Economy in Turmoil, 1929–1930* (Cambridge: Harvard University Press, 1989), pp. 451–452.

64. The OGPU was the acronym for the Soviet secret police from the mid-1920s until 1934.

65. RGVA, Yagoda to Voroshilov, March 1928, F. 33987, op. 1, d. 657, l. 196–197.

66. Thomas Nichols, *Sacred Cause: Civil-Military Conflict over Soviet National Security, 1917–1992* (Ithaca: Cornell University Press, 1993), p. 45.

67. "Delo o tak nazyvaemoi 'antisovetskoi trotskistskoi voennoi organizatsii' v krasnoi armii," *Izvestiia TsK KPSS,* no. 4, 1989, p. 43.

68. Lev Nikulin refers to the arrest in 1930 of the visible military specialists and academy professors Svechin, Snesarev, and Verkhovskii, who were released shortly thereafter. See Nikulin, *Tukhachevskii* (Moscow: Voenizdat, 1963), p. 177.

69. A. A. Kokoshin and V. N. Lobov, "Foresight (General Svechin and the Evolution of the Art of War)," *Znamia,* no. 2, February 1990, translated in JPRS-UMA-90-009, 13 April 1990, p. 16.

70. Ibid.

71. Dmitri Fedotoff-White, *The Growth of the Red Army,* pp. 308 and 324.

72. According to Voroshilov, 5 percent of military communists were expelled in 1929 as opposed to 11.7 percent for the party as a whole. In 1933 the margin was even wider, 4.3 percent vs. 17 percent. Voroshilov, "Na istoricheskom perevale," 1930, *K. Voroshilov, Stat'i i rechi,* (Moscow: Partizdat TsK VKP/b/, 1936), pp. 423–424.

73. Reese, *Stalin's Reluctant Soldiers,* p. 79.

74. Ibid., p. 308.

75. At the Sixteenth Party Conference in April 1929, a resolution, "O chistke i proverke chlenov i kandidatov VKP(b)," was adopted, because the party's ranks had tripled in number of communists since 1921 and were then in need of another purge to eliminate "unstable, careerist elements, political time servers (*prisposoblentsy)* and double dealers (*dvurushniki*)." A. A. Solov'ev, *S'ezdy i konferentsii KPSS, Spravochnik* (Moscow: Politizdat, 1983), p. 221.

76. "Chistka povysila klassovuiu boesposobnosti partiinykh organizatsii: Pervye itogi,"*Krasnaia zvezda,* 6 September 1929, p. 3. Right opportunists tended to favor a slower rate of industrialization and to maintain a good relationship with the peasants.

77. Ibid., p. 78.

78. Robert Conquest addresses the 1937-1938 purge of the RKKA in great detail. See *The Great Terror: A Reassessment* (New York: Oxford University Press, 1990), pp. 205–207.

79. For a comprehensive treatment of the distinctions among these *chistki,* see Reese, *Stalin's Reluctant Soldiers,* pp. 132–162.

80. See author's *Historical Roots of Contemporary Debates on Soviet Military Doctrine and Defense,* Note No. 3348-AF/A (Santa Monica: RAND, 1991).

81. RGVA, F. 33988, op. 2, d. 693, l. 133.

82. RGVA, F. 33989, op. 1, d. 38, l. 44.

83. Zisk, *Engaging the Enemy,* p. 4.

84. Because fascist propaganda aimed against Bolshevism was well disseminated as early as 1930, it is plausible that the Soviet leadership was concerned about German intentions as early as 1931. See Bianka Pietrow, *Stalinismus Sicherheit Offensive: Das "Dritte Reich" in der Konzeption der Sowjetischen Außenpolitik, 1933–1941* (Melsungen: Schwartz Verlag, 1983), pp. 19-20.

85. Voroshilov, "Voprosy oborony i piatiletka," Speech at the Fifteenth CPSU Congress, 13 December 1927, *Stati' i rechi,* p. 199.

86. Tukhachevsky, "Iz urokov grazhdanskoi voiny," *Pravda,* 23 February 1928, and "Voina kak problema," *Izbrannye proizvedeniia,* vol. II, pp. 12–13.

87. Tukhachevsky, "Novye voprosy voiny."

88. Manfred Zeidler, *Reichswehr und Rote Armee: Wege und Stationen einer ungewöhnlichen Zusammenarbeit, 1920–1933,* (München: Oldenbourg, 1993), pp. 171–246.

89. Parrott, *Politics and Technology in the Soviet Union,* pp. 28–29. There are many references in the press to the poor technical skills of Soviet workers at this time. For example, V. Kolesinskii wrote that in the area of nonferrous metallurgy, the situation was especially acute: "Nonferrous metals are critically important for defense. However, in this area we are exceedingly backward...herein our scientific-technical obsolescence, lack of experience and specialists, and the extraordinary low technical-manufacturing level of our factories...will make us very dependent upon foreign assistance." See

"Metallopromyshlennost' v piatiletke," *Voina i revoliutsiia*, book 5, 1929, p. 17. German military visitors to the Soviet Union at this time were also struck by the poor technical capabilities of the workers at the aircraft and motor factories there: "The further the five-year plan proceeds, the more obvious the shortcomings of the experts become. It is really curious how little—at least in those factories we visited—is being done to train apprentices." See von Schönebeck's trip report, "Bericht der Besichtigungsreise nach Moskau in der Zeit vom 8.-14. 8. 1930," BA-MA, RH12-1/56.

90. Virtually all of Voroshilov's (as well as Molotov's and Kuibyshev's) articles and speeches referred to the need to attract foreign specialists and to import foreign capital as a necessary evil. One example: "Tsarist Russia knew practically nothing about machine building and with few exceptions imported [equipment] from abroad. Therefore, we also must spend enormous amounts of gold on imports of large quantities of machines from abroad. But this is unavoidable, because without machines to equip our factories to make machines, we cannot solve the problem of machine building in general." See Voroshilov's brochure, *Na istoricheskom perevale* (Moscow: Gosizdat, 1930), p. 63. Voroshilov's calls for imports also coincided with (or perhaps purposefully aided) Stalin's collectivization campaign wherein bread was to be forcefully requisitioned and sold abroad in order to purchase imports. See Voroshilov, "Za general'nuiu liniiu partii," 5-6 March, 1929, in *K. Voroshilov, Stat'i i rechi* (Moscow: Partizdat TsK VKP/b/, 1936), p. 301.

91. The shortage of skilled Soviet workers was severe, as Voroshilov often underscored. Job announcements attempting to attract technical personnel to defense projects were periodically listed in *Red Star*, yet even the authors of them knew that the positions would be hard to fill. "One need not look through rose-colored glasses to realize that we lack skilled Red Army craftsmen, lathe operators, and milling machine operators. True, there are some, but not enough." See "Krasnoi armii nuzhny mekhaniki, slesaria, tekhniki," *Krasnaia zvezda*, 29 November 1929, p. 4.

92. N. P. Sharapov, "Deutsche Arbeiter in der Sowjetunion: über die Teilnahme deutscher Arbeiter und Spezialisten am sozialistischen Aufbau in der UdSSR 1930-1933," *Zeitschrift für Geschichtswissenschaft*, no. 10, 1976, pp. 1110-1130. Many German engineers willingly and enthusiastically volunteered their services to help in constructing the first true socialist state, having become disillusioned with the attempts to do so at home. Within the Soviet Union, the exploitation of foreign technology and expertise was a controversial theme. Some argued that too few qualified foreign experts came to the USSR, and those who were qualified were not well utilized by their Soviet hosts who failed to participate in the work the foreigners were conducting. L. Kheifets, "Ob ispol'zovanii inostrannoi tekhniki v promyshlennosti SSSR," *Torgovo-promyshlennaia gazeta*, 23 May 1928, p. 3. Some scientists went further in their criticism of the borrowing of foreign technological concepts and practices. For example, a group of chemists believed the borrowed processes to be "routine"

and "outdated." See V. D. Esakov, *Sovetskaia nauka v gody pervoi piatiletki* (Moscow, 1971), pp. 94–95, cited in Parrott, *Politics and Technology,* p. 28.

93. Parrott, *Politics and Technology,* pp. 28–29.

94. RGVA, 28 November 1929, F. 31811, op. 1, d. 1, l. 29. I also discuss details of the trips taken by various Red Army officers to the United States and Great Britain to examine and purchase weapons and equipment. Before one such trip to the United States in 1929, chief of the Red Air Force, Baranov, was handed a veritable shopping list of items to purchase there, including fifty gallons of Prestone antifreeze.

95. Anthony Sutton, *National Suicide: Military Aid to the Soviet Union,* (New Rochelle: Arlington House, 1973), p. 70. See also the Swiss edition *Der leise Selbstmord: Amerikas Militärhilfe an Moskau* (Bern: Verlag SOI, 1976), p. 80.

96. Eugene Lewis, *Public Entrepreneurship,* chapters 2 and 3.

2

Politics and Military Priorities: Building a Case for More Resources

There is a widespread view in the Western literature on organizational theory that one of a bureaucracy's primary objectives is to secure handsome budgetary resources from the state.[1] As Morton Halperin put it, "All other things being equal, [career officials] prefer larger to smaller budgets and support policy changes which they believe will lead to larger budgets."[2] Although it concerns U.S. bureaucracies, Halperin's point can easily be applied to the Soviet military in the early Stalin period as well. Without vast sums of money, the Red Army could neither have purchased equipment abroad, nor sponsored foreign specialists on its own soil, nor sent officers to study and train in Germany and other countries. In short, money was vital for military innovation in the Soviet Union.

In his analysis of military innovation in the United States, Stephen Rosen found a relatively weak correlation between money and innovation and argued that talented personnel, time, and information were far more important.[3] While these factors were also critical to successful innovation in the Red Army, it must be remembered that the Soviet Union in 1928 lagged behind most Western countries in terms of economic, and especially industrial, development. Therefore, the importation of equipment from the more advanced industrial countries and the invitation of technical experts to the Soviet Union were dire necessities. They were also extremely expensive.

With the opening of the military archives, it is now possible to examine reams of reports and statistical tables dealing with the defense five year plans, which spanned the same years as the general industrial and financial plans of the First Five Year Plan (1928/1929-1932/1933). These myriad documents have also made it very difficult to draw conclusions about the actual size of the defense budget or its "final version," and they will require a thorough going-over by skillful accountants and economists. Indeed, Lennart Samuelson argues that neither a first nor a second five year plan for defense industries was ever officially adopted, but rather a set of mobilization requests or targets served as rearmament guidelines in the 1930s.[4] But whether or not a defense procurement plan was "officially adopted" is perhaps less important than the fact that all plans were continually revised, resulting in numerous drafts. As Stalin said, "We must constantly correct [the plan] as we are fulfilling it."[5]

Upon combing the archives of the Russian Federation and the State Economy, R. W. Davies found a large discrepancy between the officially published budgetary figures and the archival figures for the Commissariat of Military and Naval Affairs (NKVM) during the First Five Year Plan.[6] The published figures were vastly understated and obscured the true picture of military expenditures considerably. Even while taking account of inflation, the "increased NKVM expenditure in both 1931 and 1932 also reflected huge real increases in military construction and armaments production."[7] Between 1930 and 1932, armaments production actually increased more rapidly than industrial production in general. Davies suggests that the Soviet authorities understated the defense budget between 1931 and 1933 intentionally, owing to sensitive diplomatic talks between the commissar of Foreign Affairs, Maxim Litvinov, and western representatives to the League of Nations' disarmament conferences. Indeed, as late as 1932, Litvinov continued to promote disarmament as *the* means of improving foreign relations and enhancing national security, and maintained that his endorsement of general disarmament was not merely a "communist slogan."[8]

But while we are gaining a better picture of how resources were allocated, problems still remain. One of the problems is that resource allocations to the NKVM in the early years of industrialization accounted for only one aspect of the defense expenditures, such as equipment and personnel, whereas allocations to capital investment, working capital, and civilian organizations contributing to defense—such as the transportation and communications commissariats—fell under the "national economy" category of the state budget.[9] Nonetheless, it is still possible to provide insight into the institutions and individuals involved in the budgeting process and illustrate the numerous revisions of the NKVM's budgetary requests by the ever-proliferating government and party commissions that participated in that process.[10]

It should also be borne in mind that the competition for resources among all economic sectors of the First Five Year Plan was extremely keen, given its grandiose or, to use Naum Jasny's term, "Bacchanalian" nature. Numerous Western scholars have written of the plan's unrealistic economic goals, which promised to serve both the state's and the consumer's needs.[11] Because the goals or "targets" of the plan were unachievable, some sectors (housing and consumer goods) suffered while others (heavy industry) thrived. As Holland Hunter put it, "All outputs were to grow, but one is tempted to paraphrase the pigs' slogan on equality in Orwell's *Animal Farm*: 'All outputs will grow, but some will grow much more than others.' The industry and construction sectors were to be expanded far more rapidly than the agriculture and housing sectors. The plan called for disproportional growth in sectoral outputs."[12]

The top priorities of the First Five Year Plan as expressed by Stalin and other party and military officials show that, at least initially, rearmament was not among them. Before 1931, it appears that there was no consensus that a large and rapid defense buildup was advisable. This reality made it incumbent upon the military, which devised new strategies and weapons, to convince the party leadership that these innovations were indispensable to the security of the Soviet state and that therefore large budgetary allocations to the military were advisable. The tactics used by two key advocates of military innovation, Mikhail Tukhachevsky and Kliment Voroshilov, to convince the party that the Red Army was a high budgetary priority are examined closely in this chapter.

In addition to the speeches and writings of Voroshilov and Tukhachevsky, the style and content of discourse used by other key members of the high command are examined in order to determine how the "war scare" of 1927 assisted the military in convincing the civilian leadership that external threats to state security necessitated more resources.

Security and the Goals of the First Five Year Plan[13]

Throughout the 1920s and early 1930s there was agreement among Soviet military and civilian leaders that enhanced security for the Soviet state would be a natural and important by-product of economic and technological progress. Through industrialization, many argued, Soviet economic and military aims coincided: Industrialization of the country connoted increased economic power and ipso facto a stronger military capability.[14] As the chief of the Gosplan's Defense Sector,[15] Konstantin Mekhonoshin, plainly put it: "We consider the entire economy to be the basis of defense."[16] Because economic and military goals overlapped, some military spokesmen asserted that military requirements would neither compete with nor contradict the "general line" of the party in the construction of socialism.[17] General Vasilii Bliukher was among those who saw the complementary nature of, rather than contradiction between, defense and civilian requirements and who made his point rather eloquently at the Sixteenth Party Congress in the summer of 1930.

> Comrades, the Red Army is a component part of our socialist organism. The correct line, which firmly and steadfastly and with Bolshevik persistence is advanced by our central committee despite all the opportunists' efforts to set us back, leads also to the strengthening of the defense of our country. The enormous growth of our industry; every new tractor sent to the fields of our villages ... every new car produced by our large automobile plants; every new blast furnace, every new open hearth furnace—all of this strengthens the defensive capacity of the country.[18]

It goes without saying that the idea of building a strong industrial base at "break-neck speed" was very attractive to the military: Without a solid steel, iron, and chemical-producing capability, the manufacture of weapons, ammunition, and aircraft was unimaginable. But while a strong industrial base was desirable in the long run, shorter-run peacetime defense production was also vital to the military. Should war break out, a certain amount of weaponry would be needed to fight the initial stages of war until such time as industries were properly mobilized for wartime production. Just how much peacetime military production to undertake—in light of budgetary constraints—was a controversial topic among both military spokesmen and economists. Konstantin Mekhonoshin believed that the existence of separate defense industries was a waste of resources because armaments could be manufactured efficiently at civilian plants at much-reduced costs and thereby free up capital for the state's industrialization objectives.[19] Mekhonoshin, it is interesting to note, also served as chairman of a special commission created by Gosplan decree to review the NKVM's 1929/1930 financial five year plan.[20] As figure 2.1 suggests it appears that there was a running battle between the War Commissariat and Gosplan, with Gosplan's defense sector—which was heavily represented by the military trying to straddle the divide.

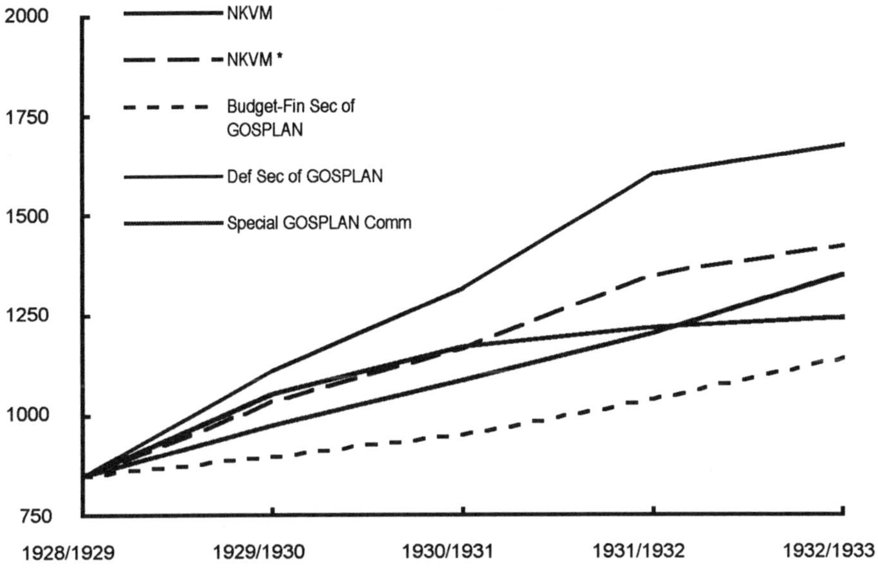

FIGURE 2.1 Versions of the Defense Five Year Plan
RGVA, F. 33988, op. 1, d. 638, l. 126

Stalin saw industrialization as a means of acquiring an economic base on which to advance technologically and thereby achieve political legitimacy for the socialist state.[21] Contrary to the interpretation of many scholars, there is little evidence that the emphasis he placed on heavy industry in the first plan was primarily a response to impending military threats to the Soviet homeland in the late 1920s requiring a rapid expansion of the war industries.[22] In a 1931 speech, Stalin, in fact, blamed the bourgeois intelligentsia for anticipating war and perpetuating the war scare, thereby disassociating himself from the very themes he used to his advantage in battling political opponents in the late 1920s.[23]

When Stalin listed the priorities of the First Five Year Plan, improving the country's defense capabilities usually occupied either last place or second to last, just above "raising the cultural level" of society; that is, improving the standard of living.[24] Eliminating the country's technological backwardness, becoming economically independent, collectivizing agriculture, and abolishing class differentiation always preceded mention of military requirements.[25] The head of the Supreme Economic Council (VSNKh), Valerian Kuibyshev, noted in 1927 that the primary goal of the First Five Year Plan was to increase the technical level of the country as much as possible, because socialism is the "technologically highest stage in the development of society."[26]

These proclamations implicitly gave the military a mandate to improve its technology along with other industrial sectors. Simultaneously, the military would have to work hard to convince the party and Stalin that rearmament was *explicitly* a high priority. Remarks made at the Sixteenth Party Conference in the spring of 1929 were an early indication that the military's battle would be uphill. This conference, during which the finishing touches were put on the First Five Year Plan's targets,[27] also included serious discussions about accelerating the pace of collectivization and intensifying the struggle against internal enemies such as kulaks and the "right deviation." Priority was assigned to these issues, while rearmament—despite the proliferation of Comintern propaganda on the collapse of capitalism and the impending Western attack—was hardly addressed.[28] Gosplan head Gleb Krzhizhanovskii stated bluntly that one of the plan's "unelaborated sections" was the military's requirements; thus the officers' complaints at the conference were legitimate.[29]

These differences boiled down to a general tension between some military and economic authorities regarding "short-run" defense growth and peacetime military production versus a "longer-run" and gradual development of civilian industries that would only in wartime begin to produce weapons. Not until 1931 did the military and the party appear to agree that defense concerns were a high, if not the highest, priority. The rest of this chapter examines how the changes came about.

Voroshilov: Criticism of the Party

Kliment Voroshilov boldly called upon the communist party to focus on defense matters. Although numerous problems attending Soviet defense industries, such as poor production quality and labor productivity, were mentioned in Voroshilov's articles throughout his tenure as war commissar, his public criticism of the party's halfhearted commitment to defense requirements seems to have lasted until approximately 1933. From this time on, Voroshilov's speeches and references were filled with praise and admiration for the party's unfailing commitment to defense and especially to Stalin's personal role. Because the defense industries fell under the purview of VSNKh, it was probably less of a political risk to attack the council than the party, until the former was abolished in 1932. However, at that time the defense industries became the jurisdiction of the Commissariat for Heavy Industry, headed by Stalin's

Georgian crony, Sergo Ordzhonikidze—which in all probability also necessitated a careful choice of words and political tiptoeing.

In a report to the All-Union Congress of Soviets in April 1927, Voroshilov rather mildly entreated the party to take into consideration the needs of defense.[30] A few months later, he sharply criticized the meager resource allocations to the military, writing that not only had the Red Army been shortchanged, but also the Imperial Army had fared much better. This was a pithy argument, ripe with sarcasm. With respect to the First Five Year Plan, Voroshilov's boldness was perhaps most evident in his insistence upon the need to amend the industrialization targets in December of the same year.[31]

Between 1927 and 1931, it appeared that little had improved. Materials used by Voroshilov in preparation for his speech to the Sixth Congress of Soviets in 1931 contained charts and tables that showed the extent to which the growth of the military budget had suffered considerably vis-à-vis the growth of the general state budget, and how military expenditures were a far lower percentage of the Soviet budget than that of other European countries. (See Figure 2.2.)

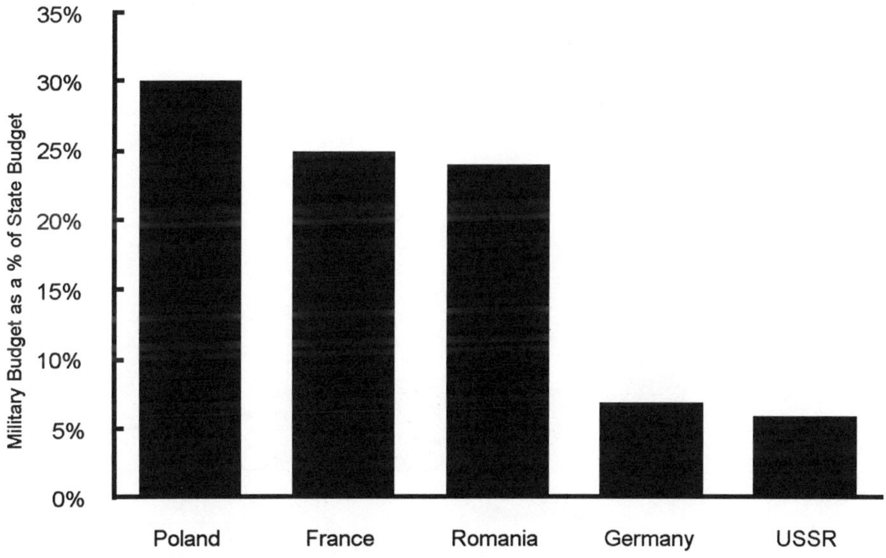

FIGURE 2.2 Countries' Military Budgets in 1931
RGVA, F. 51, op. 2, d. 405, l. 34.

The sources of Voroshilov's data for these comparisons are not revealed. However, the ordering of the countries according to their military budgets closely matches the order in which these countries were perceived as threats to the Soviet Union in the late 1920s: Poland the gravest and most probable enemy, and Germany the least certain. The data also seem to underestimate German rearmament efforts that were proceeding secretly, and therefore may reflect the official data provided by the German government that would include the Versailles Treaty's cutbacks in German military activities across the board.

In his budget for 1932, it is interesting to note, the people's commissar of finance, G. F. Grin'ko, was among the leading economists who advocated that the defense budget should decline in proportion to the general budget. (See figure 2.3.) The recent work of R. W. Davies, however, suggests that the military was winning this debate. Between 1930 and 1932—the last year of the First Five Year Plan, the production of armaments grew from 2.6 percent to 5.7 percent of total industrial production.[32] According to Davies:

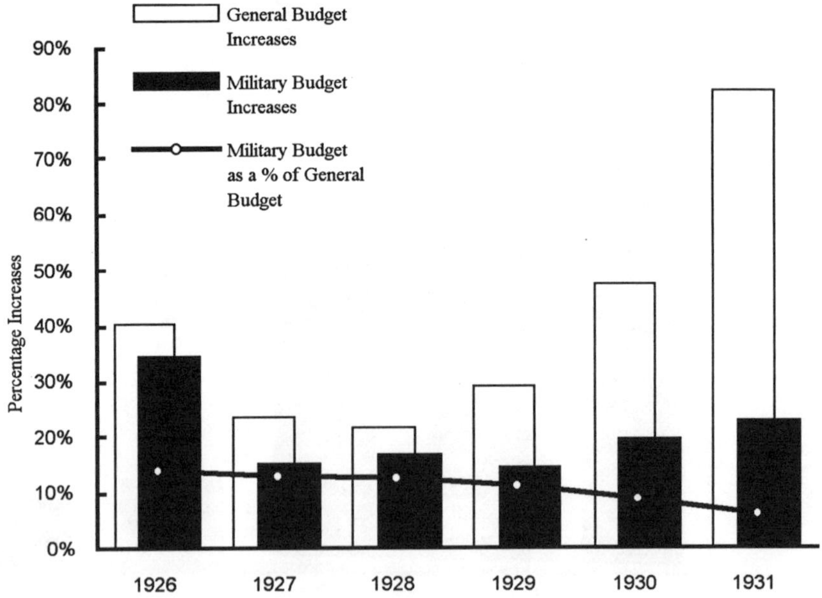

FIGURE 2.3 Soviet Military Budget Increases as Percentages of General Increases
R. W. Davies, Soviet Defence Industries, p. 13

> Budget expenditure on the NKVM, gross production of armaments, and capital investment in the arms industry all increased sharply in 1931, and increased again in 1932. The increase in both production and capital investment was much more rapid than the increase for industry as a whole; the defence sector was absorbing a rapidly increasing proportion of industrial resources.[33]

The army's share of capital investment more than doubled between 1929 and 1933.[34] And between 1930 and 1940 the defense industry's gross output grew much faster than that of the civilian industry, particularly in 1932.[35]

In his speech at the Sixteenth Party Congress in June 1930, Voroshilov seemed to implicate the party's inattention to defense matters by couching his remarks in terms of the workers' neglect. After noting that the general line of the party and that of defense coincided and that the five-year plan's breakneck pace was, in essence, a "pledge" to improve the defense capabilities of the state and Red Army, the war commissar expressed displeasure with the central committee for ignoring the military's needs.[36]

Toward the end of the First Five Year Plan, however, Voroshilov's references to Stalin's personal and direct participation in military matters and "rich combat experience" in the civil war replaced the earlier incantations about insufficient resources.[37] Indeed, Stalin was allegedly dispatched by the party to the "most dangerous and decisive fronts" during the civil war. With respect to Soviet tank development, Voroshilov was especially thankful to Stalin, going so far as to claim that there was no longer a shortage of tanks in the Red Army.

> The central committee and the government and *especially Stalin* took all the right measures and pushed all the right pedals so that the army would have tanks. ... At the present time we can consider the task of tank armament of the Red Army solved completely satisfactorily.[38]

In this same address, Voroshilov noted that the *capacity* to produce modern weapons in large quantities came about "in the course of the successful completion of the First Five Year Plan," suggesting that the manufacturing processes were now in place for mass production to unfold during the Second Five Year Plan.[39]

At the Seventeenth Party Congress, or "Congress of Victors," in 1934, references to the party's inadequate attention to defense matters had vanished from Voroshilov's speeches. By this time, the central committee did not lose sight of defense "for a single second," in Voroshilov's view. In contrast to earlier statements on the army's share of industrial production, it now did not lag at all behind the development of any other sector of the economy, "by even one step."[40] And although this "about-face" in Voroshilov's tone is somewhat circumspect, intimating perhaps that Voroshilov had a strong personal motivation for flattering Stalin at this time, the economic data seem to indicate that rearmament indeed became a higher priority sometime after 1931, as reflected in production figures.[41] R. W. Davies has illustrated that the Soviet leadership concentrated on the development of basic capital goods' (longer-term) industries until 1931. Between 1931 and 1932, the defense-related share of total machine-building and metalworking production jumped from 7.9 percent to 11.1 percent.[42] Defense industries also received an increasing percentage of capital investment, more than doubling between 1929 and 1932.[43] Despite these gains, Voroshilov continued to call for the improvement of the defense industry, which was still suffering from many production problems. Upon noting that "Bolsheviks would not be Bolsheviks" if they were satisfied with their accomplishments and failed to strive harder,[44] Voroshilov maintained that the quality of production was still wretched, factory orders were underfulfilled, production costs were astronomical, and scientific-research organizations had a long way to go in designing new prototypes, improving existing production processes, and rationalizing production.[45]

Thus, despite the sense of accomplishment and even victory that pervaded the congress's atmosphere, Voroshilov chose to underscore yet again the industry's shortcomings in a confident manner that did not smack of a "toadying conspirator and shadow, a man incapable and indeed fearful of initiating any measure of his own."[46] Rather, it bespoke a man committed to improving the Red Army—a true "Bolshevik" who was never satisfied with the accomplishments at hand.

Marshal Tukhachevsky: Optimism for Industrialization

> We encounter oversimplified and gloomy conclusions that modern war requires such grandiose forces that it is impossible to speak of military victories or achievements because the issue lies in economic competition alone. Economic competition takes place in peacetime. But if matters lead to war, then economic competition alone will not suffice. Obviously, armed forces are needed, military methods are required to add a new coefficient to economic correlation that exist. ... Only a disbelief in socialism and in our future development can

> lead to military nihilism, which rejects the possibility of changing the correlation of forces as it presently exists with military means.[47]

Perhaps the strongest advocate for large resource allocations to the military was Mikhail Tukhachevsky, who served as chief of the RKKA staff in Moscow from 1925 until he resigned from that position in 1928, then becoming the commander of troops of the Leningrad Military District until 1931. He was brought back to Moscow as deputy commissar of war and chief of armaments in 1931, promoting and overseeing numerous weapons programs for the RKKA. A more complete examination of his accomplishments is found in Chapter 6.

In contrast to Voroshilov, Tukhachevsky formulated his requests for resource allocations in an indirect fashion. Instead of blaming the party for negligence on defense matters, Tukhachevsky sang the praises of the First Five Year Plan and the colossal achievements that would accompany it, thereby enabling his ambitious rearmament schemes to be realized in the future. It is probably no coincidence that Tukhachevsky's praise for the plan earned him an invitation to a celebration at the Karl Marx factory for overfulfilling its plan in the first quarter of 1931.[48] In essence, he flattered the party for its future achievements perhaps in an effort to help his ambitious rearmament requests win acceptance by the party. The evidence suggests that Tukhachevsky's tactics were usually successful in the long run.

Tukhachevsky was generally careful to couch his discussions of defense requirements in the broader context of general industrialization, and occasionally he cited ways in which the Red Army could help the Soviet state economize and assist with various civilian initiatives, such as collectivization. In one article, Tukhachevsky proposed that the military adopt the seven-day workweek and create shift work, just as industry had done.[49] This measure would have the threefold effect of easing the overcrowded training facilities, heightening the effectiveness of cultural-political work, and, according to Tukhachevsky, "undoubtedly strengthen the anti-religious front" by limiting the soldiers' opportunities to attend worship services.[50]

A Controversial Rearmament Proposal

Despite his numerous successes in getting his ideas across and his plans adopted, by means of careful packaging and political maneuver, Tukhachevsky also made some mistakes along the way. It has become clear that he overstepped some boundaries in presenting to Voroshilov and Stalin a rearmament proposal in 1930 while he was serving as head of the Leningrad Military District. This proposal, which called for a larger number of tanks and aircraft than the economy had the capacity to produce, caused an uproar in the Revolutionary Military Council (RVS) and led Stalin to label Tukhachevsky's figures *fantastika*. But despite their poor initial reception, Tukhachevsky's figures were later incorporated into one of many defense planning drafts when he was promoted to chief of armaments.

Soviet historian Sergei Biriuzov and military theorist Georgii Isserson refer to these rearmament proposals in the articles of the early 1960s they published in conjunction with the rehabilitation of Tukhachevsky and other military victims of the Great Terror.[51] With the opening of the Russian military archives, Tukhachevsky's controversial January 1930 report to Voroshilov on the reconstruction of the Red Army became available for inspection.[52] In the report, Tukhachevsky called for a bold new approach to defense procurement, one based on the "real possibilities" of the country's industrialization successes—which had improved markedly over the past four years—and not on the incremental upward ratcheting of percentages based on the previous year's figures, a practice that had become commonplace in the central planning of the Soviet economy.[53] In contrast to his other reports and articles, Tukhachevsky provided concrete numbers of aircraft and tanks that should be produced by the end of the First Five Year Plan in hopes, perhaps, of lending more authority to his ambitious proposals.[54]

The figures that he cited, however, appear to be somewhat magically derived from a combination of sources, including the aircraft and tank production of France, England, and Germany in 1918.[55] In another section, Tukhachevsky maintained that the railroad net on the USSR's western border could accommodate some 214 rifle and cavalry divisions within 28 days of mobilization. To this the military districts in Central Asia and Siberia would also be added, bringing the total to 260 divisions.[56]

TABLE 2.1 Weapons Procurement, 1932/1933

1932/1933	Number Requested	Number in Operation *(v stroiu)*
Automobiles	350,000	
Aircraft	122,500	36,750
Aircraft motors	175,000	
Tanks	197,000	50,000

Although he called his figures "preliminary," Tukhachevksy's most flagrant political error perhaps lay in admitting to Voroshilov that he was putting forth these figures in the absence of consultation with other military and party leaders. In fact, his wording suggests that there may have been little support for his ideas among fellow officers anyway. It should be remembered that Tukhachevsky was in Leningrad at the time he wrote this and therefore was trying to influence the center from the outside.

> I should add that the following drafts are only preliminary because I was not able to enlist the services of fellow staff members (*okruzhnyi apparat*) and was confined to independent projections. However, all of these preliminary calculations are based on our real possibilities, in keeping with the adoption of the five-year plan of the people's economy and the corrections and additions to it.[57]

In essence, Tukhachevsky believed that a country's military power—as manifested in the size of its army and its technical sophistication—should reflect the economic capabilities of the state in which he saw enormous potential. He claimed that the successful realization of the plan would permit the development of mass armies and provide means of increasing their mobility and offensive capabilities.[58] Among his more specific recommendations in this report were the expansion of air transportation to overcome the country's vast geographical distances, greater tank production (one tank for every two tractors), more cavalry and rifle divisions, better lines of communication (paved highways, etc.), an improved chemical industry, and new operational methods.

According to Sergei Biriuzov, the scholar who initially exposed the quarrel between Stalin and Tukhachevsky, the problems between them started when he sent this report to Voroshilov and Stalin.[59] Upon hearing the report's proposals, according to Biriuzov, both Stalin and Voroshilov condemned them and claimed that the adoption of such an ambitious rearmament program would lead to "Red Militarism."[60] Biriuzov wrote:

> However, these proposals by M.N. Tukhachevsky were not only unfavorably evaluated by Voroshilov and Stalin, but received with enmity. In sum, Stalin, with whom Voroshilov fully agreed, became convinced that the adoption of this program would destroy socialist construction and lead to the replacement of it with some kind of peculiar system of "red militarism." *(... k zamene ego kakoi-to svoeobraznoi sistemoi "krasnogo militarizma.")*[61]

After these comments were made, an undeterred Tukhachevsky apparently requested that Stalin reconsider his proposals for the reorganization of the Red Army, while emphasizing that in a future war not only must the army win, but also the economy must preserve its strength and protect its achievements in constructing socialism.[62] With no reply from Stalin in the offing, Tukhachevsky wrote another letter to him twelve months later, in December 1930, in which he complained bitterly of having been excluded from high-level discussions of defense matters and accused the RKKA staff of "unscrupulously" misrepresenting his proposals.[63]

It appears that soon after Tukhachevsky sent the proposal to Voroshilov, who shared it with his colleagues in the RVS and with Stalin, chief of the RKKA staff Boris Shaposhnikov was asked to review the proposal thoroughly. In a thirty-page paper he apparently lambasted Tukhachevsky's proposal, charging that it was well beyond the capacity of the economy at the time to produce such numbers of weapons and providing his own estimates.[64] Upon receiving Shaposhnikov's evaluation for perusal, Stalin is said to have looked it over and attached a note claiming that Tukhachevsky's proposal was "pure fantasy.[65]" Tukhachevsky apparently found out that his proposal was critiqued in a session of the RVS in June 1930, and in the interim began writing to Stalin, countering the conclusions of Shaposhnikov, pleading his case, and buttressing his conclusions. For example, he stressed that his call for 8,000 tanks required to break through an enemy defense was quite reasonable and that his numbers were fully in line with a mobilization request for 8,000-10,000 tanks proposed by the government at an RVS meeting in April 1930.[66] He also noted that these tanks need not all be of one type, but that second- and third-echelon tanks could and should be slower, and that civilian vehicles, such as tractors, could be mounted with weapons and used in battle. In extending this logic to the collective farms, the profusion of tractors in the countryside offered tremendous combat potential. It appears that these suggestions resonated with someone in the staff and possibly with Stalin in early 1931 as Tukhachevsky's note to Voroshilov in the spring of 1931, reflected triumph and indeed a strong sense of vindication when he noted that the latest Politburo rearmament directives matched those of his original proposal.[67] While it seems uncharacteristic of Stalin to be at all charitable, Biriuzov reports that in May 1932, after Tukhachevsky had been promoted and returned to Moscow to serve as chief of armaments for the RKKA, Stalin answered Tukhachevsky's letter with a strong apology in which he accepted the blame for having judged Tukhachevsky's proposals too harshly. In closing the letter, noted Biriuzov, Stalin even apologized for taking so long to acknowledge his mistake.[68]

At approximately the same time that Tukhachevsky's proposal was being reviewed, he was at work on a variety of other projects as well. In terms of promoting the use of civilian aircraft, as the "Entrepreneurial Excursus" in Chapter 6 reveals, Tukhachevsky was also working hard to translate Stalin's wishes for a rapid expansion of dual-purpose aircraft into a well-institutionalized, realizable project.

As the record shows, this rearmament proposal was only one of many in the course of his career that provoked disapproval or bewilderment from his peers and superiors, but his persistence usually paid off. At a central committee plenum in 1933, Stalin apparently joked about Tukhachevsky "never being satisfied" and "never having enough," to which Sergo Ordzhonikidze responded, "Everything is [too] little to him. But we can say to comrade Tukhachevsky the following: when we need to move these weapons to the front, we will give the Red Army as much as it needs."[69]

The Red Army's Manipulation of the "War Scare"

The "war scare" that allegedly resulted from the rupture of diplomatic relations with Great Britain in May 1927, combined with the failure to spark communist revolution in China and the shooting of the Soviet ambassador to Poland, provided the military with a rare and extremely attractive opportunity to capitalize on impending external threats and thereby make a strong case for increased budgetary allocations for the War Commissariat.[70]

References to the threat of an imperialist war against the first proletarian state were common features of Soviet propaganda and thus predated the 1927 propaganda blitz. From the early 1920s forward, revolutionary Comintern writings had predicted the outbreak of war as the ultimate and inevitable expression of the crisis of capitalism. Because the contradictions among capitalist countries (competition for cheap labor and new markets) and within them (their class structures—rich vs. poor) had grown so profound, general war was the only recourse, according to Marxist-Leninist doctrine.[71]

Despite the military's efforts, it is unlikely to have convinced the party of the need to increase defense spending, as some scholars have suggested. This war scare had more to do with Stalin's desire to attack his political opponents. Stalin, following Bukharin's example of January 1927, grasped the utility of the "war scare" as a clever and pliable political tool in his struggle first against the so-called "left" or "Trotskyite" and later against the "right deviation.[72] " The moment he heard that diplomatic relations with Great Britain had been severed, he used the threat of war and intervention against the Soviet Union to insist on absolute party unity and attack his political opponents.[73] Stalin also used the threat of foreign intervention to justify the extremely harsh measures he undertook to force collectivization of the countryside in 1929, while his political rival, Nikolai Bukharin, viewed the overemphasis on the war scare as risky and counterproductive.[74] Threats of imminent war, to Bukharin's mind, would undermine the confidence of the peasantry and potentially lead to a disaffected rural population in the event of war.[75]

The cacophonous political tunes played by the press, at least initially, led to no consensus that the "war scare" embodied any imminent threat to the USSR's security. References to the "war scare" were often published concurrently with economic analyses emanating from prestigious economic institutes, such as the Institute of World Economic and International Relations (IMEMO) and the Executive Committee of the Comintern (IKKI) regarding the stabilization of capitalist economies in the mid- to late twenties.[76] Stable economies seldom engendered the kinds of class contradictions that were supposed to be preconditions to war in the Marxist view. Thus, such studies undermined the "war scare" propaganda. Other statements issued by party and government organs stressed that the construction of socialism "required peace" and a "breathing spell."[77] The deputy commissar of foreign affairs at this time, Maxim Litvinov, called the British anti-Soviet press campaign "as old as the Russian Revolution itself"[78] and the Soviet fears of imminent war "exaggerated and premature."[79]

In fact, a few weeks after the break in Soviet-British diplomatic relations in May, the war commissar himself wrote that the probability of war was very low—indicating that the army was clearly not the initiator of the propaganda on the imminence of capitalist attack.[80] By the end of July, Voroshilov had changed his tune and his writings and speeches began to include "war scare" slogans referring to the "international situation" at hand or to "capitalist encirclement" in his pleas for increased resources.[81] At the Fifteenth Party Congress in December 1927, Voroshilov stressed that only since last spring, when "the active policy of the Imperialists, England especially, began to threaten the USSR," had the country begun military preparations in order to defend its peace policy.[82] It was also here that Voroshilov made reference to the existence of a five year plan for defense for which resources would go toward reinforcing "technical resources and mobilization reserves."[83]

The central committee launched a major propaganda campaign in response to the break in diplomatic relations with Great Britain in June 1927. Apparently as a means of psychological motivation, an article appearing in *Pravda* on June 1 strongly advised the Soviet people not to panic but to prepare for war by expanding socialist industry.[84] This change marked the beginning of an Osoaviakhim[85]-sponsored propaganda blitz aimed at mobilizing the population under the rubric of "Defense Week." According to L. P. Malinovskii, general secretary of Osoaviakhim, the goals of Defense Week were threefold: to disseminate propaganda on military and Osoaviakhim tasks, to increase membership in Osoaviakhim, and to collect contributions for defense needs.[86] Despite its initial financial and enrollment successes, however, Defense Week also had its drawbacks. In the same report in which Malinovskii praised the celebration, he revealed that it had also ignited sharp commentary from abroad and exaggerated the threat of an impending war in the minds of the peasantry, causing unnecessary hoarding. Nonetheless, Defense Week was institutionalized and recurred annually.[87]

During the Sixth World Congress of the Comintern in the summer of 1928,[88] attendees discussed the commencement of the "Third Period" of postwar capitalism in which class contradictions were growing increasingly acute, and with these contradictions, the likelihood of revolutionary wars as well.[89] Along with this recognition came an insistence upon party unity and Stalin's attack on Bukharin and the "Right Opposition." By July 1929, at the Tenth Plenum of the Comintern's Executive Committee, the "Third Period" of the crisis of capitalism was legitimized considerably by the economic depression in the West.[90] In his report on the international situation at the plenum, Finnish Comintern official Otto Kuusinen stated that in light of the heightened internal and external contradictions in capitalist countries, "war could break out at any moment."[91]

Thus, by July 1929, the war scare had become part and parcel of the party's "general line," and any underestimation of the external threat to socialism (or at least any understatement in public) was grounds for political attack. As one military commentator wrote, "any belittling of the danger of war represents a diversion from the general line of the party and a direct association with the right deviation."[92] Months later, Voroshilov published his pamphlet called "Will There Be War?" (*Budet li voina?*), in which he predicted that the capitalist world was so replete with contradictions and hostilities that a planned attack on the USSR was just around the corner.[93]

When a British diplomat in Moscow, William Strang, asked the Soviet head of Narkomindel's (Foreign Ministry's) Press and Information Department whether the Soviet government really believed that the West would attack the USSR in 1930, he was provided with the following explanation, which he shared with Arthur Henderson, the British foreign secretary.

> The danger was a serious one and ... Soviet apprehensions were not as ridiculous as we seemed to think. He (the unnamed Head of the Press and Information Department of the Foreign Ministry) did not mean to say that foreign governments were deliberately organizing a military offensive against the Soviet Union which would one day be launched. The Soviet press undoubtedly expressed itself in these terms, but the reason was that in explaining affairs to the masses extreme simplification was necessary.[94]

But although the propaganda was presumably intended to instill fear in the minds of the Soviet citizens as a means of extracting extraordinary sacrifices from them in the construction of socialism, it was difficult to strike a delicate balance between psychological mobilization and counterproductive fear inducement. As the following analysis suggests, the internally generated "war scare" of 1927 became externally driven with the Kuomindang seizure of the Chinese Eastern Railroad, jointly owned by the Chinese and Soviet governments, in 1929 and the Japanese invasion of Manchuria in 1931.[95] These military engagements made the case for increased defense expenditures more compelling to a broader coalition of party and military figures, as hard evidence from the archives indicates.

Conclusions

Although large budgetary allocations to the military became a standard feature of Soviet politics immediately preceding, during, and following World War II, there is little evidence that this was the case in the earliest years of Stalinist industrialization. At least until 1931, the military worked very hard to convince the party leadership that it deserved to be treated as a high budgetary priority. The threat of an impending attack on Soviet soil by hostile states, despite the propaganda, was remote and the party and military knew it. Stalin's political struggle for power in 1927 and 1928 made the threat of war a useful tool for insisting on party unity. Members of the High Command, however, were not deterred from trying to convince the party and government of its combat requirements. Tukhachevsky was among those who forcefully lobbied the party on behalf of defense. As this chapter illustrates in some detail, Kliment Voroshilov, Iosif Unshlikht, Romuald Muklevich, and others—including the economist Krzhizhanovskii—were vocal critics of the paltry attention paid to defense as reflected in unelaborated military plans and defense industrial targets. Information on the defense five year plan or annual plans, until recently, was scant. Most scholars relied on secondary sources and memoir accounts to glean insights into the early defense plans that were not very illuminating. According to one secondary source, the first "official" defense five-year plan was approved in May 1927, encompassing the years 1926-1929.[96] The same source went on to suggest that the 1927 plan did not address the "fundamental technical reconstruction of the RKKA" at all, but was merely tasked with completing measures and programs initiated during the period of the Frunze reforms (1924-1925).[97] Another source claimed that the first defense five year plan for the development and reconstruction of the armed forces between 1928 and 1932 was officially adopted in July 1928.[98] In late 1927, at the Fifteenth Party Congress, Voroshilov also made reference to the plan for defense as being separate from the general economic plan and one that would focus almost exclusively on the technical rearmament of the Red Army.[99]

Because military-related industrial targets were highly classified and therefore not readily accessible to the public, it was difficult to confirm the existence of a defense five year plan. In April 1928, an article in *Torgovo-promyshlennaia gazeta* implied that a five year plan for defense had yet to be worked out and suggested that military requirements were tied to industrial branches.[100] Citing the Gosplan version of the First Five Year Plan, von Boetticher found that the position of defense was accorded rather little weight in the framework of the general economy and that, at least as of 1929, no detailed plan for military development had been drawn up.[101]

Recently declassified documents from the Russian economic and military archives, however, have shed an enormous amount of light on this issue. They have illustrated that not only did defense plans (five year, three year, and annual plan versions) exist, but that they too were revised continuously over many months by numerous commissions and sections created by the government and the party. More importantly, as the economist Gleb Krzhizhanovskii and navy head Romuald

Muklevich suggested, these plans seldom met the needs of the Red Army. As the documentation from the military's financial directorate has implied, the military's "wish list" was cut back substantially by various economic commissions over time. Indeed, as the research of Lennart Samuelson has shown, only in 1938/1937 were defense five year plans truly adopted and armaments produced in mass quantities when the threat of war to the USSR became more tangible and the economy had the capacity to underwrite the production targets adopted by the Politburo.

It should be borne in mind that 1929 was also the year during which several key domestic programs were launched. The First Five Year Plan was officially adopted, all-out collectivization was launched, and the war on the kulaks was begun. The party's focus was primarily inward, not outward. But the invasion of Manchuria by Japan in 1931, which occurred during the fourth year of the First Five Year Plan, seemingly grabbed the attention of the party and refocused it on the military's needs. Stalin remarked at this time that the invasion prompted the temporary shutdown and conversion of several civilian factories to defense production. Because of this, many civilian-related targets for the year were not met. References in the press to the threat of war became more urgent and more consistent, and concern with military threats from the East, especially from Japan, were more pronounced in official party documents, as the next chapter illustrates.[102]

In 1932, according to one Soviet military historian, Stalin apologized to Tukhachevsky for having critically appraised his rearmament proposals and instead began to back many of his operational plans and weapons procurement plans. By 1934, at the Seventeenth Party Congress, Voroshilov announced that the party had "pushed all the right pedals" and the defense industries were beginning to produce high-quality tanks and other armaments. With three years of industrialization under its belt, the country was undoubtedly better positioned to meet the challenges of rearmament and to plan more "realistically" for the mass production of weapons as the defense industries gained much larger shares of total state capital investment between 1932 and 1937. Although many materials and parts were still purchased abroad, technological processes at home were permitting the innovative ideas of Tukhachevsky and others to move from paper onto the assembly line and finally into the hands and minds of the RKKA's soldiers.

Notes

1. James Q. Wilson takes exception to this view in *Bureaucracy: What Government Agencies Do and Why They Do It* (New York: Basic Books, 1989), pp. 116-120.

2. Morton Halperin, *Bureaucratic Politics and Foreign Policy* (Washington, DC: Brookings Institution, 1974), pp. 56-57.

3. S. P. Rosen, *Winning the Next War: Innovation and the Modern Military* (Ithaca: Cornell University Press, 1991), p. 252.

4. Lennart Samuelson, "Soviet Defence Industry Planning: Tukhachevskii and Military-Industrial Mobilisation, 1926-1937" (Ph.D. diss. Stockholm School of Economics, Sweden, 1996), pp. 199 and 207.

5. Valerian Kuibyshev, *Izbrannye proizvedeniia* (Moscow: Gos. izd-vo polit. lit-ry, 1958), p. 188, and RTsKhIDNI, F. 558, op. 1, d. 3000, l. 3.

6. R. W. Davies, "Soviet Military Expenditure and the Armaments Industry, 1929-1933: A Reconsideration," *Europe-Asia Studies,* Vol. 45, No. 4, 1993, pp. 577-608. Davies used archival records in the following archives: GARF (Gosudarstvennyi arkhiv Rossiiskoi Federatsii), RGAE (Rossiiskii gosudarstvennyi arkhiv ekonomiki), and RTsKhIDNI.

7. Ibid., p. 580.

8. Henry L. Roberts, "Maxim Litvinov," in Gordon Craig and Felix Gilbert, eds., *The Diplomats,* 1919-1939 (Princeton: Princeton University Press, 1953) pp. 350-351. His tune changed considerably once Hitler came to power, and by late 1933 he declared that the era of "bourgeois pacifism" had come to an end.

9. Ibid., pp. 582-583.

10. RGVA, "Spravka ob osnovnykh meropriatiiakh po usileniiu tekhnicheskoi moshchi i boevoi gotovnosti RKKA: Finansovyi plan NKVM na piatiletie 1928/1929-1932/1933," October 1929, F. 33988, op. 1, d. 638, l. 126 and 3 Oktober 1929, F. 33988, op. 1, d. 638, l. 227.

11. Perhaps the best treatment of the first plan is Eugene Zaleski's, *Planning for Economic Growth in the Soviet Union, 1918-1932* (Chapel Hill: University of North Carolina Press, 1971). See also Holland Hunter, "The Overambitious First Soviet Five-Year Plan," *Slavic Review,* no. 32, 1973, pp. 237-257; Naum Jasny, *Soviet Industrialization, 1928-1952,* (Chicago: University of Chicago Press, 1961), and R. W. Davies, *The Economic Transformation of the Soviet Union, 1913-1945* (Cambridge: Cambridge University Press, 1994) especially chapter 7.

12. Hunter, "The Overambitious First Soviet Five-Year Plan," pp. 240-241.

13. Throughout this thesis, the "First Five Year Plan" refers to Stalin's plan (1928/1929-1932/1933) for the development of the whole economy and should not be confused with the five year plans for individual economic sectors--such as the five year plan for metals (the Khrennikov-Gatran plan) or for industry (Kalinnikov plan)--which predated Stalin's plan. For a discussion

of these early plans, see Eugene Zaleski, *Planning for Economic Growth,* pp. 42-47.

14. The lack of any contradiction between Soviet economic growth in general and an increased military capability as discussed in the Soviet press has been documented thoroughly by Manfred von Boetticher in his excellent work, *Industrialisierungspolitik und Verteidigungskonzeptionen der UdSSR 1926-1930: Herausbildung des Stalinismus und 'äusere Bedrohung'* (Düsseldorf: Droste Verlag, 1979) especially pp. 206-219.

15. For a full accounting of the creation and function of Gosplan's Defense Sector and how it related to other civilian and defense planning entities, see Samuelson, "Soviet Defense Industry Planning," chapter 2.

16. von Boetticher, *Industrialisierungspolitik*, p. 8.

17. S. Ventsov, *Narodnoe khoziaistvo i oborona SSSR* (Moscow: Molodaia gvardiia, 1931), p. 46.

18. V. Bliukher, Speech at Sixteenth Party Congress, *Stenograficheskii otchet* (Moscow: Gosizdat, 1930), p. 13.

19. K. Mekhonoshin, "Metall-baza sotsialisticheskoi industrializatsii," *Izvestiia,* 16 June 1930, p. 4. Also see M. Andrew Hulse, "Soviet Military Doctrine, Militarization of Industry, and the First Two Five Year Plans", (Ph.D. diss., Georgetown University, 1990).

20. RGVA, F. 33988, op. 1, d. 638, l. 126.

21. Bruce Parrott, *Politics and Technology,* p. 3. In Stalin's review of the results of the First Five Year Plan at a central committee plenum in January 1933, he remarked that the two most important tasks of the plan had been to transform the USSR's "middle age technology" into new and modern types and to turn the weak, agrarian, and dependent state into an industrialized one free of "capitalist caprices." I. V. Stalin, *Sochineniia,* vol. 13 (Moscow: Gosizdat, 1952), p. 172.

22. Several Soviet and Western scholars have interpreted the first plan primarily as a means of creating a powerful military capability. See, for example, John Erickson, *The Soviet High Command: A Military-Political History, 1918-1941* (Boulder: Westview Press, 1984), p. 306 According to Erickson, "Defence requirements were heavily underwritten in the First Five Year Plan, for it was to be economic development in general but war industry in particular, with the aim of consolidating Soviet defensive power and guaranteeing economic stability in time of war" p. 302. "The only consumer interest considered (during the FFYP) was that of the armed forces" p. 322. According to Merle Fainsod, "From the beginning of [the First Five Year Plan] the equipment of the Red Army was given priority over all competing demands." See Fainsod, *How Russia Is Ruled* (Cambridge: Harvard University Press, 1953), p. 403. Jonathan Haslam wrote, "they also saw a real danger that war would soon envelop themselves along with their potential adversaries. ...Indeed, it was in a desperate attempt to insulate fortress Russia from such a threat that the Soviet leadership had embarked on a five-year plan of industrial construction in 1929." See Haslam, *Soviet Foreign Policy 1930-1933: The Impact*

of the Depression (New York: St. Martin's Press, 1983), p. 1. According to Malcolm Macintosh, "This [first five-year] plan began the industrialization of Russia and attached great importance to the complete modernization of the country's defence industry and the mechanization of the Red Army." See J. M. Macintosh, "The Red Army, 1920-1936" in B. H. Liddell Hart (ed.), *The Red Army* (New York: Harcourt Brace, 1956), p. 57. Julian Cooper and Manfred von Boetticher were the first scholars to dispel the myth that foreign threats were translated into a concentrated defense buildup from the outset of the First Five Year Plan. See Cooper, "Defence Production and the Soviet Economy," CREES Discussion Paper, University of Birmingham, 1976) and von Boetticher, *Industrialisierungspolitik,* 1979. The emphasis on heavy industry was also ideologically expedient. In *Das Kapital,* Marx illustrated that heavy industrial manufacturing should grow faster than investment and that by introducing change continuously to that sector, the growth of light industries would always suffer. Therefore, Stalin could point to important ideological roots to support his ambitious and painful industrialization program. See I. Moravchik, "The Priority of Heavy Industry as an Objective of Soviet Economic Policy, "*Soviet Studies,* vol. 17, 1965-1966, pp. 245-251.

23. I. V. Stalin, "Novaia obstanovka--novye zadachi khoziaistvennogo stroitel'stva," Speech at a convention of economists, 23 June 1931, *Sochineniia,* vol. 13, part V, p. 71.

24. I. V. Stalin, "Itogi pervoi piatiletki," 7 January 1933 Report to Plenum of TsK and TsKK, in *Sochineniia,* vol. 13, p. 172. Indeed, one Soviet economist stated that during the First Five Year Plan, the standard of living fell to the level of war communism. In the areas of housing, education, health, and social welfare, the situation either remained the same or regressed. "Thus, those economists and publicists who write that the five-year plan is being fulfilled satisfactorily are deceiving their readers." See Aron Iagov, *Piatiletka* (Berlin: Sotsialisticheskii vestnik, 1931), p. 132.

25. Ibid. See also Stalin, "Ob industrializatsii strany i o pravom uklone v VKP (b)", speech at TsK Plenum, 19 November 1928, in *Sochineniia,* vol. 11, pp. 245-262.

26. V. Kuibyshev, *Itogi i perspektivy khoziaistvennogo stroitel'stva SSSR,* (Moscow: Gosizdat, 1927), p. 42.

27. Eugene Zaleski analyzed the drafting of the five year plan in *Planning.* The "official" adoption of the First Five Year Plan occurred at the Fifth Congress of Soviets in May, 1929.

28. *Shest'nadtsataia konferentsiia vsesoiuznoi kommunisticheskoi partii (b), Stenograficheskii otchet* (Moscow: Gosizdat, 1929).

29. Ibid., pp. 24-25.

30. Voroshilov, "Oborona strany i sostoianie RKKA," 25 April 1927, *Stat'i i rechi* (Moscow: Partizdat, TsK VKP, 1936), p. 129.

31. Voroshilov, "Voprosy oborony i piatiletka," 13 December 1927, *Stat'i i rechi,* pp. 210-211. Mekhonoshin was also dissatisfied with the First Five Year Plan and the failure to manufacture enough nonferrous metals, p. 51. Ferrous

metallurgy, as numerous documents underscored, was the weakest industry and at the same time the most important for defense needs. See, for example, V. Kolesinskii, "Metallopromyshlennost' v piatiletke," *Voina i revoliutsia,* book 5, 1929, p. 22.

32. R. W. Davies, *The Economic Transformation of the Soviet Union,* p. 145.

33. R. W. Davies, "Soviet Military Expenditure," p. 583.

34. R. W. Davies, *The Economic Transformation,* p. 145.

35. Ibid., p. 144 and "Soviet Military Expenditure," p. 584.

36. Voroshilov, Rech' na XVI s"ezde VKP (b), 2 July 1930, *Stat'i i rechi,* pp. 440-441.

37. See Voroshilov, "K piatinadtsatiletiiu RKKA," (RVS Order no. 24, 1933) in *Stat'i i rechi,* pp. 543-546. Voroshilov even hailed Stalin's bravery in the civil war: "The name of Stalin, the best Leninist, the *vozhd* of the Bolshevik Party, the *vozhd* of all workers, is closely tied to the armed struggle and the construction of the Red Army. In the years of the civil war the party always sent comrade Stalin to the most dangerous and decisive fronts vital to the proletarian revolution." p. 544. Voroshilov's glorification of Stalin extends to the brochures he issued on Stalin's birthdays. On the occasion of Stalin's 60th birthday see K. E. Voroshilov, "Stalin i stroitel'stvo krasnoi armii" (Moscow: Gospolitizdat, 1941).

38. Voroshilov, "15 let krasnoi armii", 23 February 1933, *Stat'i i rechi,* p. 570.

39. Ibid., p. 566. See also, *KPSS i stroitel'stvo sovetskikh vooruzhennykh sil,* 1917-1964, (Moscow: Voenizdat, 1965), p. 175.

40. Voroshilov, "Rech' na XVII s"ezde", 30 January 1934, *Stati i rechi,* p. 601.

41. R.W. Davies, "Military Expenditure," p. 585.

42. Ibid., p. 145.

43. Ibid, p. 156. Davies showed a sharp reduction in capital investment to defense in 1933, however. Thus, it was not a steady climb.

44. Voroshilov, "Eshche sil'nee budem krepit' oboronu sovetskoi strany," speech at XVII s"ezde, *Stat'i i rechi,* p. 607. Voroshilov seemed to be joking with Sergo Ordzhonikidze (then head of the Commissariat of Heavy Industries which oversaw military enterprises) and Stalin."Comrade Stalin and other comrades have said a lot of good things about industry and I think that you won't get angry with me if I (laughter), upon thanking our glorious working class, engineers and industrial chiefs for good combat equipment, say something to them that is not altogether pleasant."

45. Ibid., pp. 607-608.

46. Albert and Joan Seaton, *The Soviet Army: 1918 to the Present* (New York: NAL Books, 1986), p. 59.

47. M. N. Tukhachevsky, "Voprosy sovremennoi strategii" (Moscow: *Voennyi Vestnik,* 1926), p. 16.

48. RGVA, F. 37605, op. 1, d. 2, l. 62.

49. M. Tukhachevsky, "Nepreryvnaia nedelia v krasnoi armii", *Krasnaia zvezda,* 8 September 1929, p. 2.

50. Ibid. Tukhachevsky's article spawned controversy and debate as not all officers relished the idea of working on the Sabbath. See also "Nepreryvnaia-v krasnoi armii," *Krasnaia zvezda,* 17 September 1929, p. 2, and 29 September 1929, p. 2. Tukhachevsky also frequently underscored the importance of combat training and skillful troops because "the more skillfully troops destroy the enemy, the more economical the conduct of war will be." *Voprosy sovremennoi strategii,* 1926, p. 20.

51. S. S. Biriuzov, "Voenno-teoreticheskoe nasledstvo M.N. Tukhachevskogo", *Voenno-istoricheskii zhurnal,* no. 2, 1964, pp. 37-49, and as the foreword to Tukhachevsky's selected works: *M.N. Tukhachevsky: Izbrannye proizvedeniia,* vol. 1 (Moscow: Voenizdat, 1964). See also, G. S. Isserson, "Zapiski sovremennika o Marshale Tukhachevskom," *Voenno-istoricheskii zhurnal,* no. 4, 1963, pp. 64-78. These are excerpts from Isserson's manuscript "Sud'ba polkvodtsa." According to Robert Conquest, "the Tukhachevsky group were legally rehabilitated by the Supreme Court and posthumously restored to party membership on February 27, 1957." *The Great Terror: A Reassessment* (New York: Oxford University Press, 1990), p. 479. Other articles on Tukhachevsky that appeared in connection with his rehabilitation include: Ia. Gorelik, "O polkovodcheskoi i voenn-nauchnot deiatel'nosti Marshala Sovetskogo Soiuza M.N. Tukhachevskogo," *Voenno-istoricheskii zhurnal,* no. 7, 1961, pp. 45-55; Ia. Gorelik, "O voenno-teoreticheskom nasledii M.N. Tukhachevskogo," *Voenno-istoricheskii zhurnal,* no. 2, 1963, pp. 107-114, and one of Tukhachevsky's never-before-published works, "Novye voprosy voiny", *Voenno-istoricheskii zhurnal,* no. 2, 1962, pp. 62-77. Two biographies of Tukhachevsky were also completed in 1963 and reviewed by Colonel S. Lipitskii in *Voenno-istoricheskii zhurnal,* no. 9, September 1964, pp. 94-101: L. Nikulin, *Tukhachevskii: Biograficheskii ocherk,* (Moscow: Voenizdat, 1963), and A. I. Todorskii, *Marshal Tukhachevskii* (Moscow: Gospolitizdat, 1963).

52. RGVA, Tukhachevsky to Voroshilov, 11 January 1930, Fond 33988, op. 2, d. 693 ch. 1, l. 58-65.

53. Ibid., p. 61. Tukhachevsky wrote, "The scale of the development of air and tank forces will be determined most correctly if we use as our point of departure the production possibilities *(proizvodstvennye vozmozhnosti)* instead of increasing existing [figures] of air and armoured forces to such and such a percentage."

54. Ibid., p. 62.

55. Ibid.

56. Ibid., p. 63.

57. Ibid., pp. 58-59.

58. Ibid., p. 59.

59. S. Biriuzov, "Voenno-teoricheskoe nasledstvo," p. 39. R. W. Davies has also discussed the Biriuzov and Isserson articles in his chapter on the

armament industries in *The Soviet Economy in Turmoil, 1929-1930* (Cambridge: Harvard University Press, 1989), pp. 446-448.

60. Ibid., p. 40.

61. Ibid.

62. Ibid.

63. Ibid.

64. Lennart Samuelson, "Mikhail Tukhachevsky and War-Economic Planning: Reconsiderations on the Pre-war Soviet Military Build-up," in *The Journal of Slavic Military Studies,* vol. 9, no. 4 (December 1996), p. 829.

65. Ibid., p. 827.

66. Ibid., p. 833.

67. Ibid.

68. S. Biriuzov, "Voenno-teoreticheskoe nasledstvo," p. 40.

69. RTsKhIDNI, F. 17, op. 2, d. 514 cited in R. W. Davies, "Soviet Military Expenditure," p. 589.

70. On May 12, 1927, British police raided the premises of the Soviet trade representatives and Anglo-Russian Cooperative Society (ARCOS); two weeks later, on May 26, the conservative party, headed by Chamberlain and Baldwin, cut off trade and diplomatic relations with Russia. See M. Borisov, *Podgotovka partiei nastupleniia sotsializma po vsemu frontu, 1926-1929* (Moscow, 1961) and *Foreign Affairs* (London), June 1927, p. 1.

71. For a thorough examination of the war scare's ideological context, see von Boetticher, chapter 2, "Die Interpretation der Kriegsgefahr in der Diskussion über die weitere Entwicklung des Kapitalismus," *Industrialisierungspolitik,* pp. 17-93.

72. A. G. Meyer noted that Bukharin was the "first of the Soviet leaders to sound a war alarm" when he spoke at the Fifth Moscow Regional Party Conference in January 1927. See "The War Scare of 1927," *Soviet Union/Union Sovietique,* 5, part. 1, 1978, pp. 4-6.

73. I.V. Stalin, "Revoliutsiia v Kitae i zadachi Kominterna," Rech' na X zasedanii VIII plenuma IKKI, 24 May 1927, in *Sochineniia,* vol. 9, p. 311. See also, somewhat later, "Zametki na sovremennye temy, Chast' I: Ob ugroze voiny," *Pravda,* 28 July 1927, in *Sochineniia,* vol. 9, pp. 322-330.

74. S. F. Cohen, *Bukharin and the Bolshevik Revolution: A Political Biography, 1888-1938* (Oxford: Oxford University Press, 1980), p. 316.

75. Ibid., Sheila Fitzpatrick, "The Foreign Threat during the First Five Year Plan," *Soviet Union,* no. 5, part I, pp. 26-35.

76. von Boetticher, *Industrialisierungspolitik,* pp. 30-40.

77. Ibid.

78. *Inprecorr* 7, no. 17 (3 March 1927), pp. 344-345, cited in A. G. Meyer, "The War Scare of 1927," *Soviet Union,* vol. 5, part I, 1978, p. 6.

79. Ibid., p. 13. V. Kliuchnikov and A. Shabanin, eds., *Mezhdunarodnaia politika noveishego vremeni v dogovorakh, notakh i deklaratsiiakh,* vol. 3, part I (Moscow: Litizdat, 1928), p. 398, cited in Meyer.

80. On June 9, 1927, just weeks after the rupture of British-Soviet diplomatic relations, Voroshilov said, "I personally believe that war is highly unlikely (*maloveriatno*)," "Krasnaia armiia i trudiashchikhsia SSSR--Na cheku," *Stat'i i rechi,* p. 139. By 1930, Voroshilov was predicting the outbreak of war in 3-4 years in his brochure *Budet li voina?* (Moscow: Moskovskii rabochii, 1930).

81. According to Voroshilov, "Defense allocations must correspond to the international situation." See his article, "Nedelia oborony" in *Pravda,* 17 July 1927, *Stat'i i rechi,* p. 145.

82. Voroshilov, "Voprosy voiny i piatiletka," *Stat'i i rechi,* p. 196.

83. Ibid.

84. "Ko vsem organizatsiiam VKP(b), ko vsem rabochim i krest'ianam," *Pravda,* 1 June 1927, reproduced in *KPSS o vooruzhennykh silakh sovetskogo soiuza* (Moscow: Voenizdat, 1969), pp. 240-242.

85. Osoaviakhim (*Obshchestvo sodeistviia oborone, aviatsionnomu i khimicheskomu stroitel'stvu)* the voluntary society of aviation and chemical defense, which later evolved into DOSAAF was the locus of military training and consciousness for the civilian population as well as a disseminator of military agitation and propaganda from 1927 until 1951. See the discussion of Osoaviakhim in Fedotoff-White, *The Growth of the Red Army,* pp. 288-290.

86. RGVA, 6 April 1929, Fond 33988, op. 1, d. 633, l. 130. The first "Defense Week" during which Osoaviakhim was assisted by the trade unions and party organization was apparently so successful that it brought in 600,000 new members and 10 million rubles.

87. See the entry for "Nedelia oborony" in *Sovietskaia voennaia entsiklopediia* (Moscow: Voenizdat, 1978), p. 567. The institutionalization of "Defense Week" is discussed in Malinovsky's report and in P. Tsel'min, "Pered tret'ei nedelei oborony: uchtem opyt proshlykh let," *Krasnaia zvezda,* 3 September 1929, p. 2.

88. The Congress lasted for six weeks, July 17-September 1, 1928.

89. S. Cohen, *Bukharin and the Bolshevik Revolution,* p. 292. See also von Boetticher's detailed analysis of the "Third Period" in *Industrialisierungspolitik,* pp. 70-93.

90. von Boetticher, *Industrialisierungspolitik,* pp. 76-81.

91. Ibid., p. 81.

92. K. A. Mekhonoshin, *Oborona v piatiletke* (Moscow: Plankhozgiz, 1930), p. 6.

93. Voroshilov, "Budet li voina?" in *Stat'i i rechi,* p. 428.

94. Strang (Moscow) to Henderson (London), 30.8.30, in *Documents on British Foreign Policy 1919-1939,* vol. VII (London, 1958), document 96, cited in Haslam, *Soviet Foreign Policy,* pp. 3-4.

95. According to one author, "In 1931 Japan captured Manchuria and began to prepare an attack on the USSR." V. M. Selovokhin, *Tank* (Moscow: Voenizdat, 1958), p. 36.

96. A. Iovlev, "Tekhnicheskoe perevooruzhenie Krasnoi Armii v gody pervoi piatiletki," *Voenno-istoriicheskii zhurnal,* No. 12, 1964, p. 4.

97. Ibid., p. 278.

98. A. Ryzhakov, "K voprosu o stroitel'stve bronetankovykh voisk krasnoi armii v 30-e gody," *Voenno-istoricheskii zhurnal*, no. 8, 1968, p. 105.

99. Voroshilov, "Voprosy oborony i piatiletka", 13 December 1927, *Stat'i i rechi*, pp. 208-209.

100. "Direktivy po sostavleniiu perspektivnogo plana" (VSNKh figures), 21 April 1928; *Torgovo-promyshlennaia gazeta*, 26 April 1928, p. 4 and V. Kolesinskii, "Metallopromyshlennost' v piatiletke," *Voina i revoliutsiia*, book 5, 1929, p. 27.

101. *Piatiletnii plan narodno-khoziaistvennogo stroitel'stva SSSR*, vol. I, Gosplan SSSR, 1929, p. 11, in von Boetticher, *Industrialisierungspolitik* p. 290.

102. See, for example, V. Molotov and V. Kuibyshev, "O vtoroi piatiletke," (Moscow: Partiinoe izdatel'stvo, 1932), p. 35.

3

The Impact of the Far East Threats and Encounters on Innovation

> Events on the Chinese Eastern Railway and the possibility of a repetition of conflict in the future force us to change fundamentally our view of the Far East region as a (mere) district in the rear. The economic and political interests of Japan in Manchuria signal the possibility of a future conflict in this theater with better-organized and stronger enemies.
>
> —Inspector of Artillery Grendal', 1930[1]

Military engagements in the Far East between 1929 and 1932 affected the Red Army in a number of ways. The 1929 conflict between Chinese Nationalist troops and RKKA units from the Siberian Military District over the Chinese Eastern Railroad (CER), owned jointly by the Soviet and Chinese governments, gave teeth to repeated proclamations about impending external threats to Soviet national interests.[2] Subsequently, the Japanese assault on Manchuria in September 1931 brought the Far East threat and the prospect of a two-front war in the future more clearly into focus for the party elite, and especially for Stalin. These encounters, in which RKKA troops were both directly and indirectly involved, were also beneficial to the Red Army's innovation. Primarily they convinced the Soviet leadership that the inevitability of war was more than an overused rhetorical tenet of Marxism-Leninism. The Chinese-Soviet border area, which erupted into conflict, provided a realistic testing ground for a variety of weapons prototypes and a laboratory in which to employ several innovative operational and tactical theories that had heretofore existed only on paper. The combat experience obtained during the Sungari offensive operation, according to N. F. Kuzmin, "enriched Soviet military art" and was taken into account in the 1936 Field Regulations as well as in drawing up a new section of the Field Regulations on the joint actions of ground and naval forces.[3]

Conflict in the Far East also had a significant impact on attention paid to and resources devoted to the military.[4] According to R. W. Davies, the Kuomindang seizure of the Chinese Eastern Railway in 1929 "strengthened the argument for an immediate effort to increase military strength, reinforcing the claim for expanding the military five-year plan at a time when all sectors of the economy were pressing for higher targets."[5] It appears that the Japanese invasion of Manchuria two years later, which placed the "Imperialists" closer to the Soviet border, had an even greater impact on the party and the concern with rearmament generally than had the seizure of the railway.[6] With the rise of fascism in Germany, the Soviet Union became militarily vulnerable on two fronts: in Europe and in the Far East. This enhanced military threat in the early 1930s appears to have led to greater awareness among party leaders that defense needs must be placed higher on the agenda and given priority in economic planning. In fact, Stalin stated in his speech on the results of the First Five Year Plan that the industrial output of the fourth year of the plan did not fully meet its targets because of production redirected to the military during the Japanese invasion of Manchuria the year before.[7]

The attitudes of the party and military toward the Far East and how they may have shaped decisions over resource allocations are examined in this chapter. The seizure of the CER clearly precipitated "extraordinary expenditures" that, while improving the Red Army's case vis-à-vis competing industrial sectors, probably also diverted resources that had been earmarked for some other military R&D projects, such as shipbuilding and port construction. Official party documents are reviewed to evaluate the increasing fear of Japanese intentions and, finally, the conflicts themselves are examined for their contributions to doctrinal and weapons innovations at this time.

The Chinese Eastern Railway Conflict as Propaganda Tool

The seizure of the CER and subsequent military clashes on the Chinese-Soviet border were extremely well publicized in the party and military press during the months of the conflict. From the seizure of the railway in mid-July until an agreement was reached in late December, bold-faced references to the Far East conflict and the attacks by "Nanking Bandits" made front-page headlines in *Pravda* and *Krasnaia zvezda* almost daily. It is therefore doubtful that this conflict was, as a U. S. correspondent at the time called it, "the war that nobody knew."[8]

As is evident from an analysis of the press at this time, all members of society—workers and peasants alike—were urged to rally around the Special Far East Army (Osobaia dal'nevostochnaia armiia or ODVA).[9] Those who made special or personal sacrifices on behalf of the Far East cause were lauded in the press for their heroism. The deputy chairman of the Voluntary Society for Air and Chemical Defense (Osoaviakhim), Iosif Unshlikht, appealed to trade union and Osoaviakhim members to become Red Army volunteers in support of the Far Eastern military effort and to contribute resources—even kopecks—for new weapons and equipment.

> Workers and servants of the many thousands of enterprises and laboring peasantry are collecting resources for the "Defense Fund" to strengthen the military-technical might of the RKKA and to construct new aircraft and tanks by means of call-ups, declarations of general meetings, special *subbotniki*, contributions of monthly salaries, and in the village, contributions of harvested [grain].[10]

On November 25, *Pravda* highlighted the generous contribution to the "defense fund" made by a civil war veteran who considered it his duty to donate his gold watch to the "defense against White bandits on the Chinese border."[11] As Voroshilov pointed out on the twelfth anniversary of the October Revolution, these generous contributions—"whole echelons of coal, steel, iron, bread, salt, obtained in addition to the [first five-year] plan"—were made during workers' days off and thus served as a "prime indicator of the similarity between the interests of defense and those of the entire working class and peasantry."[12] As mentioned earlier, the solicitation of contributions by the people to the defense fund was a worthwhile endeavor. During the first year of "Defense Week" some 10 million rubles were collected this way.[13]

Numerous documents from the Directorate of Military Finance attest to the "extraordinary expenditures" associated with the Far East conflict in 1929 that had not been budgeted previously.[14] The new combat formations alone cost some 60 million rubles; additional air force costs were roughly 11 million rubles. Other expenditures included maps, repairs, political work, coats, boots, and vaccinations.[15] Particularly costly were the secret agents deployed to Vladivostok, Chita, Blagoveshchensk, and Khabarovsk to report on the strength and intentions of "eastern enemies." According to a highly classified estimate of the financial directorate, the agents cost 7,000 rubles per month, or 84,000 rubles per year.[16]

That many of the costs were not anticipated is underscored by the inspector of the Red Army Infantry, A. Sediakin, who summarized the combat experience and training of troops in the Far East in a report written a few months after the conflict.[17] One of the main problems, according to General Bliukher, was the ill-informed conviction of the "center" (presumably the party) that military action was a remote possibility.[18]

> The armaments, technical equipment, communications apparatus, transportation, horses, and automobiles used during the operations still do not meet the minimum requirements of today. The infantry is armed with heavy machine guns which are absolutely unsuitable for combat ... spare parts for the guns are lacking ... Material-technical shortages plague the ODVA with extreme operational risks.[19]

On July 15, 1929, five days after the seizure of the CER, the central committee issued a resolution on the state of the USSR's defense.[20] The resolution was, indeed, very upbeat. It claimed that the Red Army had witnessed continual growth in the two years since the last defense resolution of May 1927 was issued. The troops had become more technically proficient; the territorial organization of the army had proved its usefulness; the quality of political education and living standards of the soldiers had improved; and their moral standing, despite the "internal political situation," remained stable.

Apparently, the reconstruction did not go very far between July 1929 and June 1930, when the Sixteenth Party Congress convened. This congress witnessed perhaps the most scathing remarks made heretofore by military and nonmilitary authorities about the improvement of the country's defense posture. Despite the Red Army's participation in the Far East conflict the previous year and the optimistic RVS resolution issued soon after the seizure, military spokesmen at the congress hammered their dissatisfaction home in articles both preceding and during the congress. A rather acrimonious article appearing in *Izvestiia* on the eve of the congress highlighted the negligible military improvements undertaken since the last party congress in 1927, and urged the attendees at the upcoming congress to take the issue more seriously.[21] General Bliukher stated quite bluntly that the ODVA's success in repulsing the "Nanking Bandits" in the fall of 1929 was "not the result of the best technical equipment or the best choice of personnel—no, comrades, in terms of technical quality the ODVA is not one of the RKKA's better-equipped units."[22] The remarks of the chief of the Red Navy, Romual'd Muklevich, were similarly blunt. He made clear that fundamental military requirements were not being addressed by economic and party authorities and that they were often needlessly "shrouded in secrecy," which to him was another way of admitting that nothing was being done.

> The shortsightedness of finalizing the industrial financial plan (*promfinplan*), without completing the defense targets can be very harmful to the military. When the issue concerns "peaceful" tasks our economists have concrete plans, figures and proposals. But with respect to defense factories—nothing. And more importantly, this "nothingness" is covered in secrecy. Our basic request is for industrial workers to turn exclusive attention to military work in peacetime and to fulfilling the control (planned) batches of military orders. The failure to accumulate experience, technical habits, equipment and qualified technical personnel for wartime is impermissible.[23]

According to materials from the Russian archives, the source of Muklevich's frustration was not only incompetent industrial workers shrouded in secrecy; his naval budget was under attack and he was asked to find ways of cutting it back substantially. At a lengthy RVS meeting in May 1928, naval proponents of a large shipbuilding program were attacked rather vehemently by Mikhail Tukhachevsky and Kliment Voroshilov. Despite these attacks and the reduced expenditures for the navy that accompanied them, Muklevich worked prodigiously to convince Gosplan and the Commissariat of Finance (Narkomfin) that it made no sense to halt the funding of projects in progress, such as ships being built, and suggested eliminating funds for the last two years of the First Five Year Plan instead of reducing monies allocated for the first two.[24]

Judging by the congress resolutions, the appeals for greater party focus on defense needs had little impact. Domestic imperatives clearly superseded appeals for defense requirements, with primary concern focused on the party's approval at the congress of a policy to wage war on the kulaks according to the slogan "Liquidate the Kulaks as a Class."[25] There was more concern in 1929 and 1930 for enlisting the Red Army's participation in the collectivization campaign and in battling the state's "internal enemies and saboteurs" than in training and equipping them for foreign military ventures.[26] Indeed, a particularly amusing example of the party's propaganda was contained in a critique of several combat units within the Special Far East Army's Sakhalin regiment, whose members, although actively involved in combat against the Chinese at the time, were not able to satisfactorily answer any questions on the five year plan or collectivization put to them by their political instructors.[27] This poor performance must have been particularly irksome to the political directorate (PURKKA), which apparently allocated 50 percent more funds to the political training of ODVA troops than to any other military district.[28]

Party Documents Reflect New Concerns for Far East

It appears that a reassessment of defense requirements took place within the party leadership as a result of the invasion of Manchuria by Japan in September 1931. Stalin's report on the results of the First Five Year Plan, delivered in January 1933, is very revealing in this regard. He claimed that the plan's targets had not been met on account of the startup time required for some sixty factories[29] to convert to weapons production for the Far East. This delay, in turn, meant that production targets of the 1932 annual plan were not met.[30] Several Soviet and Western sources have referred to the approval of an abbreviated, three-year defense plan for 1931-1933, highlighting the significance of the Japanese invasion.[31] According to Marshal Zhukov, the 1931–1933 plan was the most extensive plan for military development contained within the military's First Five Year Plan and the findings of R. W. Davies cited in the last chapter certainly support Zhukov's assertion.[32] A close inspection of the speeches and resolutions of the Seventeenth Party Conference in 1932 and the Seventeenth Party Congress in 1934 also reveals a more serious attitude toward the Far Eastern threat that may have been translated into more substantial military allocations in the last years of the First Five Year Plan.[33] In his opening remarks at the Seventeenth Party Conference, the Chairman of both the Council of Peoples Commissariat (Sovnarkom) and the Council of Labor and Defense (STO),[34] Viacheslav Molotov, stated:

> The events in the Far East demand our serious vigilance and readiness for surprises from the militaristic bourgeois circles abroad ... White guardists in Manchuria and in Paris are openly making plans to divide the USSR from the Far East and create, with foreign support, a "buffer state" in the Far East, in collusion with the international scoundrels of the General Gaida type and his gang of thieves.[35]

Two years later, at the Seventeenth Party Congress, Molotov's opening remarks echoed the same concerns, and he pressed for "special attention" to improving the country's military prowess in light of the situation in the Far East.[36] Stalin also drew special attention to the Far East threat, underscoring that Japan's refusal to sign a nonaggression pact illustrated the tension in the relationship, and he called for undertaking a "number of measures" to prepare the country to defend itself from an Eastern attack and to teach potential invaders to "mind their own business."[37] Voroshilov also made reference to the fact that for the past two years, presumably 1932–1933, the central committee had devoted itself to the Far East problem and that Stalin was "completely preoccupied" with it.[38] Stalin's interest in the Far East conflict is revealed in an interesting note he sent to Tukhachevsky in November 1931, to which he attached a newspaper clipping indicating that the Japanese were purchasing English motors for their hydroplanes, and asked how the Soviet motor construction—whose horsepower he believed surpassed that of the Japanese—was coming along.[39] He also seemed to suggest that if the Japanese-Chinese conflict in Manchuria were to continue, powerful hydroplanes would be quite beneficial to the Japanese and presumably could pose a threat to the USSR. Perhaps it is "no coincidence" that "top secret" plans for the development of the Far East—including the construction of a hydroplane factory in Khabarovsk—were adopted by the Politburo Defense Commission a few months later.[40]

Vasilii Bliukher's remarks at the congress seemed to confirm that the revisions to the defense five year plan—to which Stalin refers—resulted in the shipment of equipment to the Far East sometime after 1930. In contrast to his negative portrayal of the quality of ODVA troops and equipment at his disposal in 1929, Bliukher was somewhat more satisfied with the border reinforcements he received two years later and went on to describe those measures as including the deployment of high-caliber troops and the shipment of numerous tanks, aircraft, and equipment to the Far East.[41] He noted in particular that the tanks and aircraft he received were the "fruits" of the First Five Year Plan.[42] How these tanks and aircraft were employed in the Far East encounters and how these encounters advanced military tactics and operational art are examined in the next section.

Military Encounters in the Far East

Background

A significant challenge to Soviet national interests in the Far East occurred on July 10, 1929, when Chinese Kuomindang troops seized the

Chinese Eastern Railroad in retaliation for the alleged active spreading of communist propaganda by the Soviets in southern Manchuria and because the Chinese wanted to replace the Soviet administrator of the railroad, A. I. Yemshanov, with Chinese appointees.[43] However, this aggressive act did not come as a total surprise to the Soviet leadership. Since 1924, the CER had been plagued by considerable tension between the Manchurian nationalist government and the Soviet railroad employees whose propaganda cells were feverishly recruiting Chinese communists in the area. On several occasions, Chinese General Chang Tso-lin used force to try to check Soviet communist influence around the railway.[44] In fact, Chang Tso-lin seized property belonging to the railway as early as 1924, foreshadowing the 1929 railway seizure.[45] Following the arrest of Russian and Chinese participants in a Comintern conference by Manchurian authorities in May 1929, Japanese and Chinese authorities agreed to seize the Chinese Eastern Railroad. On July 10, 1929, the plan was carried out.[46] According to *Pravda,* Manchurian authorities captured the railway's telegraph system, thereby severing all communications with the USSR.[47] They also sealed off the Soviet trade representative's headquarters and searched and arrested some 200 Soviet railroad employees.[48] Simultaneously, combat-ready Manchurian troops and Russian White Guard detachments were reportedly deployed to the Soviet border.[49] Although it was generally agreed that this "aggressive act" required a strong response, the type of response was a topic of controversy within the party and military elite for many weeks thereafter.[50] Voroshilov and Bliukher reportedly favored military intervention early on, while Stalin and Molotov opposed it until sometime in the fall of 1929.

According to Maxim Litvinov's memoirs, the seizure of the railway necessitated a military response, but this idea was initially opposed by Molotov and "Koba" (a Georgian nickname for Stalin).[51] Voroshilov's confidence in a military operation apparently echoed that of General Bliukher, who was "certain we could destroy the Chinese in the first border encounter. [The Chinese] have no troops worthy of the name. The White Guard auxiliary forces are small and riddled with our agents."[52]

It now appears that the delay in dispatching troops was due to Stalin's own reluctance. He initially opposed the operation but decided to back it in October when he realized that it could prove an auspicious opportunity for a revolutionary uprising. In a letter he wrote to Molotov in early October, Stalin recommended that instead of isolated detachments, "two double regiment brigades, chiefly made up of

Chinese," be dispatched to Manchuria to "stir up rebellion" and then occupy Harbin, overthrow the government, and create a revolutionary one.[53]

The most immediate Soviet response to the seizure of the railway was the War Commissariat's order, two days later, to concentrate units of the Siberian Military District on the Manchurian border in both the Dauri and Nikolsk-Ussuriiskii regions.[54] It was also requested that these units be fully equipped and supplied with the necessary credits immediately.[55] On August 6, 1929, Revvoensovet Order No. 227/41 was issued, calling for the creation of a Special Far Eastern Army (ODVA)[56] headquartered in Khabarovsk and commanded by the Soviet civil war hero with considerable military experience in the Far East, General Vasilii Bliukher, along with the celebrated military-political worker, N. E. Donenko, and Chief of Staff, A. Ia. Lapin.[57] The ODVA consisted originally of five rifle divisions from a variety of military districts in Siberia, the Caucasus, and the Far East, two cavalry brigades from the Kuban, the Far East, and Buriatia, and five companies of Volga Germans and a battalion of Koreans, most of whom, it was underscored, were politically reliable.[58] In addition, new formations were established in the Siberian, Byelorussian, and Central Asian Military Districts, and extra units were placed in the Moscow, Leningrad, and Ukrainian Military Districts to reinforce the western borders.[59] All told, this came to an additional 24,267 troops and 3,926 horses—figures that clearly exceeded the projected defense manpower needs of the First Five Year Plan.[60]

Throughout August and September, border raids by the Chinese were denounced daily in the Soviet press. Not until October, however, did the ODVA really swing into action with its first offensive on the Sungari River, destroying the "Manchurian militarists" with a combined ground force and naval flotilla assault-landing (*desant*) operation.[61] According to formerly classified documents, the Sungari operation resulted in 200 Chinese and 5 Red Army casualties.[62] The final and grandest offensive against the Kuomindang troops was launched on November 17 and went down in the annals of Soviet military history as the army's first encirclement operation carried out with successful airpower cover of tank units on the ground.[63] It should also be noted that these combat operations created opportunities to test some of the early Soviet tank prototypes in the field, such as the T-26 and BT (fast tank).[64]

The Sungari River Operation[65]

According to some accounts, provocation by the Chinese, manifested in the shooting of fishermen and Soviet border troops, began to escalate in August. On September 1, Chinese "diversionary bands" began to cross the border more frequently. On October 12, the enemy mined the river from the mouth of the Sungari River. Later that day, a combat group of the ODVA, composed of the Amur flotilla[66] and the Second Amur Rifle Division, received orders to launch a response strike. Specifically, these units were ordered to destroy the Sungari flotilla and break up enemy reinforcements in the city of Lakhasusu. The head of the RKKA staff, A. Ia. Lapin, was given command of the operation, which consisted of a naval infantry assault with air support. The monitor ship, *Krasnyi buriat,* opened fire on the enemies' reinforced areas. After overcoming enemy resistance, the assault team began its approach to enemy strongholds. By midday, Lakhasusu was encircled and captured. On October 30, the Amur flotilla was given another command to undertake a seventy-kilometer cruise along the Sungari River from Lakhasusu to Fukden with the aid of the rifle division and air support. Although conditions were tough because the water was becoming icy, the Chinese enemy sank six barges. Then the commander decided to conduct a raid on Fukden. Soviet air support overcame the enemy's coastal artillery attacks and sunk all the enemy ships, including a cruiser. Once on land, the assault forces took the offensive and after three hours captured Fukden.

In addition to offering a realistic stage on which to practice, the Sungari operation provided lessons for combined arms operations, especially air-ground assault-landings, which were subsequently incorporated into Red Army Field Regulations. These lessons included: the importance of supplying assault landings onto hostile shores with ground-based and ship-based artillery cover and air support, the importance of including a reinforced rifle regiment in the assault-landing force composition, and the logic of combining the actions of ground and river flotilla troops under one command when they were performing a single mission.[67]

The Dalainor-Man'chzhurskaia Railroad Operation[68]

This offensive operation was undertaken by troops of the Zabaikal group of the ODVA in the region of the Manchurian and Dalainor railroad station on November 17-20.[69] The renewed Chinese threat to the Trans-Baikal and other regions of the Soviet Far East, as manifested in the concentration of enormous forces along the border and continued provocation against Soviet vessels, impelled the central committee to choose a military response. On the morning of November 17, Soviet troops began the offensive. The fifth detachment of the cavalry brigade bypassed the Dalainor grouping and seized the railroad, cutting off the Dalainor railroad station from the central regions of the country. The units of the 35th Rifle Division fell in behind the cavalry and captured the Argun' station, thereby completing the encirclement of Dalainor. One day later, the Dalainor grouping was destroyed. Soviet troops then regrouped and launched an attack against the Manchurian grouping, eventually leading to an encirclement of Chinese troops at the Manchurian railroad station on November 19. By November 20 the garrison capitulated. The conflict ended officially on December 22, when the Khabarovsk protocol was signed by the USSR and China, restoring the status of the CER and releasing the Soviet prisoners.

One of the most innovative tactical measures employed in this operation was a mobile group composed of trains and infantry in echelons and in cars that pursued withdrawing enemy troops. This was also the first time that an encirclement operation, employing Soviet MS-1 tanks and aircraft together with combined arm formations, had been used since the civil war.

The "Manchurian Incident" of 1931

Kliment Voroshilov's trip to the Far East during the summer of 1931 certainly underscored the Red Army's readiness to defend its borders in the event of hostilities originating in Japan—which were not an idle possibility.[70] According to new research by Jonathan Bone, the Voroshilov visit transcended mere diplomatic gestures and Stalinist propaganda: Voroshilov was there on orders of the Politburo to choose a location for a new shipyard, in addition to reviewing the territory for other defense-related uses including the construction of naval bases, and to devise ways of protecting the rail links from Japanese expansion and interruption.[71] Indeed, the Japanese invasion of northern China and gradual occupation of Manchuria, which took place between mid-September 1931 and February 1932, was viewed with alarm and rapidly spurred the substantial rearming of the border with China.[72] It also marked, according to John Erickson, "the first stage of the Kwantung Army's private conquest of Manchuria."[73] Military precautions and diplomatic gestures were initiated, but Litvinov and Stalin were careful not to support either side and to declare a policy of strict neutrality. At a meeting of the Politiburo's Defense Commission in January 1932, a program responding to the Japanese occupation of Manchuria was adopted, providing for the prompt deployment of troops and equipment to the Transbaikal, Mongolian Peoples Republic, and Far East regions.[74] Rifle divisions, tank battalions, howitzer divisions, and air force squadrons were mobilized and deployed to these regions; thousands of officers were called up; and the manpower of the border and railway troops in the Far East was beefed up considerably.[75] Plans for building up coastal defenses, creating fuel depots, and laying communications lines were discussed, as well as longer-term objectives such as building munitions bases in eastern Siberia, hydroplane factories in Khabarovsk, and other naval facilities.[76] On February 1, 1932, 160 aircraft were allocated to the Far East, forming the 78th Fighter and 105th Heavy Bomber Squadrons.[77] Naval forces for the region were created with the birth of the Soviet Pacific Fleet in April 1932, submarine trials were initiated, aircraft and tanks were brought in, and by the spring of 1932 some 100,000 troops had arrived.[78] The number of troops doubled in the Far East between 1929 and 1932.[79] Indeed, as John Erickson notes, the military presence there "became a severe but profitable training school from which several senior Soviet officers gained invaluable experience."[80]

In addition to these significant military reinforcements, the RKKA troops' role gradually shifted, in the aftermath of the Japanese invasion, from a combat to an agricultural and economic orientation, with the ultimate objective of making these Far East regions into independent economic entities.[81] In March 1932, the Special Agricultural Corps (Osobyi Kolkhoznyi Korpus), of some 60,000 persons, including three rifle divisions and one cavalry division, was formed to keep the borders secure and to help with collectivization and economic development of the region generally. But harassment of Soviet citizens in the border regions continued unabated. In April 1932, Japanese police arrested 150 Soviet citizens in Harbin, accusing them of trying to explode a railroad bridge at the Sungari II station.[82]

Traditionally, these Far East encounters have been underrated by scholars of the Red Army probably because in the grand scheme of things they seemed peripheral when compared with the Polish-Romanian and later German threats to the Soviet Union's western borders. But when examined in the context of the First Five Year Plan, the profound impact of these Far East military engagements on defense prioritization is undeniable. The 1929 CER conflict was the first time that troops were committed to battle after the 1927 war scare propaganda was launched, thereby giving that initiative credence—the "threat" of war now became a tangible reality. Although the conflict did not appear to lead immediately to increased party attention to military requests and requirements, as party documents from official conferences and congresses suggest, it did provide real combat opportunities for employing new operational and tactical theories.

With the invasion and occupation of Manchuria, renamed Manchukuo in 1931, came the specter of war with Japan. As the documentation from party conference and congress resolutions and economic analyses implies, heightened concern among party members for the prospect of a two-front war, in the East and West, led to the introduction of a special, far more comprehensive defense plan for the years 1931–1933 in the short run and helped to make defense a higher priority in the long run.

Notes

1. RGVA, "Inspekora Artillerii RKKA o neobkhodimykh meropriatiiakh po podniatiiu boegotovnosti i usileniiu artillerii ODVKA," F. 33987, op. 1, d. 680, l. 76.

2. Over time these units were reinforced with those of many other military districts. See Z. Sh. Ianguzov, *OKDVA na strazhe mira i bezopasnosti SSSR* (Khabarovsk: Khabarovskoe knizhnoe iz-vo, 1970), p. 26.

3. Ibid., p. 135.

4. R. W. Davies, "Soviet Defense Industries During the First Five-Year Plan," CREES Discussion Paper, no. 27 (University of Birmingham, 1987).

5. Ibid., p. 4.

6. R. W. Davies, "Military Expenditure and the Armaments Industry, 1929-33: A Reconsideration," *Europe-Asia Studies*, vol. 45, no. 4 (1993), p. 584. Davies also links the preparation of the 1932 annual plan to the Japanese invasion of Manchuria in September 1931. He notes that W. H. Chamberlain, a British journalist who visited Soviet factories at this time, was perhaps the first to appreciate and indeed record the impact of the Japanese invasion on defense production and concern generally. W. H. Chamberlain, *Russia's Iron Age* (Boston: 1934), cited in Davies, p. 578.

7. I.V. Stalin, "Itogi pervoi piatiletki," 7 January 1933, *Sobranie Sochineniia*, vol. 13, p. 180.

8. Eugene Lyons, *Assignment in Utopia* (New York, 1937), cited in Lih et al., *Stalin's Letters to Molotov* (New Haven: Yale University Press, 1995), p. 34.

9. In February 1930 the ODBA's name was changed to OKDVA, the K (*krasnoznamennaia*, or Red Banner) awarded for outstanding combat performances in the fall 1929 offensives.

10. I. S. Unshlikht, "Bol'she sredstv v fond oborony, bol'she samoletov i tankov dlia krasnoi armii," *Krasnaia zvezda,* 5 September 1929, p. 1. It should be noted that these "contributions" (*otchisleniia)* were not really voluntary--rather, they were imposed by group pressure at factory and collective farm meetings. Osoaviakhim and other voluntary organizations were frequently reported as sending gifts to the ODVA in the form of soap, warm clothing, and cigarettes. See, for example, "Osoaviachim shlet podarki Osoboi Dal'nevostochnoi," *Krasnaia zvezda,* 29 October 1929, p. 4. According to one document in 1929, the amount spent on gifts for the ODVA troops totaled 12,700 rubles. RGVA, Fond 33988, op. 1, d. 633, l. 2.

11. "Na ukreplenie vozdushnykh sil SSSR," *Pravda,* 25 November 1929, p. 1.

12. Voroshilov, "Tov. Voroshilov—Osoboi dal'nevostochnoi," *Krasnaia zvezda,* 7 November 1929, p. 2.

13. RGVA, Fond 33988, op. 1, d. 633, l. 130. More than half of this amount was collected by the trade unions.

14. RGVA, NKVM, and RVS to STO, "Ob otpuske sredstv sverkh smety NKVM na raskhody, sviazannye s konfliktom na KVZhD," F. 51, op. 2, d. 328, l. 119-120.

15. See many of the documents from the military financial directorate, RGVA, Fond 51, opis' 2, dela 167, 328, and Fond 33988, op. 1, d. 638.

16. RGVA, F. 51, op. 2, d. 167, l. 16-17.

17. RGVA, Fond 33987, op. 1, d. 680, l. 5-27.

18. Ibid.

19. Ibid., l. 17 and 25.

20. "O sostoianii oborony SSSR," iz postanovleniia TsK VKP, 15 July 1929, in *KPSS o vooruzhennykh silakh: dokumenty* (Moscow: Voenizdat, 1969), pp. 264-266.

21. S. Ventsov and I. Petukhov, "Voennoe stroitel'stvo k XVI s"ezdu", *Izvestiia,* 26 June 1930, p. 4.

22. Bliukher, "Rech' at XVI S"ezd," *Stat'i i rechi* (Moscow: Voenizdat, 1963), p. 105.

23. Remarks by R. Muklevich at the Sixteenth Party Congress, *Stenograficheskii otchet* (Moscow: Gosizdat, 1930), pp. 506-507.

24. RGVA, F. 33988, op. 1, d. 638, l. 41-46. See especially Muklevich's inquiry about his budget cuts for 1929/1930 to Unshlikht, 12 October 1929, p. 75. He called the revised shipbuilding figure "absurd" and refused to accept the prescribed annual figure. The reductions came out of shipbuilding, port construction, and coastal defense.

25. Ibid., pp. 711-712.

26. The army's key role in assisting the collectivization, as in training villagers to become collective farmers, was often discussed in the press. See "Krasnaia armiia—rychag kollektivizatsii," *Krasnaia zvezda,* 5 September 1929; "Chego zhdet Kolkhoztsenti ot Krasnoi armii," *Krasnaia zvezda,* 22 September 1929; "Krasnaia armiia sodeistvuet uspekhu khlebozagotovok," *Krasnaia*

zvezda, 25 October 1929; *Izvestiia,* 26 June 1930. Many articles also focused on alleged wrongdoings by the kulaks in an effort to promote the soldiers' antipathy toward them. See "Mest' klassovogo vraga: Kulaki tiazhelo ranili komandira vzvoda," *Krasnaia zvezda,* 11 October 1929, and "Kak maskiruetsia kulak," *Krasnaia Zvezda,* 23 October 1929. For the fullest treatment of the Red Army's role in collectivization, see Roger Reese, "Red Army Opposition to Forced Collectivization," *Slavic Review,* vol. 55, no. 1 (Spring 1996).

27. "Kommunisty osoboi dal'no-vostochnoi na boevom postu," *Krasnaia zvezda,* 19 October 1929, p. 3.

28. RGVA, F. 51, op. 2, d. 167, l. 43.

29. Strang (Moscow) to Simon (London), 8.4.32, *Documents of British Foreign Policy,* document 184, cited in Haslam, *Soviet Foreign Policy,* p. 84. Karl Radek disseminated the line that this diversion of resources and productive capacity to defense needs was responsible for the food shortages leading to the famine of 1932–1933.

30. Stalin, *Sochineniia,* vol. 13, p. 180. Davies has recently suggested that defense expenditures in 1932 greatly exceeded the "official" version. See "Military Expenditures," pp. 581–582.

31. *Piat'desiat' Let,* p. 197, cited in Davies, *Soviet Defense Industries,* p. 11, and in von Boetticher, *Industrialisierungspolitik und Verteidigungskonzeptionen der UdSSR* (Köln: Droste Verlag, 1979), and Haslam, *Soviet Foreign Policy,* chapter 8. The plan's existence is confirmed now by archival documents: RGVA, "Perechen' orgmeropriatii po planu stroitel'stva RKKA na 1931–1933," F. 33988, op. 1, d. 638, l. 15.

32. See Zhukov's memoirs, *Vospominaniia i razmyshlenniia,* vol. 1 (Moscow: Novosti Press, 1983), pp. 142–143.

33. See, for example, A. Kadishev, *Voennaia opasnost' i zadachi oborony SSSR* (Moscow: Partizdat, 1932), pp. 18–19.

34. The STO, according to Alec Nove, was the "effective economic-military cabinet" of Sovnarkom, whose members included the chairman of VSNKh and the commissars of war, labor, transportation, agriculture, supply, and a representative of the trade unions. See Nove, *An Economic History of the USSR,* p. 100.

35. Molotov's remarks, *XVII Konferentsiia VKP,* 30 January 1932, *Stenograficheskii otchet,* (Moscow: Partizdat, 1932), p. 7.

36. Molotov's remarks at *XVII S"ezd VKP,* 26 January 1934, *Stenograficheskii otchet,* p. 6.

37. Ibid., Stalin's Report, p. 14.

38. Ibid., Voroshilov's Report, p. 235.

39. RGVA, F. 33988, op. 2, d. 700, l. 8–10.

40. RGVA, F. 9, op. 29, d. 165, l. 161–195, cited in Jonathan Bone, "Building Komsomol'sk na Amure," chapter of a dissertation-in-progress, "Socialism in a Far Country: Development and Socioeconomic Change in the Soviet Far East" (University of Chicago, forthcoming).

41. Bliukher, *Stenograficheskii otchet XVII s"ezda,* 26 January 1934, p. 630.

42. Ibid.

43. Reference to the seizure did not appear in *Pravda* until July 14, presumably because of the Chinese capture of all the railroad's communications lines, including those with Moscow. See "Reshitel'nyi protest sovetskogo pravitel'stva protiv banditskogo naleta na K.-V.Zh.D.," *Pravda,* 14 July 1929, p. 1, and Lars Lih et al., *Stalin's Letters to Molotov* , p. 147. The full accounting of political and diplomatic aspects of the conflict is contained in David Dallin, *The Rise of Asia* (New Haven: Yale University Press, 1949).

44. Dallin, *The Rise of Asia,* p. 256.

45. Ibid.

46. Ibid., pp. 259–260.

47. "Reshitel'nyi protest," *Pravda,* 14 July 1929, p. 1.

48. Ibid.

49. Ibid.

50. Maxim Litvinov, *Notes for a Journal* (New York: William Morrow, 1955).

51. Litvinov, *Notes,* pp. 126 and 180. Koba was the name of the hero from a story by Chonkadze entitled "Surami Castle," with whom Stalin identified as a young boy. See Joseph Iremaschwili, *Stalin und die Trägodie Georgiens* (Berlin, 1932), p. 18, cited in Tucker, *Stalin as Revolutionary,* pp. 79–80.

52. Litvinov, *Notes,* p. 180.

53. Lih et al., *Stalin's Letters to Molotov,* Letter no. 51, p. 182.

54. RGVA, 12 July 1929, F. 51, op. 2, d. 270, l. 1. On July 16, a dozen more reinforcements to these two regions were authorized.

55. Ibid.

56. The Special Far East Army's name was officially changed from ODVA to OKDVA (Osobaia Krasnoznamennaia Dal'ne-vostochnaia armiia or Special Red Banner Far East Army) on February 7, 1930, as a result of having been awarded in January the prestigious Order of Red Banner for the army's successful offensive operations in the fall of 1929. RGVA, Fond 33879, op. 1, introduction.

57. Ibid. See also M. V. Zakharov, *General'nyi Shtab v predvoennye gody* (Moscow: Voenizdat, 1989), p. 41; V. Dushen'kin, *Ot soldata do marshala: zhizn' i boevoi put' marshala sovetskogo soiza V.K. Bliukher* (Moscow: Gosizdat, 1960); and A. I. Kartunova, *Bliukher v Kitae* (Moscow: Glavnaia redaktsiia vostochnoi literatury, 1979). Bliukher, who was among those murdered in the purge of the High Command in 1937, remains among the most admired and revered military heroes in Russia.

58. *Krasnoznamennyi dal'nevostochnyi: Istoriia krasnoznamennogo dal'nevostochnogo voennogo okruga,* 3d ed. (Moscow: Voenizdat, 1985), p. 91.

59. RGVA, "Spravka o novykh formirovaniiakh v sviazi s sobytiiam na dal'nem vostoke i perebroskoi tuda voiskovykh chastei iz vnutrennikh

okrugov," F. 33988, op. 1, d. 638, l. 34. There is also evidence that the border troops (*pogranichniki*), who were suffering the most harm from Chinese border provocations, were being ignored by the ODVA troops. See one appeal to them in "Dal'nevostochniki—My s Vami!," *Krasnaia zvezda*, 10 September 1929, p. 4. For a fuller description of the border troops' role in 1929, see V. Bogdanov and I. Bokan, *Vsegda v boevom dozore: ocherk istorii voisk krasnoznamennogo dal'nevostochnogo pogranichnogo okruga* (Khabarovsk, 1980), pp. 50–79.

60. RGVA, Fond 33988, op. 1, d. 638, l. 34.

61. N. F. Kuz'min, *Na strazhe mirnogo truda 1921–1941* (Moscow: Voenizdat, 1959), p. 135. The first public mention of the ODVA's military action of October 12, 1929, appeared on October 18. See TASS communique, "Chasti krasnoi armii dali reshiltel'nyi otpor kitaiskomu desantu," *Krasnaia zvezda*, 18 October 1929, p. 1.

62. RGVA, F. 33988, op. 1, d. 677, l. 3. A recently published book provides the numbers of casualties suffered by Russia in its wars and conflicts between 1918 and 1989. In the 1929 conflict, according to this book, the Chinese had 1,035 total casualties and the Soviets had 143. See G. F. Krivosheev, ed., *Grif sekretnosti sniat: poteri vooruzhennykh sil SSSR v voinakh, boevykh deistviiakh i voennykh konfliktakh* (Moscow: Voenizdat, 1993), pp. 65–66.

63. Kuz'min, *Na strazhe*, p. 134. Kuz'min also pointed out that there were numerous organizational mistakes in both operations; the experience was not purely one of combat successes.

64. V.D. Mostovenko, *Tanki* (Moscow: Voenizdat, 1956), pp. 48-49 and 80. See also John Milsom, *Russian Tanks* (London: Arms and Armour Press, 1970), p. 29.

65. The description of this operation is drawn from Dushenkin, *Ot soldata do Marshala;* TASS report in *Krasnaia Zvezda,* 18 October 1929, p. 1; and Ianguzov, *OKDVA*, pp. 46-60.

66. The history of the Amur flotilla, including its role in this operation, is discussed in detail in V. N. Bagrov and N. F. Sungorkin, *Krasnoznamennaia amurskaia flotiliia* (Moscow: Voenizdat, 1976), pp. 90–102.

67. Kuz'min, *Na strazhe,* pp. 134–135.

68. See the lengthy discussion of this operation in Ianguzov, *OKDVA*, pp 77-96, and the memoirs of Marshal V. Chuikov, "O konflikte na KVZhD," *Voenno-istoricheskii zhurnal,* no. 7, 1976, pp. 53–57.

69. This description of the Dalainor operation is drawn chiefly from the entry "Man'chzhuro-Chzhalinorskaia operatsiia 1929" in the *Soviet Military Encyclopedia* (Moscow: Voenizdat), pp. 127–128. See also Dushenkin, pp. 110–111, and the front page reports in *Krasnaia Zvezda* and *Pravda* , 23 November, 1929.

70. John Erickson, *The Soviet High Command,* p. 335. Japanese sources admitted that a war plan against the Soviet Union was drawn up in 1930.

71. Jonathan Bone, "Building Komsomol'sk-na-Amure" (forthcoming).

72. Ianguzov noted the enthusiasm with which the demobilized RKKA troops in the Far East signed up to assist with collectivization drives there. See *OKDVA* p. 104.

73. Erickson, *The Soviet High Command,* p. 335.

74. Bone, "Komsomol'sk na Amure," p. 7. Bone cites the top secret resolution concerning the defense buildup in the Far East region from RGVA, F. 9, op. 29, d. 165, l. 161–195.

75. Ibid.

76. Ibid., p. 8. Bone goes on to discuss what happened to these projects in the ensuing years. Even the most enthusiastic of Stalin's youth were put off by the miserable conditions of the region, and "unfree" convict laborers were sent to complete many of the construction projects begun by them.

77. *Krasnoznamennyi,* p. 106.

78. Haslam, *Soviet Foreign Policy,* p. 83.

79. Ianguzov, *OKDVA,* p. 155.

80. Erickson, *The Soviet High Command,* p. 337. Among those talented commanders trained were: I. F. Fed'ko, V. K. Putna, K. A. Meretskov, and V. I. Chuikov.

81. *Krasnoznamennyi,* p. 106.

82. Ianguzov, *OKDVA,* p. 145.

4

The Clandestine Collaboration Between the Reichswehr and the Red Army

Information about enemy intentions and weapons development programs is a key ingredient of military innovation. Information concerning a state's military capability, however, is usually highly classified and is thus acquired by intelligence collection means, which are imperfect. As Stephen Rosen has illustrated in great detail, there is good and bad intelligence, and the bad usually, but not always, occurs in wartime.[1] In the interwar period, however, Rosen shows that "political barriers constrained intelligence collection and review for strategic target analysis in the [U.S.] Army Air Forces."[2]

The clandestine military collaboration established between the Red Army and the Reichswehr in the aftermath of World War I was unusual indeed.[3] Instead of relying on espionage and other means of intelligence collection to keep abreast of foreign military developments, the Red Army worked face to face with its former enemies who, ironically, would become its future adversaries as well. Indeed, for the "pariahs" of Europe to come together secretly, despite the risks of violating the Treaty of Versailles, was itself a novel means of innovation. And while these covert military ties were plagued with many problems and appear to have aided the Germans in rebuilding and retraining the Reichswehr more than they benefited the Red Army[4], they launched the Red Army's chemical weapons program and aided Soviet tank and aircraft programs. The collaboration also enabled Red Army officers to observe German exercises and to participate in General Staff Academy exchanges for the purpose of studying German tactics and strategy. Although influence per se is hard to measure, there is little doubt that these opportunities contributed to conceptual and technical innovation in the Red Army in the late 1920s and early 1930s.

Drawing on extensive research of both German and Russian military archives, this chapter first reviews what the Red Army commanders were looking for in the collaboration, and then examines the actual course of events as revealed in various reports, protocols, and correspondence issued by members of the Red Army and Reichswehr in order to evaluate whether their needs were met. In so doing, the major forms of cooperation are studied: tank and aircraft schools for testing weapons and training in tactics, chemical weapons R&D and testing, and high-level officer exchanges that occurred at this time. These topics are divided, where possible, into theoretical training (the officer exchanges) and the practical, hands-on testing of aircraft, tanks, and chemical weapons.

The Background and Context of the Secret Collaboration

The Treaty of Versailles (1919) contained a military statute whose aim, in part, was to prevent further aggression by the German army in the aftermath of World War I by imposing restrictions on German military training and weapons production. For example, the Reichswehr was given a cap of 100,000 men including officers; a demilitarized zone in western Germany was drawn; the German General Staff and war academies were to be abolished; mobilization measures were prohibited; and the production of tanks, dirigibles, aircraft, and gas for employment in war was strictly forbidden.[5] Needless to say, the threat to the Weimar Republic's security that such an emasculation of its army entailed led Reichswehr leaders to find alternative and even covert means of maintaining and improving their armed capability, especially in the areas of weapon testing and production.

At the same time the Reichswehr was reeling from the treaty's "punitive measures," the Red Army was recovering from an array of combat defeats and wartime devastation. World War I, the civil war, and the Polish campaign in 1920 had not only taken their toll on the Soviet populace and army, but had also highlighted the tactical and technical backwardness of the RKKA and its need for reform. Although it would seem ideologically incorrect for the communist party to align itself with a capitalist foe for the purpose of rebuilding its army, Russian historians D'iakov and Bushueva point out that "taking advantage of contradictions in the capitalist world in order to improve relations with Germany was fully in keeping with the Leninist foreign policy line." It must be recalled that the KPD (German Communist Party) was still very much a political force at this time to be nurtured and encouraged by the Comintern.

The intensity of the cooperation between Russia and Germany, which began with casual and exploratory contacts in 1921 in Moscow and Berlin between Captain Oskar Ritter von Niedermeyer and Colonel Otto Hasse on the German side, and with Red Army staff chief Pavel Lebedev, commissar of Foreign Trade, Leonid Krasin and Comintern functionary Karl Radek, on the Soviet side, grew gradually over time. In early 1924, a special group of German representatives from the Reichswehr, headed by Oskar von Niedermeyer, were housed in Moscow in order to facilitate closer contact with their Russian counterparts. Herewith the contours of the collaboration took shape.[6] By 1926, Reichswehr General Hans von Seeckt headed up the effort in Berlin, and deputy head of the Main Political Directorate, Iosif Unshlikht, was the Red Army's contact person in Moscow.[7]

Before turning to an examination of the substance of the collaboration and the areas in which it contributed to the innovation of the Red Army, a few remarks about the context of the collaboration are in order. Many aspects of the military collaboration were tainted throughout their duration by the secrecy and suspicion of both parties. Historically, the Soviets had little reason to trust the Germans and their political and/or military intentions vis-à-vis Russia. Mikhail Tukhachevsky was one of the most vocal High Command leaders to articulate concerns for German intentions and at the same time demand full cooperation from the Germans on the test sites. Because of the highly sensitive nature of the military ventures in the USSR, which clearly violated the Treaty of Versailles, the Germans were understandably cautious about sharing information with their Soviet counterparts for fear that they would carelessly expose the German military presence in the USSR to the outside world.[8] Their fears were not unfounded. For example, some Soviet military journals described in detail the technical aspects of the Reichswehr's military status in 1926, causing much embarrassment for the Germans.[9]

Later that year, reports concerning the shipment of Soviet-made grenades to Germany found their way into the British *Manchester Guardian.*[10] These and other threats to security appear to have resulted in the establishment of a strict code of conduct for German officers serving in the Soviet Union at various testing sites. For those Germans engaged in the testing of chemical weapons, fraternization with the Russians was strictly forbidden outside of supervised functions, curfews were imposed, and travel restrictions enforced.[11] Soviet security precautions were also missing on the test fields, according to the German military attaché in Moscow, General Ernst Köstring. While observing a chemical exercise, Köstring objected to the testing of poisonous gases in fields adjacent to the homes of Soviet citizens without warning them in advance. The attending Soviet officer replied, "When our neighbors smell the gas, they will leave."[12]

It is interesting to note, however, that such breaches in security did not seem to apply to the Soviet weapons design programs which were so tightly held that even the Germans—with whom they were collaborating on various tank components—were hard-pressed to identify some of their prototypes.[13] As far as the tank program was concerned, elaborate security schemes were implemented by the War Commissariat and the OGPU for transmitting information to the designer[14]—whose whereabouts were classified—and special rules were set up by the Directorate of Mechanization and Motorization to ensure that the designer's technical assistants would also keep the program under wraps. For example, in 1929, Khalepskii authorized two engineers, Braverman and Pavlovskii, to scrutinize the blueprints of three German tanks from the Daimler, Krupp, and Rheinmetallwerke firms at the OAT's (Orudiinyi-arsenal'nyi trest) design bureau.[15] The OAT would in turn select a small group of technicians to examine the blueprints only in the presence of Braverman and Pavlovskii, in a closed-off and fireproof area. Special provisions were also established for copying the German blueprints: The copying was to take place in a secluded area, no traces of their German origin were to be left on the copies, and each copy was to be coded.[16] Copies that were not handled properly would be burned post haste in the presence of the chairman of the main political administration and other individuals named by the chairman of the trust or the director of the factory.[17]

The Soviets were similarly mistrustful of their German counterparts. Having been bred on the belief that capitalists were untrustworthy and dangerous—despite the aforementioned Leninist dictate condoning the need to exploit capitalist contradictions—the Red Army officers found themselves in a very awkward position working and negotiating with their traditional Teutonic foes. Worries as to whether or not the Germans were really telling them the truth and sharing with them all they knew constantly plagued the relationship and probably affected the Soviet assessment of German tactics and weapons. Both the official and personal documentation retrieved from German and Soviet archives indicates that these suspicions persisted throughout the period of collaboration. One particularly piquant example of this is an excerpt from Voroshilov's letter to the Soviet political representative in Berlin: "The entire 'friendship' and cooperation of the Reichswehr consisted in their efforts to give us less and worse, while exploiting us to the hilt."[18] When speaking with his German counterparts, however, Voroshilov was rather diplomatic. In a conversation with the Head of the German Heeresleitung Kurt von Hammerstein-Equord, and Head of the Reichswehr's statistical department, Erich Kühlenthall, in 1929, Voroshilov said:

> I will not conceal that there were some bumps in the road ... but in general the results were good. ...[Therefore] the issue is not about trust or distrust, but about whether we can find new paths for improving and solidifying our relationship to the benefit of both Germany and the USSR.[19]

The Red Army's Objectives in the Collaboration

It is difficult to evaluate the impact of the German-Soviet collaboration on Soviet military innovation until we establish the areas in which the Red Army sought change and modernization with the Reichswehr's help. Most of the documentation from the Russian side indicates that there were some problems getting their joint ventures off the ground between 1926 and 1929. At the outset of the collaboration in 1926, Unshlikht sent a lengthy report to Stalin in which he stated the following objectives.

> I believe that in continuing to cooperate with the Germans, we should strive to use their tactical and operational experience of the [first] world war with the participation of our specialists in German war games, maneuvers, etc. and also [to exploit] the most important technical innovations of the Germans in communications, artillery, aviation, tank matters.[20]

The chief of the Fourth Directorate of the RKKA staff, Jan Berzin, noted his frustration with the "first period" of the collaboration, which failed to produce satisfactory results, and went on to outline the subsequent improvement of the situation in a lengthy report from 1928. Stating that the Red Army's relationship with the Reichswehr could now be expressed in concrete terms, Berzin included among those areas of collaboration: familiarization with the condition of one another's armies by participating in maneuvers, field exercises, and academic courses; joint chemical warfare experimentation at "Tomka," tank training at

"Kama," and aircraft training at Lipetsk; and permitting Soviet representatives from different directorates, such as the Air Force and Scientific-Technical Commission, to travel to Germany for study.[21]

In Berzin's view, the most positive impact on the army was derived from the trips taken by members of the High Command to maneuvers, field exercises, and academic courses in Germany. According to Berzin, the study of the organization and employment of individual combat arms and how to train them, as well as German military tactics and strategies, contributed not only to the acquisition of knowledge and expansion of the commanders' horizons, but also helped them to learn how to adapt these ideas to Soviet conditions.[22] This sentiment was underscored one year later in a draft of a Politburo resolution on cooperation with the Reichswehr.[23] In addition to requesting that the Germans "guarantee" that they would not speak to the press about the collaboration (which seemed highly unlikely anyway) and demanding monetary compensation for their use of Soviet buildings and other facilities in Lipetsk, Kazan, and Tomka, it was also decreed in the draft resolution that "to the maximum degree possible, use the opportunity [provided by the German-Soviet collaboration] to improve our command staff by sending [our officers] to German military academies, to participate in maneuvers, field exercises, games, and firing drills."[24] Reichswehr General Werner von Blomberg underscored the Red Army's pressing need for officer training during his trip to Russia in 1928.[25] According to von Blomberg, the High Command suffered from a poorly organized Russian General Staff.[26]

German Influence on Theoretical Training

> The tendency to grab onto foreign experience without taking into proper account our own situation was a trait of the old Russian army. One can point to the influence of the Swedes and the Germans on the birth of our regular army and the ever-increasing German influence during the 18th and 19th centuries [continuing] right up to the [first] world war. Field regulations and tactical writings are testimony to this. [But] we must reject unconditionally such blind transfers of foreign experience... . [Instead] we must exploit the sum of all experience while considering our peculiarities.[27]

The influence of German tactical, operational, and strategic theory on the formulation of Red Army air, chemical, and ground force doctrine is difficult to measure, yet some generalizations can be made. Air force doctrine in the interwar years in Europe was influenced considerably by Italian air force strategist Guilio Douhet. German air doctrine, like that of the French and British, was largely a reflection of Douhet's ideas and thus, to the degree that there was European "influence" felt in this area by the Russians, it was inherently Italian. With respect to tank doctrine, the Red Army appears to have preceded the Germans in the systematic formulation of innovative tank employment tactics and strategies in their "deep battle" and later "deep operations" theories contained in the 1929 Field Regulations. In the sphere of chemical weapons experimentation and production, however, there is less evidence that the Soviets had developed either a doctrine for chemical weapons employment or produced the poisonous chemical substances themselves. Thus, their dependence on German military assistance in the area of chemical weapons development and tactical employment appears to have been especially profound.

Officer and General Staff Exchanges

> The Russians were "students"; at least, that is how we were inclined to view them! They "studied" in our schools in Russia; their technical personnel were trained by German specialists. They studied the developments that German research and technology provided with tremendous enthusiasm... . They also "studied" in Berlin; they studied and mastered German tactical regulations better than most of the German General Staff officers. They acquired our tactical and [our] operational ideas.[28]

It appears that the exchange of members of the General Staff for officer training, troop inspection, and observation was the most successful aspect of the collaboration for the Red Army and the Reichswehr. Red Army officers uniformly hailed these officer exchanges and continually strove to expand them.[29] In contrast to other areas of the collaboration, many of the Reichswehr officers who observed troop maneuvers were impressed with the Red Army's "openness."[30] According to a few German officers, the Russians let them see everything they wanted. One of the Soviet participants went so far as to note, "The German officers were shown more than we showed our own allies during the [First] World War."[31]

The motives for the General Staff's cooperation were, according to Unshlikht and von Seeckt, the Soviets' desire to gain insight into German training methods in exchange for information regarding Russian mobilization and deployment plans vis-à-vis Poland.[32] Among the first Soviet High Command visitors to German General Staff courses were Ieronim Uborevich and two of his General Staff professors, Sergei Krasil'nikov and Mikhail Svechnikov, in 1926.[33] According to Manfred Zeidler, the RVS issued Order no. 227 in 1927, which provided for an expanded number of Soviet General Staff and/or Frunze Academy officers to participate in trips to Germany for academic study.[34] Archival documentation listing the participants in the exchanges also illustrates the diversity of the training in which the Red Army officers took part. Table 4.1 summarizes this information for 1929-1933.[35]

Uborevich was a frequent visitor to Germany who appeared to have a special and unusually close relationship with his counterparts in the Reichswehr. Throughout the period of collaboration, Uborevich attended various courses in German academies and obtained valuable data on German weapons developments, such as air defense cannons and flame-throwers.[36]

Air Force Doctrine and Theory

The German military archives are rich with materials related to the training of Soviet officers and pilots by the Germans in Moscow and Lipetsk. Manfred Zeidler has exploited much of this material in his work describing the experience of seven expert German pilots from World War I, "Gruppe Fiebig," who were sent to the USSR to serve as special air force advisers and instructors in various air force facilities around Moscow in the mid-1920s.[37] In May 1925, Martin Fiebig was requested by the head of the Red Air Force to work as a specialist and adviser to the Command Staff (Kommandeursfakultät) of the Moscow Zhukovsky Air Force Academy for several months. His experience there is partial testimony to the limited impact the German experts had on Red Air Force (Rote Luftflotte) activities in general, and on doctrine in particular. Although Fiebig was considered a member of the academy's staff, taking part regularly in meetings and discussions and often expressing his opinions, he was not permitted to draw up strategic and tactical exercises for the classes and thereby had no influence on the lesson and exercise plans of the academy.[38]

What Fiebig saw of the workings of the academy did not impress him. Compared with German air force training, he found that of the Russian academy lacking in rigor and called it a personnel "assembly line in the true sense of the word" (*Schnellpresse im wahrsten Sinne des Wortes*).[39] Among the deficiencies he encountered there were the limited amount of theoretical training (only five months), instruction

TABLE 4.1 Russians in Germany

Russian Participants	Activities
1929	
Jakir, Zomberg, Stepanov, Lazis, Longva	General Staff training (*Führergehilfenlehrgang*), Reichsarchiv, field exercises (*Truppenübungen*)
Kalmykov, Fedotov, Dannenberg	Field exercises and Trips to Military Districts (*Wehrkreisübungsreisen*)
1930	
Chernobrovkin, Dubov, Malakhitskii	Clarification of Technical Issues
Belov, Germanovich, Velikanov, Kotov, Kapulovskii, Kokadeev, Mikhailovskii, Belianov	Trips to military districts; field exercises
Lepin, Admin, Dreier	Logistics course (*Nachschublehrgang*)
Potapov	Clarification of technical issues
Filipovich; four additional unnamed assistants in Würzburg and Berlin	Visits to field hospitals and infirmaries
1931	
Egorev, Dybenko, Belov, Kushinkin	General Staff Training
Efimov, Shilesniakov, Siniavskii	Defense industry course
Appoga, Pavlov, Nikitin, Enokian, Lemberg	Military railroads course
Putna, Ventsov, Belitskii, Merezhkov, Kuchinskii, Chatsov, Obysov, Dobrovolskii, Nemirov	(als Ia und Stabschefs)
Chiefs of Staff course	
Maksimov, Demianovskii, Fedorov, Shchukov, Martiagin	Military topography course
Timoshchenko, Gorbachev, Ushchinskii	Military district exercises
Kokadeev, Orlov, Sakrier, Struselba	Discussions on artillery and communications (*Nachrichtwesen*)
Simonov, Khailov	Industrial matters; chemical weapons
1932	
Lunev, Saborovskii, Kaiukov, Eliseev, Rudnev, Sokolov, Baikov, Vladimirskii, Nikolin	Course led by General Ludwig
Koltunov, Grunde, Fedorov, Berner, Pavlov	Railroad Course
Appoga, Lemberg	Railroad war game and trip to cargo stations in Hamm and troop deployment using mobile troops in Wehrneuchen
Tukhachevsky, Feld'man, Sediakin, Gasukin, Garkavyi, Fesenko, Vainer, Khoroshilov, Klein-Bursy, Trifonov, Piatkevich	Fall exercises, September
Medvedev, Chernobrovkin, Rogov	Air raid drills (*Luftschutzübung*)
Mezheninov, Putilov, Babkin	Unspecified visits
1933	
Levandovskii, Primakov, Dubovoi, Uritskii	
General Staff training and various field exercises	

requiring little thought on the part of students because it was confined to questions and answers, nonmandatory class attendance, and formulaic exams without time limitations.

Fiebig's observations of the ill-prepared air force candidates were confirmed and appraised even more harshly by the Soviet deputy director of the Military Academy, R. A. Muklevich, in a paper entitled "Our Tasks."[40]

> It is a disgrace to say that some of the pilots have astonished the academy's examining committee by their limited horizons and inability to think on their feet. There have been candidates who have had no idea which country has the strongest air force, what kind of aircraft our neighbors use or which types [of aircraft] our industry produces, no knowledge of the Red Army and a very weak familiarity with the military regulations. Such a situation can no longer be tolerated. We must shake up our pilots and force them to read and think!

Although Fiebig exerted little influence on instruction, he was in a perfect position to observe and study the academy's course offerings and especially the sources of its air doctrine. Standard sources used in the classrooms of the Zhukovsky Academy included a wide variety of foreign texts, including translations of U.S., British, and Polish field manuals, a study of World War I by Russian theorist Alexander Zaionchkovsky, and translations of French and German military journals. Muklevich underscored the importance of studying the experience of foreign air forces and foreign languages in order to improve the quality of the Red Air Force.

> In working out our own tactics and strategy we do not want to spurn the experience of foreign armies and air forces. We must attentively and untiringly follow [the developments of] other countries' air forces and learn from them [emphasis mine].[41]

According to Muklevich, the most important languages for air force personnel to study were English, French, German, and Polish. He suggested sending air force candidates to London and Paris for language preparation.

Fiebig found little agreement among the academy's professors as to the composition of current Soviet air doctrine. Thus, no clear conception of air doctrine was being conveyed to the students. The root cause of this confusion, according to Fiebig, was the lack of any historical tactical basis on which to build.[42] The Red Army's air force experience in World War I was extremely limited, and its experience in the civil war, which Fiebig felt was overemphasized in the classroom, would in no way prepare the Red Air Force for a future war against one of the more technologically advanced Great Powers.[43] Although he conceded that the Red Air Force was eager to learn and improve its standing, he believed that it would be a long time before its quality would reach the level of other countries' air forces. In addition to the substance of the students' lessons at the academy, the head of the Red Air Force, Iakov I. Alksnis was equally concerned with teaching methodology and pedagogy that he felt was not up to snuff. Alksnis said as late as 1931 that it was not enough to know the subject; one must know how to teach it.[44]

During the 1920s, all military academies used Alexander Svechin's *Strategiia* as the official textbook of Soviet doctrine and strategy. Its emphasis on the preparation of a defensive war of attrition for a large and economically weak country, such as the Soviet Union, was applied to the air, as well as the ground, dimension. As Fiebig observed of Red Air Force exercises, the air force traditionally played a "reactive role" in which, some six hours after the beginning of mobilization, it would move out from its rear bases to forward ones, where it would wait until the second or third day of mobilization to begin attacks on the enemy. This passive orientation of air force strategy contrasted sharply with German doctrine at this time. Influenced to some degree by Giulio Douhet, European air doctrine envisioned a future war to be three-dimensional with the air force launching a preventive or surprise air attack on enemy air forces, while the defense of land and sea was carried out by ground and naval forces simultaneously.[45]

Eventually, Douhet's ideas caused controversy within the Red Air Force as Soviet theorists began to challenge the ideas of the more defensively oriented theorists, such as Svechin and Andrei Sergeev, who commanded the air force during the civil war and authored a book on air force doctrine.[46] Both theorists advocated the use of aircraft primarily in an auxiliary role of air support to ground forces along the front. The reform of air doctrine was also impeded by the composition of the Red Air Force, some 40 percent of whose personnel had been recruited from the army.[47]

Red Air Force chief inspector, Vasiliy Khripin, chief of staff of the Red Air Force, Sergei Mezheninov, and airpower theorist Alexander Lapchinskii were among those influenced by Douhet and were therefore more optimistic about the potential technological gains for the air force and the expanded roles that would accompany them.[48] In keeping with the Western views of this time, these theorists favored the early employment of the air force in order to protect friendly aircraft and troops during war mobilization and the launching of bombing raids against the enemy's important political and industrial centers at the outset of war. But such ideas were not warmly embraced by all. The employment of preventive strikes against enemy political centers was considered provocative and risky by some air force theorists. Victor Novitskii believed that such early air strikes would be viewed by the Soviet citizenry as an "inadmissible act" and fail to rouse the spirit and patriotism that normally accompanied the massive employment of ground troops.[49]

Nonetheless, in the late twenties, Douhet's and other Western air theorists' views of the importance of a separate and independent air force doctrine, in addition to the traditional doctrine by which the air force facilitated ground force movement, gained considerable ground.[50] By the early 1930s, these views of air force employment, now firmly supported by Lapchinskii, Khripin and Soviet air force theorist Aleksei Algazin, supplanted the defensive view of air power's combat role that predominated in the 1920s.[51] The daunting task that faced the air force was to construct enough heavy bombers to employ these more offense-oriented missions; in 1930 the prospect of possessing a large fleet of bombers for such strategic and deep missions must have seemed a long way off.

Tank Doctrine and Theory

> The Red Army arrived at deep tactics of its own accord. [These tactics] were not the natural continuation of the bloody combat school of the world war. The experience of the Tsarist army was shattered by the 1917 Revolution. According to Russian custom the Red Army adopted deep tactics from the Vikings. It has not yet been established which source was the first to stimulate this revolutionary turn in our tactics—the Fedorov submachine gun or the translation of French infantry regulations. Nonetheless, it is certain that the Red Army arrived at deep tactics carefully, parting from the accustomed linear tactics with reluctance.[52]

The evidence suggests that in the area of tank theory, the Red Army's concepts of tank employment in a future war were just as innovative, if not more innovative than those of the Germans and certainly more fully systematized by the early 1930s. According to David Glantz, "the Soviets formed their mechanized corps in the fall of 1932, three years before Germany created its first panzer division."[53] German armored warfare theorists simply were not supported as strongly as airpower theorists and aircraft production took priority. Nonetheless, the utility of tanks was appreciated in both continental states which would have to rely largely on ground forces in a future war. As Allan Millet writes:

> By the 1930s the concept of armored warfare received official sanction in the school systems of both nations and had entered the doctrinal publications on land warfare. The critical development, however, was an army commitment to further operational experimentation. Germany created its first armored division in 1935; the Soviet Union its first in 1931.[54]

The theory of the deep battle, which envisioned important roles for the tank in developing breakthrough attacks and operating independently in the rear of the enemy's defense, was developed by Soviet military theorists in the 1920s and found expression in the 1929 Field Regulations. These ideas for tank employment developed by Konstantin Kalinovskii, Mikhail Tukhachevsky, and Vladimir Triandafillov, were incorporated into the 1929 Field Regulations, thereby preceding the formulation of a systematic tank theory by the Germans.[55] John Erickson also refers to the Red Army's 1932 Field Regulations as evidence that Soviet tank employment concepts were in place well before the Germans codified their own.[56] In fact, both the Germans and the Soviets, judging by their writings, were most interested in and influenced by the work of British tank theorist J.F.C. Fuller, who insisted that mechanized units assume the leading roles and missions in war while other combat arms, such as the infantry and artillery, support them.[57] Indeed, the significance of Fuller's influence on the thinking of Marshal Tukhachevsky in particular, and on Soviet armored doctrine in general, has been well documented in recent scholarship.[58]

The eminent German panzer theorist Heinz Guderian wrote in his memoirs that it was the British theorists, J.F.C. Fuller and B. H. Liddell-Hart, whose ideas about expanded roles for the tank beyond infantry support struck a chord with him.[59] When asked to teach a course on panzer tactics in 1928, he claims to have relied on British military regulations translated into German for his course preparation, which "served for many years as the theoretical guide for the evolution of our thinking."[60] In 1929, Guderian's ideas began to take shape as he grew convinced that the tank should play a primary role in combat accompanied by the other service arms. Instead of a tank supporting an infantry division, the reverse should occur. In his view, tank divisions must be created and supported by the infantry and all other combat arms. Guderian initially encountered considerable opposition from his superiors, such as the chief of the general staff, Ludwig Beck, who scorned the idea of creating tank divisions and relegating the infantry to a support role.[61] Only in 1933 did Guderian's ideas receive full endorsement by Reichswehrminister Werner von Blomberg, Colonel Walter von Reichenau, and indirectly, Adolf Hitler.[62]

In contrast, the Red Army theorists, with Tukhachevsky at the helm, were somewhat ahead of the game. They recognized in the late 1920s that the tank would have "decisive influence" on the course of future battles, given its increased speed and survivability, and would require the support of infantry and artillery to carry out many of its missions.[63] Thus, while the importance of creating operational-level tank units for high-speed and often independent tasks was generally agreed upon, the extent to which the infantry would become motorized in order to keep up with the rapidly moving tank units was a topic of debate. Some saw the motorization of the infantry as a dangerous and risky proposition that would result in a battlefield cluttered with armored cars and tanks restricting combat mobility and speed.[64] Others were convinced of the need for motorized infantry and tanks to operate together and support one another in combat, but insisted that the tank units remain ultimately under the command of the infantry group.[65]

At the tactical level, too, much controversy surrounded the specifics of the tank-infantry unit relationship, including issues such as the distance at which the two units should be separated from one another during combat, the proper composition of infantry and tank units, and how the units should be echeloned. Although these technical matters were discussed frequently, the general assumption that both infantry and tank units were needed on the battlefield in support of one another was agreed upon universally.[66]

A comparison of the 1925 and 1929 Red Army Field Regulations illustrates the degree to which tank employment concepts had evolved in the course of four years. The 1925 manual contained only a brief reference to tanks, whose main mission would be to assist the forward movement of the infantry by destroying obstacles and suppressing enemy machine-gun fire.[67] The infantry, in turn, would protect tanks from enemy antitank weapons using artillery and Maxim machine guns. No mention of tank missions beyond infantry support is found in this edition of the RKKA's Field Regulations.

The 1929 manual, in contrast, devoted a much larger section to tank employment and discussed several new missions for the tank.[68] Although infantry support still topped the list of tank missions, the following were added: to perform independent tasks in the depths of the defensive belt, to operate with cavalry on enemy flanks, and to operate within motorized units on flanks and during breakthroughs of the enemy's defense. Many tank echelons in support of the infantry (*PP—podderzhka pekhoty)* would be created for the battle at the forward edge of the enemy's defense, and tank echelons for long-range operations (*DD—dal'nego deistviia*) would also be sent to combat the enemy's artillery in the rear. Tanks were also assigned a more prominent and "decisive role" in developing the breakthrough of an enemy defense by following on the heels of the infantry attack. The coordination of tanks and infantry units in the course of a breakthrough operation, however, had not been fully worked out. Although the ideas of the deep employment of tank units into the enemy's rear and in developing the breakthrough found fuller expression in the 1936 Field Regulations, their roots at the tactical level can be traced to the 1929 manual.

Chemical Doctrine and Theory[69]

The Soviets appear to have willingly followed the German lead in the development and production of chemicals for use in peace and war. This is not too surprising, because the German chemical industry was world-renowned and the German army had hands-on experience in employing chemical gases successfully in the First World War. The Red Army had good reason to take an interest in procuring chemical weapons for themselves, as well as in developing means of defending themselves from chemical attack, given their losses in World War I. According to one record, the Soviets were second only to the Italians in terms of casualties suffered from poisonous gas in that war, having lost some 11.7 percent of their combat troops.[70]

Soviet admiration for the German chemical industry and eagerness to exploit contacts with it can be traced to the tsarist period. Vladimir Ipatiev, the esteemed Soviet chemist and academic who oversaw the development of chemical compounds for peaceful and military application, studied in Munich, Germany, following the completion of his dissertation. Throughout the 1920s, Ipatiev served as a guest chemist of the Bayerische Stickstoff Werke, where he spent two-month stints three to four times per year.[71] Ipatiev is said to have set up 150 chemical factories in the USSR based on his original methods and to have developed the first Russian chemical explosives for use in World War I.[72] His participation in the testing of chemical compounds and machine guns until at least 1925 has recently been confirmed by declassified Soviet archival sources.[73]

But despite Ipatiev's valuable pioneering work, the Soviet Union lagged well behind Germany, France, Great Britain, and the United States in the creation of indigenous chemical industries. Throughout World War I, the Imperial Army received most of its chemical weapons, artillery, and explosives from France and the United States. Only with the adoption of the First Five Year Plan did the Soviet Union begin to redress this problem with an all-out chemicalization drive.

In terms of chemical warfare doctrine, many Soviet military journal articles and books published in the 1920s and early 1930s discussed the likelihood that chemical weapons would be employed in a future war, despite the international conventions prohibiting their use, and stressed above all the utility of using aircraft for the delivery of poisonous gases deep into the enemy's rear in the early stages of mobilization.[74]

> The combination of aviation and chemicals can have the most effect on morale. During the period of mobilization, the actions of aviation and chemicals will be directed chiefly at the destruction of army command and control centers and train nets. The results of air attack at the outset of war can be compared with the results of a cavalry attack on dispersed infantry forces that have not succeeded to repulse the cavalry.[75]

One classified handbook on chemical warfare stated that, as of 1928, chemical weapons were comprised of smoke and incendiary devices employed by special troops and artillery, air force, and infantry units, and that chemical troops were to be employed exclusively for chemical attacks on the enemy.[76] Of these employment methods it was aircraft, in the Red Army view, that had "fundamentally changed" the methods of defending the country from enemy attack and had presented new and effective methods of delivering chemical weapons on enemy soil.[77] Unlike ground and naval forces, which were constrained by territorial and maritime borders, aircraft had revolutionized the battlefield, rendering a country's entire territory vulnerable to attack in the very early stages of war.[78] The only constraint on the depth to which chemical weapons could penetrate an enemy's defense was the delivery vehicle's—that is, the aircraft's range and sustainability. In order to defend against this threat, Pavlovich recommended placing air defenses closer to the front, organizing the defense early and even before the official outbreak of war, and defending important military, industrial, and political centers from attack. Pavlovich maintained that even the strongest infantry with the most technologically advanced equipment could be paralyzed easily by aircraft-delivered poisonous chemicals. Tanks were vulnerable to chemical penetration and measures were taken to ensure that tank drivers would be properly protected.[79] According to the chemical directorate, however, the speed and maneuverability of the light tank and tankette would be compromised by hermetization, and therefore, the drivers would have to use gas masks and other individual means of protection.[80]

The seriousness with which the Red Army regarded the threat of chemical war was also reflected in the establishment of voluntary chemical defense organizations, Dobrokhim and its subsequent incarnation, Osoaviakhim, to prepare the population for the employment of poisonous gases and the creation of an extensive literature on chemical warfare for the layperson and the specialist.[81] According to one catalog of military publications, roughly as many books and pamphlets were published on chemical warfare and weapons as on infantry or air force employment.[82] Perhaps the most comprehensive work published on chemical warfare in the Soviet Union was *Voenno-khimicheskoe delo,* edited in 1929 by the head of the Military-Chemical Directorate, Iakov Fishman.[83] It should be noted, however, that this lengthy tome described chemical weapons and the history, employment, and production thereof in countries other than the Soviet Union and served in actuality as a catalog of foreign, rather than Soviet, chemical developments and wartime experiences in employing poison gases.

With respect to chemical warfare tactics, Fishman stressed that much work remained to be done in coordinating chemical and infantry units, working out air and projectile delivery of gases, and employing smoke.[84] Because the allies had been caught unawares by the German employment of gas in World War I and lacked any effective means of protecting themselves, he noted, the study of the wartime experience was of limited value.[85] Since World War I, virtually all countries were training and preparing for chemical warfare and developing more reliable and sustainable protective gear for their troops and horses.[86] The following quotation from Fishman's work sums up the Soviet view.

> The USSR, having signed the Geneva protocol, will fulfill its obligations but the RKKA must be ready to confront the enemy, in

> the event that he violates the signed international agreement and employs weapons of mass destruction against us. That is why we may under no circumstances allow the attention of the RKKA and the entire country to stray away from the problems of chemical warfare.[87]

Lipetsk, Tomka, and Kama: Weapons Development, Testing, and Tactical Training

During the years of the German-Soviet collaboration, three centers were established in the USSR for testing aircraft, tanks, and chemical weapons and for training troops to use all three: Lipetsk (near Voronezh) for aircraft,[88] "Tomka" (Volsk—on the middle Volga)[89] and Uchtomskaia (near Moscow) for chemical weapons, and "Kama" in Kazan (on the Volga) for tanks. This was the part of the bargain most highly valued by the Germans, who were by treaty prohibited from testing weapons on their own territory. The degree to which the aircraft and tank sites contributed to Soviet military innovation, however, is a topic of controversy. Some Western authors, such as former Luftwaffe General Wilhelm Speidel, insisted in their memoirs that "large numbers" of Soviets participated in the exercises and profited mostly in the area of theoretical knowledge.[90] A competing image that emerges from Reichswehr and Red Army documents, however, is one of restricted Soviet access to the development and testing of equipment and participation in exercises. In many cases, Soviet officers served as observers of German exercises or as assistants[91] to the German experts who actually flew the aircraft and tested the chemicals.[92]

Aircraft Testing: Lipetsk[93]

The degree to which the aviation school at Lipetsk benefited the Red Air Force is perhaps more ambiguous than for any of the other schools and joint German-Soviet enterprises. Documents concerning the flight training and aircraft testing performed at the school are often contradictory, and it is very difficult to draw conclusions about their impact on Soviet Air Force innovation. Although it appears that the Reichswehr achieved its goals of training a large cadre of its pilots while also testing new aircraft models in Lipetsk, it is less clear that Soviet pilots achieved the same satisfaction. There is evidence, however, that Soviet technical personnel learned a considerable amount in the area of testing and repairing aircraft. Manfred Zeidler argues that by 1930, interest in tactical training subsided and both sides were more interested in the testing of new aircraft models. The school at Lipetsk essentially turned into a test field, in his view. Iosif Unshlikht, the aforementioned point of contact in Moscow for the clandestine operations, wrote (after the school had been in operation for about one year) that in December 1926 the Soviet side had sent some sixteen pilots through training in fighter aircraft and some forty-five full-time and temporary technicians had undergone the extensive study of Neper-Lion aircraft motor construction. Highly qualified technicians were placed in groups of up to forty persons under the direction of German engineers. Training in the school focused on new tactical methods that were considered extremely useful.

> The study of tactical innovations is for us invaluable because tactical methods of various aircraft types are studied by German instructors who [in turn] have spent time in America, England, and France.[94]

Unshlikht went on to list the areas in which he foresaw continued benefit: providing the Red Army with a well-equipped and modern air base; well-trained and competent Soviet specialists, mechanics, and workers; new air tactics for various aircraft types; knowledge of the newest technical developments in aircraft development via the testing to occur at Lipetsk; and all-around improvement of Red Air Force pilots. Yet, two years later, Berzin was complaining that the promised site modernization had not yet occurred and the school was still operating with obsolete equipment. But he also pinned some of the blame on the Russian side for failing to take full advantage of the test site.[95]

Criticism of the restricted Soviet access to experimentation and testing of aircraft equipment at Lipetsk is encountered in Soviet and German documents written by many members of the Soviet High Command and the German Reichswehr who participated in this joint venture. One unpublished Soviet source describes the number of pilots being trained in Lipetsk as early as 1925, yet says nothing of Soviet pilots; in fact, the only reference to the Russian staff is in terms of technical personnel.[96] The Soviet deputy head of the Red Air Force, Iakov Alksnis, informed Reichswehr officer Oskar von Niedermeyer that the air force had learned nothing from the Germans at Lipetsk in the course of the year (1928), chiefly because the Russian technical staff was so much poorer than the German staff.[97]

Several meetings took place in September 1929 in which Soviet dissatisfaction with the lack of progress and limited Soviet participation in the flight training at Lipetsk on the part of members of the Soviet High Command was expressed by the chief of the RKKA's Main Administration, Boris Feldman, and the head of the Red Air Force, Petr Baranov. Feldman scoffed at the idea that the school at Lipetsk could be considered a valuable source of exchange of air force technology and methods. He complained that the school had not been equipped with the newest aircraft nor had it provided all the other German-built equipment, such as weapons, radios, and compasses earlier promised by the German side.[98]

Later that month, in a similar meeting, Baranov reported that the present activity of the school at Lipetsk satisfied neither Soviet War Commissar Kliment Voroshilov nor him, insisting that the "German side takes more than it gives."[99] Not only must the range of the tests be enlarged, but also "they must be conducted in closer connection with the Russian side."[100] In addition to outdated equipment, noted Berzin, the school offered little in the realm of tactical training for aircraft formations and served only to improve the prowess of individual pilots.[101] Other reports have referred to Soviet artillery batteries operating in concert with German-flown aircraft,[102] but little indication of intensive Soviet flight training per se is revealed.

Regardless of the degree to which Soviet Air Force pilots participated in fighter aircraft tactical training, it appears that the bulk of Red Air Force officers and engineers in attendance at the Lipetsk aviation school gained considerable technical knowledge and training and learned about aircraft developments in the process. Excerpts from Tukhachevsky's technical requests of the German officers at Lipetsk engaged in constructing the aircraft are not only testimony to the seriousness with which Tukhachevsky approached the matters, but also provide further insight into the specific features of aircraft design that interested the Soviet side. In 1931, for example, Tukhachevsky requested the following items: observation of Junkers aircraft flight tests at high altitudes with the use of infrared radar in both combat and noncombat in foggy weather conditions,[103] use of heavy-fuel motors in military aircraft, and use of wireless photographic transmission (*drahtlose Bildübermittlung).*[104]

The extent to which the Germans tried to satisfy the technical demands of the Russians is illustrated by a particularly interesting report on aircraft testing at Lipetsk in the summer of 1931.[105] According to this report, a navigational device (*Kursvisier*)—despite objections by the Germans—was dismantled at the request of Red Army commander-engineer Frolov so that he could inspect its parts. But owing to the instrument's complexity, once it was put together again, it never operated as well as it had beforehand.[106]

Whether or not Tukhachevsky's requests for tactical training in air defense, combined arms operations, and offensive maneuvers were actually met is less clear. Because of the rather high incidence of German deaths resulting from various flight-related accidents at Lipetsk, however, Tukhachevsky and other Soviet officers may not have minded the exclusion from extensive hands-on testing and training of aircraft. According to D'iakov and Bushueva, the corpses of the German test pilots were returned to Germany in boxes labeled "aircraft parts" in order to preserve secrecy.[107]

Chemical Testing: "Tomka"

The Soviet collaboration with the Germans at the chemical weapons testing ground, "Tomka," was indisputably beneficial to the Red Army and ranks as perhaps the single biggest contributor to its innovation in the early Stalin period. In 1926, Unshlikht had the following upbeat remarks on chemical weapons testing.

> Concerning the results, I must say that these tests have benefited us greatly. Aside from the fact that the dispersion methods were unknown to us previously, we obtained all of the material and methodology related to this work immediately. Our specialists worked one-on-one with [the Germans] and soaked up experience like a sponge. ...As a result of this, our specialists who were collaborating with the most highly qualified German specialists, learned a lot in a short period of time these experiments should be seen through, because, thanks to them, we will receive top-notch weapons for modern war.[108]

Berzin wrote in a report on the collaboration with the Reichswehr two years later:

> The chemical experiments in Podosinkakh and later in "Tomka" have yielded good results and the continuation of these experiments in the course of next year has been advised by the Chemical Directorate. The objectives of these experiments include the testing of new equipment and new methods of chemical weapons employment (by artillery, aviation, special chemical projectors etc.) and also new methods and means of decontaminating affected areas.[109]

One month later, Berzin listed the new chemical weapons developments that were undergoing testing; these included: cisterns for contaminating areas, "Minimako" and "Nag" portable decontamination equipment, devices for spraying chemical weapons from the sky, prototypes of long-range chemical weapons bombs, equipment for spraying mustard gas, chemical flame-throwers that explode in the air, decontamination equipment, protective gear, and means for treating and healing mustard gas wounds.[110]

In a field dispatch to Voroshilov a few years later, Berzin stated quite frankly that while the tank and aircraft schools were not living up to the expectations of either the Directorate of Mechanization and Motorization or the Directorate of the Air Force, the gas school at Tomka was performing admirably in the eyes of the Chemical Directorate. The head of the Chemical Directorate and codirector of operations at Tomka, Iakov Fishman, went on to list several areas in which experimentation should continue, including various employment methods of mustard gas, the development of new lethal chemicals, and liquid decontamination based on automatic tanks manufactured by Krupp.[111]

Reports from Fishman provide new insights into the depth and multifaceted nature of the collaboration in this area. A 1929 trip to Germany by three Soviet chemists permitted the observation and evaluation of laboratories for testing and repairing gas masks and other protective gear; the polygon in Kümmersdorf for decontaminating equipment; the laboratories of several chemists, including Professor Wirth at the Higher Technical School in Charlottenburg, where research on equipment for determining the presence of mustard gas in soil and the decontamination of cloth was taking place; and numerous other laboratories and facilities.[112] In addition, there were preliminary discussions with the Germans regarding the construction of a factory for processing *tiodiglikolia* (raw material for mustard gas).

The Soviet chemists also obtained secret materials during their visit: data on the production of various chemical weapons in the First World War at the factories of the largest chemical conglomerates and data on the application of chemical weapons in World War I (and their mixtures with physical and chemical constants, reaction to metals, etc.). These data were viewed as especially valuable because they allowed the Soviet chemists to accelerate the lab work.

Not all the assessments of the chemical collaboration were positive, however. Mikhail Tukhachevsky demanded that the Soviets be privy to more of the German experiments, tests, and weapons developments.

With respect to the chemical procedures at Tomka, Tukhachevsky insisted that Russians be allowed to work alongside Germans in their laboratories in order to become acquainted with new chemical substances, as it was important to share the chemical processes with German specialists "and not only to be shown the buildings."[113] Tukhachevsky's complaints about limited Soviet access to experiments in Tomka have been contradicted, however, by the chemist who ran the chemical warfare school, Ludwig von Sicherer. Sicherer insisted that the two sides worked very closely (*Hautnah)* and that two Soviet specialists were assigned to each of the forty German chemical experts.[114] Where the truth lies may never be known. However, it does appear that Soviet interest in developing air-delivered chemical weapons was great given their emphasis on the disruption of the enemy's rear using air-delivered chemical poisons.[115] Fishman enthusiastically viewed the prospects of air-delivered chemical weapons, calling them the "Super guns of the future" and the end of classical artillery.[116] Thus, Tukhachevsky's complaints about restricted Soviet access to the development of chemical weapons may have reflected his own eagerness and impatience with the length of the development procedures.

The Germans were equally annoyed with the impatience and naiveté of the Soviets and the lack of skilled engineers on the Soviet side. A long list of complaints concerning transportation, sanitation, and communication problems in the Soviet Union, which were costing the Germans "precious time" was filed by the leader of German air-delivered chemical testing, Amberg,[117] in a letter to Lieutenant Colonel Helmuth Wilberg in Lipetsk. In addition to complaining of the isolation, lack of telephone connections, delayed deliveries of important equipment from the Soviet Union, and poor hygiene at his test site, Amberg opposed the idea of permitting Russians aboard each German test flight, as this would invariably "complicate the test."[118]

Other German officers were bothered by the impatience of the Soviets, who did not appear interested in testing the new chemical weapons and equipment properly—who "just wanted to get their hands on it quickly."[119] The Soviets also apparently tried to obtain confidential documents and drawings from the German personnel without permission and often were on the verge of violating German patent laws.[120]

Tank Testing and Development: "KAMA"[121]

The "Kama" tank school in Kazan, where most of the testing of tank parts and full prototypes took place, seems to have provided the Soviets with unique opportunities for tactical growth as well as frustration regarding their access to German tank-related technical developments. Perhaps one of the best illustrations of this mix of sentiment is contained in a report from Berzin to Khalepskii issued in March 1930.

> If technical issues are characterized by a light digression in the area of internal combustion engines, electro-technology and ballistics, then the work on tactics is taking place in a much more serious fashion and in all tasks a course of detailed work has been chosen.[122] ...At our first meeting, Colonel Lutz[123] said that it is clear that Moscow is mistrustful of what's going on at the courses. Superficially, they are very polite to us, but they do not show us everything that we want [to see] or, more correctly, they do not show us everything that they show the German cadets. For example, in Kummersdorf, Pirner shoved us off in the direction of an installation for testing track chains, while the German cadets were led to another place to see, judging by the remarks of the Germans, 8- and 10 mm. wheeled vehicles of some kind of special construction by Krupp and a tractor by Bussing. When we asked not to be separated from the German cadets, [Pirner] said that there would not be enough time.

Unlike the chemical and flight-training schools, the Kazan tank school suffered several delays in getting started partly because of ambivalence within the Soviet leadership about opening another clandestine school in the Soviet Union,[124] German misgivings about transporting tank prototypes to the USSR in light of the political risks involved, and the lack of a Soviet industrial basis upon which to rely. Only in 1929 did tank prototypes arrive in Kazan for inspection and field exercise.[125]

Once under way, according to Zeidler, the tank school witnessed enormous and enthusiastic Soviet participation, wherein fifty to sixty Soviet mechanics and engineers supported the forty-man-strong German contingent.[126] As for training, the number of Soviet participants climbed steadily from year to year. While in 1929 only five cadets participated, by 1931 forty officers were in attendance. Between 1929 and 1933, some ninety Soviets had received training in Kazan.[127] According to a Soviet source from early 1932, sixty-five highly ranked tank and motorized rifle unit officers participated in the Kazan tank school courses during a three-year period.[128] Of these, a large percentage were line commanders and teachers of tactics at the tank higher schools. Griaznov was especially enthusiastic about the impact of the tank school on Soviet tank technicians as well as on tactical training.

> Our engineers' familiarization with the material aspects of German combat machines and also the study of all German materials, such as blueprints and test results, has allowed us to exploit the experience of TEKO. The courses are a research laboratory for technical, tactical, and methodological improvement of our commanders.[129]

Major General Otto von Stülpnagel, who visited the Kazan school in the fall of 1930, gave a mixed review of Kazan's training procedures. The chief problem, as he saw it, was that the Russians wanted to train a large number of students right away and from that pool select the most promising students for more advanced training. The Germans, on the other hand, wanted to gradually enlist a small core of competent instructors by training them fully before opening the training opportunities to a large group of students. While Stülpnagel was optimistic about meeting future goals, such as the increased participation of both sides, he admitted that tank shortages and defects, poor Soviet preparedness, and "personnel and organizational" problems prevented training goals from being achieved in 1930.[130]

Impediments to Interpreting Influence: A Closer Look

Throughout this chapter we have encountered conflicting views and evaluations of the clandestine military ventures by Reichswehr and Red Army officers during the interwar years. Perhaps one of the most startling contradictions uttered concerns aircraft operations in Lipetsk. The German pilot Wilhelm Speidel stated in no uncertain terms that the "Germans gave and the Russians took," while Petr Baranov, head of the Red Air Force claimed on a separate occasion that "the German side took more than it gave." Such contradictory statements might be expected of the two somewhat antagonistic partners, yet there are many examples of German officers who held differing views among themselves on the nature and impact of the military collaboration. For purposes of illustration, two views of the benefit accorded to the Red Army by two German participants, Reichswehr Generals Werner von Blomberg and Ernst Köstring are discussed in the following paragraphs.

The memoirs of Reichswehr General Ernst Köstring are particularly insightful vis-à-vis the German-Soviet military ventures of the interwar years, as they reflect on all aspects of the collaboration by someone who had considerable experience residing within, and knowledge of, the Soviet Union.[131] Köstring served as the first German "Military Attaché" in the Soviet Union from roughly 1931 to 1941.[132] Born in Russia and fluent in the Russian language, Köstring often interpreted for his fellow German officers during the negotiations over the military ventures and served as an observer to many of the training exercises in the Soviet Union both during his tenure as military attaché and for several years beforehand. The overall conclusion of his memoirs was that the value of the secret collaboration for both sides was greatly exaggerated. In his view, the Russian mistrust of the Germans and the latter's "angst" over its responsibility for conducting these illegal operations on foreign soil, not to mention in collusion with communists, kept the work from becoming what it could have "between friends."

Köstring believed that the common assertion that the Germans trained the Russian Army was simply wrong. The Russian officers who participated in the yearly exchanges in Germany served only as observers of German exercises and General Staff courses. Thus, according to Köstring, "The training of Russian troops by German officers never took place." He noted that the training at the Kazan tank school involved more joint participation than at the flight school, yet the availability of tanks with which to train was limited. The flight school involved minimum Soviet participation where "close cooperation with Russian air forces did not occur." As for the development of poisonous gas at Tomka, Köstring noted in particular the Soviet mistrust of the Germans who, they believed, were holding back new discoveries from the Soviets. The Russian Chemical Troop inspector apparently told a Reichswehr official, who had complained during a meeting in Moscow that the German scientists had not discovered any new compounds that year, that "Germany has the most famous chemical industry in the world. We do not believe that your men cannot develop anything new. Shut yourselves up in a house and don't come out until you have found something new. Then you'll develop something quickly."[133] Although this quotation reveals Soviet mistrust of the Germans, it also underscores the Soviet's willingness to allow the German experts the privacy to undertake chemical experiments, presumably without Soviet participation.

However, despite his bleak assessment of the collaboration in general, Köstring was very impressed with the keen interest that Soviets displayed in German military ideas, and claimed that he was constantly sought after for his advice on military questions when he visited Soviet military facilities. He recounted in detail one visit in 1931 to Tschkalov, a town near Orenburg in the southern Urals, where he was to observe a Soviet cavalry division. En route to Tschkalov, a trip that lasted four days by train, one of the accompanying Soviet officers spent many hours hypothesizing various cavalry scenarios, playing them out, and then asking Köstring to comment on them. Much to the Soviets' dismay, Köstring interrupted them, saying that he could not comment because he was only a lieutenant.[134] This trip prompted Köstring to send General Hans von Seeckt a letter praising the extent to which German ideas were beginning to penetrate the thinking of the Red Army.[135]

Köstring's impressions of the German-Soviet collaboration by stand in sharp contrast to the highly optimistic appraisals of the collaboration in the 1928 trip report of General Werner von Blomberg. His trip included visits to the three clandestine schools, Ukrainian Military District exercises, and Moscow and Leningrad. Von Blomberg's report, perhaps because of its accessibility, has often been cited by Western scholars as evidence of the value of the secret collaboration for the Soviets and the Germans.[136]

Von Blomberg was impressed, during his 1928 visit, with many aspects of the military undertakings in the USSR—especially with the Red Army's thirst for knowledge and willingness to accommodate the German guests.

> The value of the collaboration for the Red Army was often reiterated, as was the desire to learn from the Reichswehr and to hear the opinions and evaluations of the respected German officers about the Red Army's [military] accomplishments.[137]

He was so impressed with what he saw that he sought expansion of the existing programs. With regard to flight training at Lipetsk, von Blomberg perhaps erroneously interpreted Voroshilov's silence on the topic as evidence that the Soviets were satisfied with its progress. Although the Red Air Force lacked combat experience, von Blomberg underscored that its pilots were vigorous students of current air force literature and were well aware of the important new roles for fighter and bomber aircraft in combat.[138] Von Blomberg's strong advocacy of the continuation of the military ties was supported by his identification of areas in which the Reichswehr could learn from the Red Army and Air Force, including pontoon-building, aviation, chemical weapons, and propaganda, although he is not specific about Soviet contributions in these areas.[139]

Given von Blomberg's position as chief of the general staff, it is possible to suggest institutional reasons why he would want to preserve the German-Soviet military relationship. If the Reichswehr were benefiting from the collaboration, as he believed it was, he and other generals would presumably build a strong case for its continuation, enabling them to defend it before skeptical German political and diplomatic authorities who were unsure whether the Reichswehr's military gains from the collaboration outweighed the political risks.

Conclusions

These selections from the German military archives illustrate not only a variety of viewpoints regarding the value of the interwar military collaboration for the Soviets, but also the difficulty in attempting to assign primary importance to German military ideas and technologies and their impact on the Red Army's innovation.

Soviet air doctrine was influenced initially by the work of its own theorists, but later drew on ideas concerning independent air force operations as expressed in Guilio Douhet's seminal work, *The Command of the Air*. It appears that the Soviets desired greater access to the flight training opportunities at Lipetsk, but because it was tightly controlled by German pilots who were more interested in training their own cadres than Soviet ones, few Soviet pilots could benefit from the tactical exercises. Nonetheless, technical training does appear to have been achieved, as well as familiarization with and testing of German aircraft models.

The tank school at Kazan may have provided some unique tactical and technical training opportunities for Red Army attendees. Like Lipetsk, the tank school was perhaps the most beneficial to the Red Army in terms of familiarizing its technical staff with new tank prototypes, tank parts, and teaching them how to test and repair tanks. With a few exceptions, the tanks used in Kazan were British models purchased by the Russians.

Of undeniable importance to Red Army innovation were the chemical school and laboratories at Tomka wherein chemical weapons for air and ground delivery deep into the enemy's rear were developed by German and Soviet chemists. German expertise in this area was world-renowned, and Vladimir Ipatiev, father of the Soviet chemical industry, frequently traveled to Germany for training well before the clandestine ties developed. Although a few Red Army officials complained of limited access to the laboratories, they had enormous confidence in German chemical expertise and capability to produce new poisonous substances. In fact, they seemed perfectly willing to give the Germans free rein to conduct experiments even without Soviet participation. The Germans were probably delighted to have access to a field on which to test their poisonous gases.

Finally, judging by the remarks of Soviet participants throughout the collaboration period, the visits to German military academies and courses were treated with the greatest enthusiasm. General Staff-level exchanges enabled Red Army officers to observe maneuvers and receive training in the operational art of the Reichswehr which was highly respected by the Russians. Through its contacts with the Reichswehr, the Red Army officers could study many of the Western concepts and new weapons designs—not only German—that were difficult to come by at home. This access to German laboratories and know-how accelerated Soviet military innovation because the Soviets readily obtained some processes and pieces of equipment that were impossible or difficult to replicate in the USSR. There is little doubt that the German-Soviet collaboration contributed to the innovation of the Red Army during its most intensive phase (1928-1933), despite the prevailing secrecy and suspicion.

Notes

1. Stephen Rosen, *Winning the Next War: Innovation and the Modern Military* (Ithaca: Cornell University Press, 1991), pp. 186-190.

2. Ibid., p. 253.

3. Manfred Zeidler's choice of the word *ungewöhnlich* (unusual) in the title of his book on this subject is quite appropriate. Manfred Zeidler, *Reichswehr und Rote Armee 1920-1933: Wege und Stationen einer ungewöhnlichen Zusammenarbeit* (München: Oldenbourg, 1993).

4. This is clearly the view of Dia'kov and Bushueva, whose collection of excerpts from the Russian military archives on the German-Soviet collaboration bears the title: *The Fascist Saber Was Sharpened in the USSR* (Moscow: Sovetskaia Rossiia, 1992).

5. These and other restrictions are discussed in great detail in General E. Requin, "The Armaments and Military Power of Germany," *Foreign Affairs,* Winter 1932/33, pp. 230-231. The author goes on to illustrate how these restrictions were subsequently undone at the Conference of Ambassadors.

6. D'iakov i Bushueva, *Fashistkii mech,* p. 13. For a fuller reconstruction of the establishment of the collaboration see the first two chapters of D'iakov

and for the fullest treatment see Zeidler, *Reichswehr und Rote Armee,* pp. 29-82.

7. Ibid., p. 17.

8. The Germans complained that the Russians were responsible for losing books on chemical war that they feared would invariably end up in the hands of some German civil servant--many of whom were unaware of the clandestine military cooperation and who, if they did know, would strongly object to it. They also accused the Russians engaged in chemical tests of speaking about their work privately, and "even in the presence of women." See *Schlußbericht 1926--Arbeiten der Gruppe Amberg,* Berlin, 21 December 1926, Bundesarchiv-Militärarchiv, Freiburg, Germany (hereinafter abbreviated as BA-MA), RH2/2304.

9. J. Erickson, *The Soviet High Command,* p. 248. One can find detailed references to Reichswehr developments in many Soviet military journal articles in 1926 and 1927. See, for example, G. Girs, "Nemetskaia taktika," *Voennyi Vestnik,* no. 20, 1926 (translated from the French *Belges des Sciences Militaires* vol. II, no. 3) One excerpt: "Although the German cavalry, in accordance with the Versailles Treaty may not be equipped with Maxim guns, the Germans have succeeded, nonetheless, in getting around this restriction with help of special circumstances" p. 36.

10. BA-MA, RH8/3621. Unidentified German correspondents, "Aus Manchester Guardian vom Freitag, den 3 Dezember 1926." "Geheime Abmachungen zwischen Reichswehr-Offizieren und Sowjet. Ueberraschende Enthüllungen."

11. Ibid. "Instruktion für die Gäste," *Anlage zur Wochenbericht Amberg,* no. 5, 28 October 1926. BA-MA, RH2/2304.

12. Ernst Köstring, cited in Rolf-Dieter Müller, "Die deutschen Gaskriegsvorbereitungen 1919-1945: Mit Giftgas zur Weltmacht?," *Militärgeschichtliche Mitteilungen,* no. 1, 1980, p. 31.

13. A German source describing the "Medium D" noted that in one Soviet handbook mention was made of the Vickers Model 1927 as being superior to the Medium D. Thus, the author guessed, "It is possible that the Medium D tank was purchased in the USSR before the contract with Vickers was concluded." BA-MA, RH2/2746, the German report, "Kampfwagen Medium D in der Roten Armee, Bericht Nr. 12/1," Berlin, 21.3.1931.

14. RGVA, F. 31811, op. 1, d. 31, l. 27, and d. 425, l. 10.

15. RGVA, F. 31811, op. 1, d. 331, l. 5.

16. Ibid., l. 17-18.

17. Ibid., l. 18.

18. RGVA, F. 33987, op. 3, d. 342, l. 180.

19. RGVA, "Iz besedy Voroshilova s deiateliami Reikhsvera Generalom Gammershteinom i Polkovnikom Kiullentalem," 5 September 1929, in D'iakov, *Fashistskii mech,* pp. 98-99.

20. Unshlikht to Stalin, 31 December 1926, F. 33987, op. 3, d. 151, l. 18-23, cited in D'iakov, *Fashistskii mech,* pp. 72-73.

21. Ibid.
22. Berzin, p. 86.
23. RGVA, F. 33987, op. 3, d. 329, l. 146-147, in D'iakov, *Fashistskii mech*, p. 103.
24. Ibid, p. 103.
25. Reisebericht von Blombergs, 17.11.1928, in Handakten Direktoren, Dirksen Akten, Russische Militärische Angelegenheiten, Politisches Archiv des Auswärtiges Amtes, Bonn, H276185, pp. 158-168. Portions of von Blomberg's trip report were reprinted by Francis Carsten in the *Slavonic and East European Review*, no. 41, 1962, pp. 217-244.
26. Ibid., p. 168.
27. S. S. Kamenev, "Osnovnye voprosy sovremennoi taktiki," *Voennyi vestnik*, no. 8, 27 February
1926, p. 1.
28. German General Staff Project #6, Wilhelm Speidel, "Training and Development of German General Staff Officers," vol. XXVI, part I, Landsburg, 1949, p. 44.
29. RGVA, O podgotovke ofitserov Reikhsvera. Belov Voroshilovu, 7 Oktober 1930, F. 33987, op. 3, d. 348, l. 104, cited in D'iakov, p. 272. See also above-mentioned remarks by Unshlikht, Berzin, and Voroshilov and similar remarks by Tukhachevsky, Uborevich, and others cited in Zeidler, *Reichswehr und Rote Armee*, pp. 262-265.
30. Ibid., pp. 247-248.
31. Aufz. Stephanys vom 17.9.1927, PA-AA (Politisches Archiv des Auswärtiges Amtes, Bonn), Geheimakten, Militärangel., Bd. 5, cited in Zeidler, p. 247. Hermann Geyer, Otto von Stülpnagel, Ernst Köstring, and Werner von Blomberg were similarly impressed with Russian openness as per their own trip reports.
32. Zeidler, *Reichswehr und Rote Armee*, p. 217.
33. D'iakov, *Fashistskii mech*, p. 85.
34. V. I. Savostianov and P. Ia. Egorev, *Komandarm pervogo ranga I.P. Uborevich*, Moscow, 1966, p. 162f., cited in Zeidler, *Reichswehr und Rote Armee*, p. 222.
35. BA-MA, RH2/2417, pp. 208-214.
36. Uborevich Voroshilovu, "Doklad o prebyvanii v Germanii," 13 January 1929, F. 33987, op. 3, d. 295, l. 141-183, cited in D'iakov, pp. 249-258.
37. Manfred Zeidler, "Luftkriegsdenken und Offiziersausbildung an der Moskauer Zukovskij-Akademie im Jahre 1926. Die Gruppe Fiebig und die sowjetische Luftstreitkräfte," *Militärgeschichtliche Mitteilungen*, no. 1, 1987.
38. BA-MA, RH2/2296. Zusammendfassender Bericht Martin Fiebigs vom 31 März 1926 an D.v.d. Lieth-Thomsen.
39. BA-MA, RH2/2217. Fiebigs Allgemeine Bemerkungen von betr. Strategische Aufgabe Nr. 1 und ihre Durchführung bei der Kommandeur-Fakultät der Luftakademie, Moscow.

40. BA-MA, RH2/2294. Abschrift von Muklevich, "Unsere Aufgabe," 1926.

41. Abschrift von Muklevich, "Unsere Aufgabe."

42. BA-MA, RH2/66, "Die russische Rote Luftflotte" vom 14.1.1927.

43. Ibid.

44. V. Ia. Kremlev, ed., *Akademiia imeni Zhukovskogo* (Moscow: Voenizdat, 1990), p. 45.

45. Giulio Douhet (German translation), *Luftherrschaft* (Berlin: Drei Masten Verlag,1935), p. 7. In the foreword to the book, Bülow called Douhet the "Clausewitz of the 20th century" and the "Schlieffen of the Air." See also R. Kohn and J. Harahan, (editors of English translation), *The Command of the Air,* USAF Warrior Studies (Washington: Office of Air Force History, 1983).

46. A. Sergeev, *Strategiia i taktika Krasnogo Vozdushnogo flota,* Moscow, 1925.

47. Zeidler, *Reichswehr und Rote Armee,* p. 117.

48. Ibid.

49. V. Novitskii, "Deistviia aviatsii v nachal'nom periode voiny," *Voina i revoliutsii,* book 9, 1929, pp. 23-24.

50. E. Tatarchenko, "Vozdushnyi flot v budushchei voine", *Krasnaia zvezda,* 2 October 1929, p. 2. In this article, Tatarchenko made a strong case for the independent air doctrine, drawing on the work not only of Douhet, but also of Foche, Robertson, Fuller, and Ritter.

51. Zeidler, *Reichswehr und Rote Armee* p. 117.

52. A. Vol'pe, "Spornyi moment v atake pekhoty," *Voennyi vestnik,* no. 22, 1926, p. 17.

53. David Glantz and Jonathan House, *When Titans Clashed: How the Red Army Stopped Hitler* (Lawrence: University Press of Kansas, 1995), pp. 9-10.

54. Murray and Millet, *Military Innovation in the Interwar Years* (Cambridge: Cambridge University Press, 1996), pp. 349-350.

55. As early as 1924, Kalinovskii was advocating the massive employment of tank in deep waves and in surprise attack. Konstantin Kalinovskii, "Bronevoe delo v mirovoi voine," *Voennyi Vestnik,* no. 28, 1924, p. 64.

56. Erickson, *The Soviet High Command,* p. 351.

57. TAY, "Samostoiatel'nye bronevye soedineniia," *Voina i revoliutsiia* book 5, 1930, p. 120.

58. Alaric Searle, "J.F.C Fuller, Tukhachevsky, and the Red Army: The Question of the Reception of Fuller's Military Writings in the Soviet Union," *Journal of Slavic Military Studies,* vol. 9, no. 4 (December 1996), pp. 848-884.

59. Heinz Guderian, *Errinerungen eines Soldaten* (Heidelberg: Kurt Vowinkel, 1951).

60. Ibid., p. 17.

61. Seatons, *The Soviet Army,* pp. 87-88.

62. Guderian, *Erinnerungen,* p. 23. The Seatons describe the disagreements between Guderian and the infantry generals, but fail to provide the source of these discussions. Seatons, *The Soviet Army,* pp. 87-88.

63. K. Kalinovskii, "Bystrokhodnye tanki vo vstrechnom boiu," *Voina i revoliutsiia,* book 5, 1929, p. 61.

64. S. Chikalin, "Ob osnovakh primeneniia i organizatsii operativnykh tankovykh soedinenii," *Voina i revoliutsiia,* book 4, 1930, pp. 25-35.

65. I. Kiselev, "K voprosu o primenenii bronevykh sredstv" (K stat'e t. Chikalina), *Voina i revoliutsiia,* book 11, 1930, pp. 84-93.

66. An example of discussion at the tactical level regarding infantry and tank employment was spurred by the translation of a French journal article by Velpry. See Velpry, "Pekhota i tanki," *Voennyi vestnik,* no. 20, 1928, and the response of I. Kiselev, "Tanki i ikh rabota," *Voennyi Vestnik,* no. 33, 1928.

67. *Vremennyi Polevoi Ustav RKKA, Chast' II* (Moscow: Voennyi vestnik, 1926), pp. 266-267.

68. *Polevoi Ustav RKKA: 1929* (Moscow: Gosizdat, 1929), pp. 126-131. These field regulations officially replaced those of 1925 by RVS Order no. 154 of 21 June 1929.

69. There is evidence of a biological weapons program in Soviet labs under the auspices of VOKHIMU--Voenno-khimicheskoe upravlenie--that was studying strains of Siberian ulcers/sores *iazvy* and plagues at a microbiological institute in Saratov. It is not clear, however, to what degree the Germans were involved in this effort, if at all. It is also interesting to note that R. Muklevich (head of the navy) was asked to come up with some unpopulated islands on which to test these substances. See Fishman's report, "Rabota bakteriologicheskoi laboratorii VOKHIMU," RGVA, Fond 33987, op. 1, d. 657, l. 143-144, 10 February 1928.

70. E. Fradkin, "Chemical Warfare: Its Possibilities and Probabilities," in *International Conciliation: Documents for the Year 1929,* no. 248 (Worcester: Carnegie Endowment for International Peace), p. 150. The author notes that these percentages are very rough estimates. According to this table, the Italians lost 34.7 percent of their troops through chemical poisoning.

71. Ipatieff, V.N., *Zhizn' odnogo Khimika* (Oxford: Oxford University Press, 1946).

72. E. Barsukov, "Grazhdanskaia promyshlennost' v boevom snabzhenii armii," *Voina i revoliutsiia,* book 10, 1928, p. 19.

73. RGVA, F. 33987, op. 3, d. 98.

74. Triandafillov, V.N., *Kharakter operatsii sovremennykh armii,* (Moscow, Voenizdat, 1929), pp. 17-19.

75. Ia. Ia. Alksnis, "Nachal'nyi period voiny," *Voina i revoliutsiia,* book 9, 1929, pp. 19-20.

76. RGVA, "Spravochnye dannye po voenno-khimicheskomu delu," Fond 33987, op. 2, d. 340.

77. M. P. Pavlovich (M. Vel'tman), *Khimicheskaia voina i khimicheskaia promyshlennost'* (Moscow: Moskovskii rabochii, 1925), pp. 84-85. As of 1928,

"the basic chemical weapon of the air force was the 8-32 kg. mustard-gas bomb capable of covering up to 300 square meters, F. 33987, op. 2, d. 340, l. 7.

78. Ibid.

79. Memorandum on chemical defense capabilities of the light tank from Chief of the Military-Chemical Directorate to Chief of the Directorate of Mechanization and Motorization, 4 December 1930. RGVA, Fond 31811, op. 1, d. 344, l. 59-60.

80. Ibid.

81. Dobrokhim was an acronym for Dobrovol'noe obshchestvo druzei khimicheskoi oborony i promyshlennosti (Volunteer Society of the Friends of Chemical Defense and Industry) formed in 1924, which later, in 1927, joined with the OSO (Obshchestvo sodeistviia oborone SSSR) to become Osoaviakhim (Obshchestvo sodeistviia oborone, aviatsionnomu i khimicheskomu stroitel'stve). In 1951, voluntary organizations for the army, air force, and navy joined together to form DOSAAF.

82. See A. Roginskii and A. Shleming, *Katalog voennoi literatury* (Moscow: Biblioteka tsent. doma krasnoi armii imeni Frunze, 1931). The catalogue lists sixty-two books on chemical warfare as compared with seventy on infantry and sixty-four on air force employment.

83. Ia. M. Fishman, *Voenno-khimicheskoe delo: posobie dlia nachal'stvuiushchego sostava RKKA* (Moscow: Gosizdat, 1929). Excerpts from the book were translated and published in Germany a few years later: *Der kriegschemische Dienst in der Roten Armee,* München, Zeitschrift für das gesamte Schieß-u. Sprengstoffwesen, 1933.

84. Ibid., pp. 10 and 30.

85. Ibid., p. 30.

86. In addition to Fischman, see Ia. L. Avinovitskii, *Protivogazy: Ikh ustroistvo i primenenie*
(Moscow: Osoaviakhim, 1928), and *Khimiia v sisteme sovremennykh vooruzhenii imperialistov,* (Moscow: Osoaviakhim,1936).

87. Fishman, *Der Kriegschemische Dienst,* p. 47.

88. The cover names for the school at Lipetsk used frequently in German military documents were "Schule Stahr" and "Wivupal" (Wissenschaftliche Versuchs und Personalausbildungsstation--Scientific Testing and Personnel Training Station).

89. "Tomka" was the chemical site's cover name, earlier referred to as Podosinskii.

90. Wilhelm Speidel, "Reichswehr und Rote Armee," *Vierteljahrshefte für Zeitgeschichte,* München, 1953.

91. BA-MA, RH2/2214. For example, at Lipetsk, according to one report, there were some 267 Russian personnel serving the 35-man-strong German officer group in the capacity of technical assistants and office workers.

92. Albert and Joan Seaton also maintain that the flight school at Lipetsk was entirely run by the Germans and that "The Russians took no part in the

instruction at all but merely serviced and guarded the camp" *The Soviet Army,* p. 83.

93. Lipetsk was the site of a Red Air Force pilot-training school up until 1924 , when it was unexpectedly closed. There the Reichswehr set up its own aviation school, which was camouflaged by the fourth Red Air Force Squadron where it trained pilots and tested German aircraft (e.g., Fokker D-7 and D-13) for some ten years. See D'iakov, *Fashistskii mech,* pp. 17-18.

94. Unshlikht to Stalin, 31 December 1926, F. 33987, op. 3, d. 151, l. 18-23, cited in D'iakov, *Fashistskii mech,* pp. 72-73.

95. RGVA, F. 33987, op. 3, d. 295.

96. RGVA, "Protokol sovetsko-germanskogo soglasheniia ob aviatsionnoi shkole v Lipetske", 15 April 1925, in D'iakov, *Fashistskii mech,* pp. 162-165.

97. Niedermeyer's Besprechung mit Alksnis, 12. October, 1928, BA-MA, RH2/2214.

98. BA-MA, RH2/2303.

99. BA-MA, RH2/2303, Bl. 44. It is interesting to note that Helm Speidel wrote the same about the Russians. They took in knowledge but shared none with the Germans: "Der Austausch der geistigen Grundlagen auf dem Gebiet der Kreigführung war somit durchaus einseitig; die Deutschen gaben, die Russen nahmen." See Speidel, p. 56.

100. BA-MA, RH2/2303.

101. "Lipetsk, in any event, could serve the training of singles, [but] as far as tactical training of formations is concerned, the school could offer nothing." BA-MA, Auszug aus der Besprechung zwischen Herrn Oberst Fischer und Herrn Bersin am 13.4.32, BA-MA, RH12-1/61, S. 170.

102. Reisebericht von Blomberg, p. 146.

103. During World War I the Germans were producing experimental IR devices for detecting objects and targets in the dark. See *Engineering Design Handbook: Infrared Military Systems,* HQs, US Army Materiel Command, Washington, DC, April 1971, pp. 1-2, 1-3.

104. BA-MA, RH 12-1/61, S. 11. "Protokoll der Besprechung vom 22.11.1931 zwischen Alksnis, Feodoroff, Hoffmeister, und Niedermeyer." These requests are repeated in the following summary of various meetings with the Russian side in the fall of 1931: "Stellungnahme In1 zu den Ru. Vorschlägen," Berlin, 18.1.1932, RH 12-1/61, S. 125. See also D'iakov, pp. 122-123.

105. BA-MA, RH12-1/61, S. 113. Betr. Sommerversuche 1931.

106. Ibid., p. 113.

107. D'iakov and Bushueva, *Fashistskii mech,* p. 19.

108. Ibid., p. 74.

109. Ibid., p. 87.

110. Ibid., pp. 195-196.

111. Ibid., p. 200.

112. Ibid., pp. 241-244.

113. BA-MA, RH12-4/v.54. Memorandum von Deutschen Botschaft Moskau an Chef des Truppenamts, Berlin, 16.5.33.

114. Zeidler, *Reichswehr und Rote Armee*, p. 200.

115. See Müller, "Die deutschen Gaskriegsvorbereitungen," p. 31.

116. Fischmann's letter to Voroshilov describing the cooperative work in 1928 with "our guests" (Germans) also seemed rather upbeat about the training aspects. See RGVA, Fond 33987, op. 1, d. 657, ch. 2, l. 152-156.

117. Amberg was a pseudonym for the German engineer and pilot Hans Hackmack.

118. BA-MA, RH2/2213.

119. BA-MA, RH12-4/54.

120. BA-MA, RH12-1/61.

121. "Kama" was an acronym for Kazan (the location of the school) and Malbrandt (the school's director). Sometimes the school was also referred to as "Katorg" by the Germans (Kazaner technische Organisation). Zeidler, *Reichswehr und Rote Armee,* p. 189. On the Soviet side, the school was officially placed under the auspices of Osoaviakhim and renamed accordingly in 1928 in order to conceal the "real sponsor of the course," D'iakov, p. 182.

122. RGVA, Berzin to Khalepskii, 18 March 1930, F. 31811, op. 1, d. 331, l. 72. The German officers who were conducting lectures on tanks included Pirner, Esser, Baumgardt, Bukhardt, and von Leist.

123. General Lutz was the head of the tank school and became head of the Reichswehr's motorized and mechanized troops in 1933.

124. Erickson, *The Soviet High Command*, p. 257. While most Western sources date the opening of the Kazan tank school in 1928-1929, a recent Soviet source dates it from 1926. See Major Boitsov, "Reichswehr i Krasnaia Armiia", *Krasnaia zvezda*, 25 November 1990.

125. Milsom, *Russian Tanks: 1900-1970* (London: Arms and Armour Press, 1970), p. 30. Voroshilov seemed quite willing to take the risks. According to him, "I proposed that we proceed [to purchase German tanks], because the "tank purchase" cannot cause us damage. A fictional agreement could be concluded either with Voenprom or with Berlin trade representation. The agreement should state that money for the tanks has already been spent. The speedy delivery of tanks to the USSR for the RKKA extremely desirable." Voroshilov to Stalin, March 1929, in D'iakov, *Fashistskii mech*, p. 186.

126. Zeidler, *Reichswehr und Rote Armee*, Bl. 191.

127. BA-MA, RH1/14, s. 8. Otto von Stülpnagel, "Bericht über meine Reise nach Rußland," 1930.

128. Griaznov to Voroshilov, 14 March 1932, cited in D'iakov, pp. 186-187. I. K. Griaznov was the deputy head of the Directorate of Mechanization and Motorization.

129. Griaznov, p. 187.

130. BA-MA, RH1/14. Stülpnagel, "Bericht über meine Reise nach Rußland vom 16.9 bis 13.10. 1930," Berlin, 12.11.30.

131. Ernst Köstring, *Erinnerungen,* BA-MA, Nachlaße 123/6. (These memoirs were written between 1948 and 1953.)

132. Köstring noted with dismay that because the Reichswehr was prevented by the Foreign Ministry from having a military mission abroad, he could not officially be called a military attaché, as were the representatives of other countries serving in Moscow. Rather, he was named a "Representative of the Reichswehr in the Red Army Staff" and denied many perquisites, including a diplomatic pass.

133. Köstring, *Erinnerungen,* pp. 52-53.

134. Ibid., p. 67.

135. Brief Köstrings an Seeckt vom 27.8.1931, BA-MA, N 247/88, cited in Zeidler, *Reichswehr und Rote Armee,* p. 262. This is the quotation that numerous scholars have used to drive home the point that German influence on Red Army thinking was great. The translation from the German is, "The effects of what we taught the [Russians] are manifold (*vielfach*); our ideas are like a leitmotif (*der rote Faden*) in what we have observed."

136. Both Manfred Zeidler and John Erickson cite von Blomberg's trip report to substantiate their convictions that the German-Soviet military collaboration was vital to the modernization of the Red Army. For a more unfavorable evaluation of the Red Army, see "Rußlandreise Gruppe Geyer" 14 October 1929, BA-MA, N221/10.

137. Reisebericht von Blomberg, p. 143. (In German, "*Der Wert der Zusammenarbeit für die Rote Armee wurde immer wieder betont, desgleichen der Wunsch, von der Reichswehr zu lernen und das Urteil der als massgebend angesehene deutschen Offiziere über das von der Roten Armee Geleistete zu hören.*")

138. Ibid., p. 180.

139. Ibid., In von Blomberg's own words, "We can also learn alot about various areas from the Red Army, especially in the areas of pontooning, air force operations, chemical weapons, propaganda activities, civilian air defense, and the involvement of the population in defense-related activity."

5

The Acquisition and Adaptation of Foreign Models The Case of Tank Development

> In matters of technical assistance we follow neither an English, nor a German nor an American orientation. Our orientation is a Soviet orientation. In every country we are ready and willing to learn in those areas in which that country is most advanced. When we had the problem of modernizing the petroleum, automobile and tractor industries we turned to the United States, as America is the leading country in these industries. When it came to the chemical industry we asked for German help and it is no fault of ours if we were forced to go elsewhere for some of our technical assistance.
>
> —*Ekonomicheskaia zhizn'*, 1929

Integral to the Red Army's successful and relatively rapid innovation during the First Five Year Plan period, in addition to financial resources, talented military theorists, and combat experience, was its access to foreign markets for purchasing equipment and parts for its weapons research and development programs and to foreign military advice and expertise. Although "economic autarky" or independence from foreign markets was the ultimate objective of the Soviet leadership, it was widely recognized that in the short run, Western expertise and the importation of foreign models for study would help to "jump-start" the nascent Soviet R&D process by providing it with many well-established, proven technical processes that would take an enormous amount of time to develop at home.

The documentation provided here challenges the views of Anthony Sutton, who has cast the Soviets as aggressive imitators of Western models who were incapable of designing their own high-quality weapons. Sutton accused the United States of helping to construct the Soviet military industrial complex because of all the assistance it rendered in areas of heavy industry.[1] While there is no doubt that the Soviets purchased equipment and expertise from abroad to accelerate their R&D programs, one cannot deny the existence of successful indigenous R&D projects in the USSR.

Upon returning from a visit to the Aberdeen Testing Grounds in the United States in early 1929, the head of the Military-Technical Directorate, Innokentii A. Khalepskii, made the following observation in a trip report to Voroshilov:

> The American Army and industry spent tens of millions of dollars on research and all we have to do is to purchase the finished product. Therefore we should concentrate on preparing our manufacturing base, ... familiarizing ourselves with the experimental work of the United States Army.[2]

This "shortcut" sentiment was confined not only to defense-related R&D programs. Dependence on technical assistance from the West for numerous industrial branches, a feature of Lenin's regime as well, was extolled and expanded by Stalin during the First Five Year Plan.[3] Although there were some dissenters, especially scientists who scoffed at the idea of learning anything new from the West, this was a minority view. As Bruce Parrott notes, "More orthodox interpreters of official policy, by contrast, felt that the essential first step toward self-sufficiency was a massive draft on foreign technology with a minimum of indigenous innovation."[4] Indeed, it seemed senseless, as Stalin's commissar of trade put it, "to invent that which has already been discovered and tested abroad."[5] But although the military leaders were interested in finding ways to expedite their R&D processes, especially in the area of tank development, it is not obvious that there was a conscious effort to borrow Western technology instead of creating indigenous designs, as was the case in nondefense research.[6] Rather, it was an integrative approach by which some foreign tank features were borrowed and assimilated, while others were dropped in favor of indigenous design concepts.

Perhaps more than in any other area of weapons design, the Red Army lagged behind other countries in tank procurement owing chiefly to its nascent automotive industry, poor infrastructure,[7] and severe shortages of engineers knowledgeable in tractor and tank design and unskilled factory workers manning the production facilities. The nagging "cadre problem" led Soviet authorities to send technicians and workers to study designs and production methods in more technologically advanced countries and then apply them at home. Trips abroad by Red Army officers to examine and purchase tanks and tank parts, especially in Great Britain and the United States, are well documented.[8]

Many of the newly declassified materials from the Russian military archives shed light on several issues concerning military research and development during the Stalin era. Documents regarding the tank features that were purchased or borrowed and adapted by the Soviets in the R&D process, and those that were ignored or dropped in favor of Soviet indigenous designs, are particularly interesting. They convey that the skillful combination of foreign and indigenous tank characteristics not only went far to aid the Soviets in weapons innovation, but also aided them in a speedy fashion. Access to foreign technical assistance indisputably expedited the Russian R&D process and the production of tanks.[9]

In addition to the refreshing insights these documents offer in terms of the "nuts and bolts" of tank R&D, many of them illustrate the heated exchange of blame between economic and military authorities for failing to fulfill tank plans on schedule. The OGPU also made its presence known in the R&D community by complaining in 1928 about the "gentry" social status of the personnel filling the research organizations who were either "incompetent" or "dangerous."[10] It should be recalled that this was the same year the arrest of German engineers accused of sabotaging industrialization, culminating in the famous "Shakhty Trial," and the atmosphere was rife for the arrest of alleged "saboteurs."[11] In a letter that OGPU chief Genrikh Yagoda wrote to Voroshilov in March 1928, he listed the percentages of gentry, merchant, and "blue blood" backgrounds of the members of each technical committee, which he believed were far too high, and went on to say:[12]

> Our institutes, committees, bureaus and laboratories are controlled by old, so-called "exclusive" specialists. ...The majority of these specialists are not familiar with the RKKA or its requirements and do not understand the technical issues associated with modern combat and weapons...some members of the *Tekhomov* are incompetent in technical matters and do slap-dash work...politically, many of the "exclusive specialists" are dangerous.

It is clear that Yagoda was grasping for reasons to "cleanse" the technical committees of these specialists—one's background is unlikely to predetermine one's intelligence or ability to comprehend modern forms of warfare. Yet, if we look beyond the shouting matches, preoccupation with quotas, lack of coordination among R&D efforts, and complaints about scientists' social backgrounds revealed in these pages, many positive attributes of the Soviet military R&D system emerge. Unsuccessful efforts to centralize military R&D elements translated into relatively high levels of autonomy for weapons designers, as is evidenced by the records of at least two indigenous tank designers, Dyrenkov and E. Grotto. Complaints about delays and other problems in tank production were frequent and shrill because tanks were one of the RKKA's highest procurement priorities, as many military records underscore.

The Birth of Research and Development Bureaus

> Up until now we have had no kind of plan for weapons systems in the RKKA and really in such circumstances the supply directorates and technical committees are working out alot of issues connected to weapons independently and according to the initiative of individual workers without ...a plan and without ties to separate arms resources among themselves.[13]

Right after he assumed his new post as chief of the Mechanization and Motorization Directorate in 1929, Innokentii Khalepskii issued a "state of the tank R&D" progress report in which he clearly threw his support to the R&D community.[14] He recommended increased budgetary allocations to R&D, including large sums of hard currency for the purchase of equipment and tank prototypes from abroad, in an effort to end "tinkering" and get down to business. That such budgetary enhancements took place is evidenced by reports on the War Commissariat's financial plans.[15] High on Khalepskii's list of recommendations was the creation of a centralized design bureau for tanks, tractors, and armored cars at the Central Scientific-Research Automotive and Motor Institute (NAMI).[16] He believed that too many design forces were dispersed among industrial trusts without any solid and cohesive leadership. Awards, prizes, and travel abroad were also advocated by Khalepskii as means of instilling competitiveness in Soviet tank designers.[17]

Although the lines of responsibility between industrial and military authorities were clearly drawn in reports and military orders from

1928,[18] some members of the military proposed concentrating all military research in the scientific-research bureau of the RVS,[19] instead of continuing the practice of consolidating designs and inventions in the Main Directorate of the Defense Industry (GVPU) within VSNKh.[20] GVPU itself came under criticism for failing to possess a "special scientific-technical organ" that would coordinate technical research matters more speedily and make final decisions.[21] There were also proposals for organizing a military research institute in the military section of the Communist Academy and creating a similar institute within the NIS (*nauchno-issledovatel'skaia sektsiia*) of Osoaviakhim.[22] Tukhachevsky proposed setting up a NIID for dirigible construction *(nauchno-issledovatel'skii institut pri dirizhablestroeniiu)* within Leningrad's Institute of Civilian Air Forces,[23] and military-scientific bureaus (*voenno-nauchnye biuro)* were subsequently established at the military academies.[24]

This sampling of the various research elements that were coming into being at this time, both at the "macro" level and within each service arm,[25] contrasts sharply with the "highly centralized" depiction of the entire process by some scholars[26] and the utter "simplicity" of it by others.[27] Many R&D bureaus, institutes, commissions, and other entities were created that, at least in the years 1928-1931, appeared to suffer from an acute lack of coordination among themselves, with the armament factories, and with civilian scientific-technical institutions. This lack of coordination was partly responsible for delays and other bottlenecks that occurred in the tank procurement process, which inevitably led to some frustration on the part of the designers.

Ostekhbiuro: Where Civil and Military Goals Overlapped

Perhaps the oldest and least controversial R&D bureau was VSNKh's Ostekhbiuro (*osobyi tekhnicheskii biuro po voennym izobreteniiam spetsial'nogo naznacheniia pri VSNKh*—special technical bureau of special military inventions attached to VSNKh), created in 1921 by STO order and headed by Georgian scientist Vladimir Ivanovich Bekuari.[28] Its appears that Ostekhbiuro was the locus of all military inventions—regardless of service.[29] Upon completing and approving an invention, for example, it would officially grant permission for that invention to be exploited by a given industrial trust. In one recorded instance, a prominent naval officer named Duplitskii complained that Ostekhbiuro had not given permission to the appropriate trust (in this case, Trest Slabykh Tokov) to begin working on its invention of quartz adapters for radio installations.[30] S. S. Kamenev, deputy chairman of a governmental commission overseeing Ostekhbiuro, intervened on behalf of Duplitskii and asked Bekuari to check on the problem and presumably to speed things up. Bekuari responded that he had already agreed to release this particular invention.[31] It is also interesting to note that Kamenev urged the RVS not to burden the Ostekhbiuro with small problems so that the bureau could retain its independence and unique character.[32] Thus, this particular R&D organ seems to have enjoyed the support of the military.[33] It also appears to have been fairly successful in obtaining needed parts for its projects via a contract with a Paris firm called VISSNER and was well funded by the state.[34]

The Acquisition and Alteration of British and American Tanks

Before turning to the specific features of tank design that were adopted, altered, or rejected by Soviet R&D authorities, a few words should be said about early tank trends in general. During World War I, the tank was seen as "primarily a machine gun destroyer, which can be employed as an auxiliary to an infantry assault," according to the British World War I tank commander E. D. Swinton.[35] Indeed, only very gradually did the tank assume greater roles and responsibilities in combat beyond infantry support. Because its chief function was to transport anti-artillery fire, the most controversial issues in early tank design and development were the tank's armor thickness, the appropriate number of turrets and weapons mounted on them to ensure steady and continuous fire, and tank weight/speed ratios. The Soviet Union developed multiple-turreted tanks to accommodate their 76.2 mm guns. The Soviet T-28 had two turrets and the T-32 and T-35 had five turrets each.[36] Tank speed was enhanced by high-powered engines and new suspension systems, such as the Vickers Medium tank. The Soviet BT, modeled after the American Christie, whose speed was increased by its capability of running both on wheels and on tracks, became "what was probably the most effective tank of the mid-1930s."[37]

The influence of British tank design on early Soviet tank programs is well documented in Soviet, German, and British sources. The Directorate of Mechanization and Motorization ordered twenty Carden-Lloyd tankettes, fifteen six-ton Vickers, fifteen twelve-ton Vickers from Great Britain, and two Christie tanks from the United States, along with dozens of other pieces of foreign equipment, in 1930.[38] In a letter to the RVS from June 1930, Khalepskii described the tank features to be changed in the recently or soon-to-be-acquired British and American tanks and also set deadlines for the completion of prototypes based on them.[39] As demonstrated in the following sections, substantial changes were made to the foreign imports, and in some instances the resulting Soviet prototype represented an amalgam of features from more than one foreign design. In particular, the Soviets were attracted to the higher-speed American engines (such as Ford) and to British turret, hull, and chassis configuration. As a rule they relied on their own tank armaments, such as the DT (Degtiarev tank) machine guns. Some of the recommended changes to British, U.S., and some German tanks are discussed.

The Carden-Lloyd Tankette

According to Khalepskii, the British Carden-Lloyd tankette, with the exception of its weapons system, compared favorably with Soviet prototypes in several areas, including its speed, its Ford motor, and its ease in adjusting to a self-propelled mount.[40] In a confidential letter to Uborevich, then chief of armaments, Khalepskii recommended that industry alter the Carden-Lloyd's all-round traverse and then proceed to the serial production of parts such as hulls. His goal was to oversee the production of 290 tankettes based on the Carden-Lloyd whose motors would be purchased abroad. The hulls were to be manufactured at the Izhorskii factory, and other parts procured from the Stalingrad factory, where the bulk of its production was based.[41]

According to John Milsom, one of the foremost British authorities on early Soviet tank development, the Soviets' first T-27 prototype built in 1931 was almost identical to the Carden-Lloyd MkVI machine-gun carrier, thanks to concessions granted by Vickers-Armstrong Ltd. to manufacture these carriers in the USSR.[42] Subsequent prototypes, however, differed from the first in several areas. Namely, the hull was redesigned, and the armored fairing was riveted to the top of the hull to improve communication between the driver and the gunner. The tank's superstructure was widened to allow more room for storing ammunition and equipment and many of the Model A GAZ truck components were included.[43] Among the tankette's drawbacks, however, were its poor ventilation and cramped conditions, which made it very difficult to operate and necessitated the recruitment of short tankmen. These problems eventually led to work on light amphibious tanks with machine guns mounted on rotating turrets used primarily for reconnaissance purposes.[44]

6-Ton Light Vickers Tank

The production of a prototype based on the six-ton (light) British Vickers, but with changes to its turrets and armed with Soviet weapons, was given a deadline of August 1931. The alterations to the Vickers were not to interrupt the work already proceeding on other indigenous light tanks, such as the successor models to the MS-1 (T-19[45] three-seater and T-20 two-seater with a more powerful motor and gearbox).[46] Only after extensive testing of the Vickers might it be placed on the production line, according to Khalepskii in a memorandum to Uborevich.[47] "We can produce the engines, transmission, and bodies but not the motors—even with the aid of a model," claimed Khalepskii.[48] Although Milsom concludes that "apart from the armaments, there were virtually no changes made to the original Vickers design between 1931 and 1933,"[49] the German officers studying Soviet tank design in Berlin saw things differently. They reported in 1933 that the Soviet Vickers (T-26) was an amalgam of British and American design features.

> If one compares the Soviet light Vickers tank with the English light Vickers and the American TJ-EL (German acronym), one can see that the Russian chassis and tracks are identical to those of the American TJ-EL ...[and] both turrets are similar to the English Vickers. Vickers [influence] consists in the form of the chassis and the external fuel container. The similarity between the Russian and the American tanks consists in the design of the chassis, the caterpillar track, in the uniformity of the diameters of the rear and front wheels, in the similarity of the surface and in the wings.[50]

Mostovenko called the T-26 "the second type of light tank (after the BT series—*Bystro-khodnyi tank* or fast tank) and the basic tank for combined units and tank units."[51] Its chief drawback was insufficient speed compared with the BT, which led to the initiation of work on other light tanks, such as the T-46. Nonetheless, the T-26 remained a model for future self-propelled weapons and special-mission car designs.[52]

The American Christie

Although the American Christie (M3) tank was initially hailed by Khalepskii as "unbeatable in terms of its speed,"[53] features such as its armaments were incompatible with Soviet design and production capabilities.[54] According to Western analysts of the early tank program, the Christie was too complex to be replicated, but a simplified version appeared as the BT-1 in 1931.[55] Like the Vickers, the BT ran on wheels or tracks with the capability of switching back and forth at a cost of thirty minutes. Its speed in the tracked mode—in which it normally operated—is what earned it the name "fast tank."[56]

Vladimir Mostovenko also described the wheel-track drive as its most innovative feature which enabled the tank to reach a heightened speed of 52 km/hour on tracks and 70 km/hour on wheels.[57] But in terms of armaments, Mostovenko insisted that there was nothing to be learned from the Americans: "When some of our tankists examined the American light M3 tank in 1942, they were shocked by its primitive design features, steering gear, and turret bearings."[58] Despite Khalepskii's initial enthusiasm for the Christie, however, he later believed that with regard to its motor and engine design, the Grotto tank prototype compared favorably with the Christie.[59]

> Comparing the construction of the Grotto tank with the construction of the Christie in the United States also using large cylinders, which I saw [when I traveled there] leads me to believe that all the advantages lay with the Grotto [tank], because the Grotto's motor group and engines are better thought-out and more expedient. ... I exchanged opinions with Soviet engineers and designers regarding the mass production of tanks. Our engineers, who work with Grotto, also believe that there will not be any particular production problems.[60]

12-Ton Vickers Medium Tank/ T-12 (28)

Owing to its incompatibility with Soviet weapons and armour systems and its poor passability, the British Medium Vickers would only be replicated, according to Khalepskii, if the Soviets' own T-12 and T-24 were unsuccessful.[61] But the Soviet program to develop the T-24 appears to have been quite successful, as it built on several Soviet prototypes; this history is discussed in the next section.

Excursus: Soviet Design Analyses of German Tank Models

The German firms of Daimler, Krupp, and Rheinmetallwerke (whose corresponding designations were D, K, and 4)[62] allowed the Directorate of Mechanization and Motorization to copy blueprints of their tank prototypes for perusal by Russian engineers if strict security measures were observed.[63] These measures included sharing the documents with a small group of engineers hand picked by the OAT, viewing the material in the presence of Braverman and Pavlovskii in a closed-off area, and storing the material in a fireproof case. The directorate was similarly cautious about the copying of German blueprints and attached the following instructions on their handling: They must be copied in a secure, secluded area; no traces of their German origin or evidence of the documents having been copied should be present; and each copy must have a code. Any copies found that did not comply with these regulations would be swiftly burned in the presence of the GPU chairman and either a representative of the trust or the factory director.[64]

Upon reviewing these documents, the Soviet designers concluded that all the German models needed extensive testing.[65] The design concept of the Rheinmetallwerke tank (RM) was viewed as impractical, while the epicyclical steering mechanisms[66] of K and D tanks, they believed, deserved further study. The production of K and D tanks, though characterized by complicated casting techniques, could be adapted to Soviet manufacturing processes, in their view.[67] Other aspects of the "R" tank were considered adaptable at Soviet factories: the body of the weapons and breech piece, semi-automatic loading system, cradle, compressor, counterrecoil mechanism, and more.[68]

Indigenous Tank Programs and Prototypes: Dyrenkov and Grotto

> It goes without saying, that the assimilation of foreign designs absolutely must not impede work on our own prototypes whose production must proceed at increased paces in order to meet all of the requirements of the RVS in tank and tractor rearmament.
>
> —Innokenty Khalepskii

In addition to assimilating foreign models, the Red Army was actively engaged in developing its own tank prototypes, some of which predated the purchase of British and U.S. ones. Two medium tank prototypes named after their designers, Dyrenkov (DRS) and E. Grotto (T-G), were apparently predecessors to the T-12 (24) medium tank issued in 1930.[69]

A fair amount has been written in the East and West about some of the Red Army's early tank programs at the Krasnoe Sormovo factory, where the first Soviet tank was produced in 1920, the "Borets za svobodu Lenina" (Freedom Fighter Lenin). The Soviets' successful MS-1 light tank, based on the French Renault and later known as the T-18—

the first tank to enter serial production in the late 1920s—was also constructed there.[70] But little has been written—and undoubtedly until recently little was known—of the Dyrenkov and Grotto medium tank prototypes designed in the late 1920's and tested in 1930.[71] The Dyrenkov tank[72]—named after the Russian engineer and weapons designer whose official title was "representative to the RVS for special orders"—was constructed at the Izhorskii state factory (Izhzavod) in Leningrad under the directorship of I. Marchenko.[73] The Grotto tank was named after its German designer, E. Grotte, who, on loan from Rheinmetallwerke, built the tank prototype at Leningrad's Bolshevik factory at approximately the same time.[74] These R&D programs were so highly classified, that not only were the projects' names, whereabouts, and characteristics shrouded in complete secrecy, but even the Germans—with whom the Soviets were also collaborating in the area of tank training and development—may not have identified the DRS tank properly, speculating that it was purchased before the contract with Vickers of Great Britain was signed.[75]

An examination of the progress of these two prototypes, as revealed in recently declassified Soviet sources, is worth undertaking for two reasons. First, the two tanks offer insight into the intricacies of early Soviet tank research and development. The Dyrenkov and Grotto prototypes appear to have been designed and produced prior to the purchase of English tanks in 1930 and thus were, for the most part, indigenous designs—the Grotto albeit developed by a German. Whereas Dyrenkov encountered many of the problems associated with the defense industry in general, including shortages of qualified technicians, delays in receipt of equipment, and red tape, Grotto appears not to have been so burdened. In fact, the Grotto team was lauded by Khalepskii for its success in training competent technicians in the process of designing the tank who could be sent to factories to oversee production later on.[76]

Whereas little was recorded in terms of the DRS's combat and technical qualities, perhaps because it suffered from technical problems,[77] the Grotto was viewed as enormously successful by Voroshilov and Khalepskii and hailed by chief of Armaments Uborevich, in a letter to Stalin, as a model superior to the T-24.[78] According to one document, the Medium T-G was rushed by the OGPU and NKVM as the most important special weapons project for 1931.[79] The T-G's features differed in its streamlined hull configuration, 76 mm cannon, four machine guns, and—what was new for that time—pneumatic servocontrol and herringbone gear in the gearbox.[80]

Second, interactions among Voroshilov, Khalepskii, head of VSNKh Kuibyshev, Uborevich, and Dyrenkov regarding these tank prototypes provide interesting insights into the politics and priorities of tank design and production at the turn of the decade. Khalepskii was a fervent proponent of research and development and proved generally supportive and complimentary of the tank designers he oversaw,[81] while Voroshilov was preoccupied with the business of the matter: meeting deadlines, watching budgets, and coping generally with the industrial bureaucracy. Voroshilov was not afraid to pounce on Khalepskii and Kuibyshev when he perceived too many delays in production. Unnecessary expenditures on hard currency imports also called for reprimands.[82] In 1931, foreign technical assistance contracts in the civilian sector were cut back, and between 1932 and 1933 a sharp decline in the percentage of the imported capital goods occurred.[83]

At least initially, work on designing the Dyrenkov tank proceeded ahead of schedule, to the delight of all concerned. In a report to Unshlikht about the progress of the DRS, Khalepskii wrote with pride that the work was completed two weeks earlier than expected and that the designs were ready to be transferred to the factories.[84] Two days later, Voroshilov was issued a protocol by those reviewing the Dyrenkov project.[85] It was decreed:

> To recognize the expediency of putting the tank system Dyrenkov to a comprehensive test with the aim of sending an urgent order to the Izhorskii factory for six experimental models (prototypes) of the tank in two variants, with a deadline of testing the first tank no later than April 1, 1930 and the rest no later than August 1, 1930.[86]

However, the auspicious beginnings of the program were short-lived. Within a few weeks a telegram was sent to Dyrenkov from Khalepskii asking the director of the Izhorskii factory, Marchenko, to be informed that the "delays have been fraught with unpleasantness" and urging Marchenko to take a personal role in ensuring that the calendar plan, presumably for tank development, be met.[87] A few days later, Marchenko responded with a comprehensive accounting of the preliminary calendar plan for manufacturing one DRS prototype. He provided dates for the completion of various parts of the tank, such as the tank hull, whose blueprint would be ready December 20 whose turret casting would be prepared by January 5 and whose technical processing would be ready by January 20, 1930.[88] He also listed the cost of each prototype at 95,000 rubles.[89]

Despite the somewhat desperate tone of Khalepskii's telegram to Dyrenkov, Voroshilov seemed generally pleased with the progress that Izhzavod was making and wrote a note to Marchenko wishing him well with his production of six D tanks.[90] So long as he met his deadlines, wrote Voroshilov, the War Commissariat would cooperate with him in every way. But Dyrenkov was growing impatient with delays in the delivery of equipment and advances of funds vital to the success of his research. In December he complained to Bokis, chief of the Technical Directorate, that he was still waiting on the delivery of a light automobile and funds for experiments.[91] By February 1930, Dyrenkov's tone had grown much shriller.

> The elaboration of the design of the turret wall was delayed first by a shortage of cannons and now by the shortage of machine guns which, despite my requests (I sent you four telegrams!) I have not yet received...The 45 mm cannon will not be manufactured this year. ...I am requesting that you send me one reinforced 37 mm cannon...and I will repeat my request for a Degtiarev tank (DT) machine gun with a ball mount.[emphasis mine].[92]

While Dyrenkov initially pinned the blame for slowdowns in tank D development primarily on the shortages of and delays in receiving equipment—especially guns—Marchenko tended to criticize the shortage of designers and draftsmen at the Izhorskii factory.[93] He claimed that his factory was promised ten such specialists but only received eight, and believed that this would lead to a significant delay in the production of blueprints and "hinder greatly the work associated with the details of the first experimental model."[94] Later, Dyrenkov was found complaining directly to Voroshilov—who was very aware of the "cadre" problems and constantly wrote and made speeches about the need for more qualified technicians—that the technical diversity of factory workers was lacking and that he needed far more man-hours than he had been given for manufacturing the tank hull and forging the armor.[95]

Conclusions

These early tank designs and prototypes were important to the evolution of tank development in the Soviet Union and ultimately paved the way for the creation of the legendary T-34 heavy tank employed in World War II.[96] As this chapter illustrates, the judicious borrowing of specific features of foreign weapons technologies and industrial processes, what could be called "emulative innovation," assisted and indeed expedited the Soviet R&D process in the early 1930s. In addition to weapon parts and equipment borrowed and purchased, the influx of technical experts from abroad was invaluable, given the dearth of Soviet technical expertise, the so-called cadre problem. This foreign assistance should not be overstated, however. As this examination of Soviet tank development indicates, the Soviet R&D establishment was well on its way to designing and producing a formidable arsenal of high-quality indigenous weapons.

Notes

1. Anthony Sutton, *National Suicide: Military Aid to the Soviet Union* (New Rochelle: Arlington House, 1973), p. 70.

2. RGVA, 8 April 1929, F. 33988, op. 1, d. 637, l. 15. One area in which Khalepskii wanted technical assistance was nonrupturing automobile tires and tire covers. He also wrote about negotiations he had with Goodyear Tires during his visit to the United States.

3. Bruce Parrott, *Politics and Technology in the Soviet Union* (Cambridge: MIT Press, 1983), pp. 27-34.

4. Ibid., p. 28.

5. *Piatnadtsatyi s"ezd VKP(b): Stenograficheskii otchet* (Moscow: 1962), vol. II, pp. 1099-1100, as cited in Parrott, *Politics and Technology,* p. 29.

6. Ibid. Parrott cites the work of a prominent industrial journalist, A. F. Khavin "During the First Five-Year Plan the party instructed economic officials and engineers to concentrate on assimilating foreign technology rather than on devising novel designs."

7. The author of an article in *Krasnaia zvezda* cites Osinskii's remarks at the Sixteenth Party Conference in order to underscore just how far behind the USSR lagged in number of cars per capita. Whereas there were 5 people per car in America and 137 per car in Germany, there were 7,000 per car in the USSR. P. Ionov, "Armiia, avto i piatiletka," *Krasnaia zvezda,* 16 October 1929, p. 2.

8. For example, Baranov was assigned the tasks of aquiring blueprints to American cars and tanks and purchasing 50 gallons of "Prestone" antifreeze on his trip to the United States in late 1929. RGVA, 28 November 1929, F. 31811, op. 1, d. 1, l. 29. See also, Milsom, *Russian Tanks,* p. 34.

9. Sutton, *Western Technology* p. 322. Sutton correctly points out that technology transfers to the USSR were not without their own set of problems: Inefficiences invariably occurred, equipment went unused, and the Soviets were not legally protected from the foreign supply of inferior goods. Sutton goes too far, however, in assuming that Soviet engineers were hopelessly at the mercy of foreign equipment and expertise because they lacked any indigenous capabilities.

10. RGVA, March, 1928, F. 33987, op. 1, d. 657, l. 196-197.

11. In March 1928 German employees of AEG were arrested while delivering turbines to Soviet coal miners in Kharkov and accused of "sabotage, industrial espionage, and attempts to establish contact with the former owners of the mines, now in emigration," according to Hilger. The purpose of the trial, he went on to say was, "most important, to blame all such troubles on bourgeois specialists and foreign capitalists, thus distracting the workers' attention from the serious blunders of Soviet policy." Gustav Hilger and Alfred Meyer, *The Incompatible Allies: A Memoir History of German-Soviet Relations, 1918-1941* (New York: MacMillan, 1953), p. 218.

12. RGVA, F. 33987, op. 1, d. 657, l. 196-197.

13. RGVA, Prikaz No. 422/77, F. 33988, op. 1, d. 616, l. 108.

14. RGVA, Spravka to Chm. of the Commission on tank and tractor production, Narkom RKI, Ordzhonikidze from Khalepskii, 27 November 1929, F. 31811, op. 1, d. 1, l. 18-22.

15. RGVA, F. 33988, op. 1, d. 638, l. 126.

16. RGVA, F. 31811, op. 1, d. 1., l. 21. It is interesting to note that some seven months later, Khalepskii was advocating that VATO (All-Union Society for Auto-Tractor Industry) replace NAMI as the centralizing locus.

17. RGVA, F. 31811, op. 1, d. 1, l. 21.

18. RGVA, F. 33988, op. 1, d. 616, l. 111.

19. RTsKhIDNI, Voroshilov Fond 74, op. 1, d. 367, l. 2-8.

20. RGVA, Kalinovskii's report, 31 December 1929, F. 31811, op. 1, d. 82, l. 2-3.

21. "O nauchno-tekhnicheskom obsluzhivanii voennoi promyshlennosti." *Torgovo-promyshlennaia gazeta,* 30 May 1928, p. 4.

22. RGVA, F. 33988, op. 1, d. 633, l. 8.

23. RGVA, F. 33987, op. 2, d. 346, l. 25-31.

24. RTsKhIDNI, F. 74, op. 1, d. 367, l. 7.

25. Scientific-Technical Committees, or NTKs/Tekhkomy, performing research on military technology were attached to each service arm. In a protocol from May 1928, it was decreed that the NTKs--whose abolition was debated--were to remain within the air force and naval directorates and were to be better tied to civilian research institutions. RGVA, F. 33988, op. 1, d. 614, l. 24. In another report issued by Unshlikht to Voroshilov a few months later, the NTKs were stated to reside within the Supply Directorate, as well as the air force and naval directorates. RGVA, "Dokladnaia zapiska," 18 July 1928, F. 33988, op. 1, d. 616, l. 170, and RGVA, March 1928, F. 33987, op. 1, d. 657, l. 198.

26. Mikhail Tsypkin, "The Origins of the Soviet Military Research and Development System" (Ph.D. diss., Harvard University, 1985).

27. Jerry Hough, "The Historical Legacy in Soviet Weapons Development," in Jiri Valenta, ed.,*Soviet Decisionmaking for National Security* (London: Allen and Unwin, 1984).

28. RGVA, F. 33989, op. 1, d. 38, l. See also I. Artem'ev, "Ostekhbiuro," *Voenno-istoricheskii zhurnal,* no. 4, 1967, p. 71.

29. Some of the military inventions worked on in 1928 by Ostekhbiuro included ultra shortwave and light beams, antitank mines, long-range aviation bombs, and mobile smokescreens. RGVA, F. 33989, op. 1, d. 38, l. 1-2.

30. RGVA, 27 September 1928, F. 33988, op. 1, d. 38, l. 33.

31. RGVA, 12 December 1928, F. 33989, op. 1, d. 38, l. 34-35.

32. RGVA, F. 33989, op. 1, d. 38, l. 44.

33. Tsypkin viewed this organization noteworthy for its lack of civil-military squabbling as well in "Origins of the Soviet Military Research and Development System," p. 53.

34. RGVA, F. 33989, op. 1, d. 38, l. 4-7. Its budget for the year 1928/1929 was 5,219,456 rubles.

35. Richard Ogorkiewicz, *Technology of Tanks* (Surrey: Janes Information Group, 1991), p. 7.

36. Ogorkiewicz, *Technology of Tanks*, pp. 14-15.

37. Ibid., p. 17.

38. RGVA, F. 31811, op. 1, d. 99, l. 1-8. Some of the other items to be imported included Harley-Davidson motorcyles, Packard cars, Hercules motors, German levels (*uklonomery*), and Austrian bullets.

39. RGVA, F. 31811, op. 1, d. 83. The shipment of the Carden-Lloyd and Vickers tanks was confirmed by official British sources on May 31, 1930, according to a German report, "Zur Klärung über die Anzahl der englischen Kampfwagen in der Sowjetunion," BA-MA, 1931, RH 2/2746.

40. RGVA, F. 31811, op. 1, d. 1, l. 83.

41. RGVA, F. 31811, op. 1, d. 1, l. 99.

42. Milsom, *Russian Tanks, 1900-1930* (London: Arms and Armour Press, 1970), p. 82.

43. Ibid.

44. Vladimir Mostovenko, *Tanki* (Moscow: Voenizdat, 1958), p. 99.

45. Note that the T-19 was criticized as being too heavy and should be considered a transitional model, RGVA, F. 31811, op. 1, d. 344,

46. RGVA, F.31811, op. 1, d. 1, l. 101.

47. RGVA,28 June 1930, F. 31811, op. 1, d. 1, l. 102.

48. Ibid, l. 103.

49. Milsom, *Russian Tanks*, p. 83. Ogorkiewicz also stated that the T-26 was a copy of the Vickers.

50. BA-MA, 26.4.33, RH2/2746.

51. Mostovenko, *Tanki*, p. 91.

52. Ibid., pp. 93-94.

53. RGVA, Khalepskii to RVS, 16 June 1930, F. 31811, op. 1, d. 1, l. 83.

54. RGVA, Khalepskii to Uborevich, 28 June 1930, Ibid., l. 99.

55. Alexander, p. 21, and Milsom, *Russian Tanks*, p. 96.

56. Milsom, *Russian Tanks*, p. 96.

57. Mostovenko, *Tanki*, pp. 86-87.

58. Ibid., p. 95.

59. RGVA, F. 31811, 12 November 1930, op. 1, d. 425, l. 10.

60. Ibid. Khalepskii's unfavorable reviews of the Christie's motor and engines are probably connected to the report from Berzin of the fourth directorate of the RKKA staff to Uborevich at approximately the same time, which listed the German General "L" (Lutz's) complaints about the Christie's technical characteristics in great detail: "General L informs us that our friends, having studied the Christie's data (via information received from their people in America) and correlating them with the construction data on their own tank, have come to very sober conclusions regarding the construction of the Christie. The Christie has a motor of 400-420 horsepower which gives it a speed of 100 km/hr., whereas the German model of 150 HP renders a speed of 80 km." RGVA, 13/15 November 1930, Fond 31811, op. 1, d. 340, l. 21.

61. RGVA, 28 June 1930, F. 31811, op. 1, d. 1, l. 99.

62. RGVA, 1 November 1929, F. 31811, op. 1, d. 331, l. 12.

63. RGVA, 2 December 1929, F. 31811, op. 1, d. 331, l. 9. For a full description of the security measures to be undertaken when viewing the highly classified documents on German tanks, see RGVA, 20 January 1930, F. 31811, op. 1, d. 331, l. 17-18.

64. Ibid.

65. RGVA, "Zakliuchenie o mashinakh marki RM i K," F. 31811, op. 1, d. 331, l. 25.

66. Ogorkiewicz, *Technology of Tanks,* especially pp. 280-281.

67. RGVA, "Otzyv o tankakh D, RM, K konstruktorskogo Biuro zavoda Bolshevik," F. 31811, op. 1, d. 331, l. 29.

68. RGVA, F. 31811, op. 1, d. 331, l. 35.

69. Mostovenko, *Tanki,* pp. 81-82.

70. Ibid., pp. 75-83; Ryndin, *Tank MS-1* (Moscow: Redizdat TsS Osoaviakhim, 1938); Rotmistrov, *Vremia i tanki* (Moscow: Voenizdat, 1972), A. Alexander, *Armor Development in the Soviet Union and the United States,* R-1860 (Santa Monica: RAND, 1976), pp. 17-26, and A. Ryzhakov, "K voprosu o stroitel'stve bronetankovykh voisk krasnoi armii v 30-e gody", *Voenno-istoricheskii zhurnal,* no. 8, 1968, l. 106.

71. RGVA, "K rabotam Dyrenkova," Fond 31811, op. 1, delo 31, and "Po postroiki srednego tanka T-12," Fond 31811, op. 1, d. 425. The Izhorskii factory, also known as "Izhzavod," belonged to the metal and metal-processing industry trust under the auspices of VSNKh. Ibid., l. 29. Only one western source has mentioned the Dyrenkov and Grotto tanks: John Milsom, *Russian Tanks,* p. 33. p. 33. Milsom mislabeled the T-G a "heavy tank." Rather, it appears to be a successor to the T-12 (24) Medium tank. See P. Rotmistrov, *Vremia i tanki* (Moscow:Voenizdat, 1972), p. 46 and 82.

72. The "S" is presumably for Medium (*Srednyi tank*).

73. Dyrenkov was also responsible for designing an automobile with an internal combustion engine. F. 31811, op. 1, d. 455, 2 June 1930.

74. Ibid. The reference to E. Grotte was found in Lieutenant Colonel V. V. Zakharov, "Voennye aspekty vzaimootnoshenii SSSR i Germanii, 1921- 1941

gg." (Ph.D. diss., Armed Forces Humanities Academy, Moscow, 1992), p. 91. Both spellings, Grotte and Grotto, occur in the literature.

75. RGVA, Fond 31811, op. 1, d. 31, l. 1, and the German report, "Kampfwagen Medium D in der roten Armee," Bericht Nr. 12/1, Berlin, 21.3.1931, BA-MA, RH2/2746. The Germans may have also been referring to the British Medium D tank, which appeared to be in the Soviet arsenal as well. The extensive list of measures associated with preserving the tank's secrecy is found in a letter from Khalepskii to the special department of the OGPU and to Unshlikht, 28 November 1929, F. 31811, op. 1, d. 31, l. 22-23.

76. RGVA, Fond 31811, op. 1, d. 425, l. 10.

77. Indeed, in a letter from Dyrenkov to the RVS on the shortcomings of the Dyrenkov tank, he noted its inability to operate effectively on any surface other than highways or railroads--that it could not travel long distances without breaking down. F. 31811, op. 1, d. 31, l. 6., 5 October 1929.

78. RGVA, F. 31811, op. 1, d. 82, l. 50, 19 February 1931. It is unclear, however, what ultimately became of the T-G.

79. Ibid., l. 32.

80. TG discussed by Mostovenko, *Tanki*, p. 82.

81. According to Khalepskii, Dyrenkov's impressive capabilities and achievements made him the perfect candidate to embark on two other design projects: the tankette with a Ford motor A and the small tank with a Hercules motor. These projects also took place at the Izhorskii factory. Ibid., l. 2. Later, Dyrenkov was also responsible for the design of the self-propelled wagon with an internal combustion engine. RGVA, F. 31811, op. 1, d. 455, 2 June 1930.

82. RGVA, F. 31811, op. 1, d. 31, l. 58-59. In a letter to Kuibyshev and Khalepskii, Voroshilov criticized the importation of grinding machines for riveting purposes at the Izhorskii factory and suggested that welding would prove a lot cheaper and reduce the weight of the armor by 5 percent. In switching to welding the fulfillment of orders would also be accelerated.

83. Parrott, *Politics and Technology*, p. 36. But capital investment in domestic scientific research tripled by the end of the Second Five Year Plan.

84. RGVA, F. 31811, op. 1, d. 31, l. 2, 16 November 1929.

85. Ibid., l. 5. The following Red Army officers comprised the commission of the RVS reviewing Dyrenkov's progress: Unshlikht, Khalepskii, Kamenev, Postnikov, Shaposhnikov, Kalinovskii, and Rogovskii.

86. Ibid., l. 5, 18 November 1929.

87. Ibid., l. 26, 7 December 1929.

88. Ibid., l. 29-32, 10 December 1929.

89. Ibid., l. 35,"Opytnyi zakaz no. 900510," 14 December 1929. This figure of 95,000 rubles was the cost of the order for one DRS tank and not the final cost (*okonchatel'naia stoimost'*).

90. Ibid., l. 49, December 1929. On December 18, funds were released for the manufacture of six DRS tanks, the first of which was due no later than January 25, 1930. "Ob otpuske kredita na spets. zakaz," 18 December 1929, F. 31811, op. 1, d. 31, l. 44.

91. Ibid., l. 60, 28 December 1929.

92. Ibid., l. 102, 1 February 1930.

93. RGVA, F. 33988, op. 1, d. 638, l. According to a report issued by Voroshilov two months earlier, he mentions that because of cutbacks in the tank program, the orders for Degtiarev machine guns in each service were also reduced.

94. Ibid., l. 85, 12 January 1930. Here Marchenko was referring not only to the DRS, but also to the T-18 and T-12. Voroshilov officially adopted the T-12 for the RKKA and congratulated the KhPZ factory for a job well done. RGVA, F. 31811, op. 1, d. 425, l. 3.

95. RGVA, 9 June 1930, F. 31811, op. 1, d. 31, l. 119-120.

96. P. A. Rotmistrov, *Vremia i tanki*, p. 49.

6

Marshal Tukhachevsky: Enigmatic Military Entrepreneur

> It was not Tukhachevsky's fate to live until the Great Patriotic War. But Tukhachevsky and his heroes annihilated the fascist armies. The technology that Tukhachevsky constructed, along with the party and the people, brought down the enemy. Guided by Soviet military doctrine, to which Tukhachevsky made major contributions, the soldiers and generals destroyed the adversary.
>
> —Alexander Todorskii, 1963

The chief catalyst of the RKKA's innovation, in my view, was the former Imperial Army lieutenant-turned-Red Army commander, shrewd strategic thinker, and savvy politician, Mikhail Nikolaevich Tukhachevsky. Drawing on a combination of skills and experiences obtained through the vigorous study of foreign and indigenous military histories and technological developments, the command of a front in the civil war, and possessing an uncanny ability to synthesize past combat lessons and to forecast future combat scenarios, Tukhachevsky articulated a vision of the RKKA that was compelling to a large audience of party, government, and military leaders. Keen political acumen—as manifested especially in his ability to use Stalinist ideology to his advantage—enabled him to gain acceptance for many of his ambitious and sometimes controversial operational and technological ideas among the powerful party and military elite and to challenge and indeed discredit the views on military strategy long held by the eminent and prolific General Staff Academy professor, Alexander Svechin.

My conviction that a powerful reformer from within the ranks of the military was capable of bringing unprecedented degrees of innovation to the Red Army is shared by very few authors. Most scholars of bureaucracies, as discussed in the Introduction, have traditionally viewed reform-minded bureaucrats as a contradiction in terms. Bureaucrats, in the common view, are said to be resistant to change and protective of the status quo. Military bureaucrats are thought by some to be especially entrenched and incapable of instigating changes on their own behalf.[1] Kimberly Marten Zisk challenged this view in her study of the Red Army in the post-Stalin era. In examining how the Soviet military establishment reacted to NATO's Flexible Response Doctrine in the 1960s, Zisk uncovered a wide range of views—including politically risky ones—held by various Soviet military officers.[2]

Going somewhat further than Zisk, I illustrate in this chapter that Tukhachevsky was not only one of the catalysts of innovation in the Red Army, but the predominant one. I draw loose comparisons between Mikhail Tukhachevsky and the American "Father of the Nuclear Navy," Hyman Rickover, borrowing from Eugene Lewis's concept of "public entrepreneurship," in order to identify some of the personal characteristics, organizational practices, and environmental conditions shared by these two individuals that contributed to their respective successes.[3] In addition to Lewis's study, I base my discussion of Tukhachevksy on available biographies of him,[4] his own writings,[5] and relevant archival documents.[6]

Tukhachevsky as Public Entrepreneur

In explaining the subjective factors that led to Tukhachevsky's success as the Red Army's key military innovator, Eugene Lewis's study of public entrepreneurs offers a useful framework. Lewis focused on the common characteristics of three successful American entrepreneurs—Hyman Rickover, J. Edgar Hoover, and Robert Moses—who were able to bring about significant and unprecedented changes within their respective institutions. Of the three cases investigated by Lewis, I focus on the similarities between Tukhachevsky and the legendary American naval engineer and father of the nuclear navy, Admiral Hyman Rickover.

Before examining the similarities between Admiral Rickover and Marshal Tukhachevsky, some of the reasons that Lewis's framework fits "loosely" and not "tightly" should be mentioned. First, U.S. military bureaucracies differed from Soviet ones. For example, historically there has been far less interservice rivalry in the Red Army than in the U.S. military establishment. The Soviet General Staff traditionally has discouraged such rivalry and rewarded holistic thinking about strategic objectives in a combined arms sense, whereas its U.S. counterpart, the Joint Chiefs of Staff, remains a virtual battleground in which the army, navy, air force, and marines compete for combat missions and the resources to underwrite them.[7] In spite of these institutional differences, both Rickover and Tukhachevsky operated effectively in their respective milieus. Rickover was extremely adept at accumulating resources for his branch of the Navy's Bureau of Ships and the Naval Reactors Division of the Atomic Energy Commission, while Tukhachevsky was similarly skillful at making his case for the costly modernization of the Red Army in the General Staff (and combined arms) context.[8] It goes without saying that Tukhachevsky's position as chief of armaments in the early 1930s aided this process.

Another problem endemic to study of the Soviet Union generally was the quantification of budgetary allocations, especially to the military. One of the key characteristics shared by Lewis's entrepreneurs was their ability to alter the existing pattern of resource allocations in their favor. As several biographers demonstrate, Rickover did so admirably. While there is plenty of evidence that Tukhachevsky was granted many of the resources he requested, there is also evidence of cutbacks in the army that may or may not have had something to do with him.[9] The difficulty of making a final determination about the defense budget arises from the numerous revisions that the five year plans underwent as a result of the tugging and hauling between civilian and military authorities. Based on my data, it would be an overstatement to say that Tukhachevsky alone altered the existing pattern of resource allocations, even though many of his operational and technological programs were launched.

An additional and obvious discrepancy between these two entrepreneurs was their physical longevity. While directing the navy's nuclear propulsion program for three decades, Rickover served fourteen defense secretaries, fifteen navy secretaries, and eleven chiefs of naval operations and went kicking and screaming into retirement at the ripe age of eighty-two.[10] When asked how he got projects accepted, Rickover reportedly quipped, in reference to his opponents in the defense department, "You just outlive them."[11] Indeed, as Duncan notes, Rickover's longevity enabled him to secure support for his nuclear propulsion projects from key legislators in Congress "while secretaries of the navy came and went."[12] Among Rickover's most ardent supporters was Senator Henry "Scoop" Jackson, who urged President Kennedy to permit Rickover to stay on despite his retirement age.[13] When the navy decided it was time to retire him when Ronald

Reagan became president, the "plot" to get him out was filled with political intrigue but was certainly not life-threatening.[14]

Unfortunately, this was not the case for Marshal Tukhachevksy. Despite all of his talents and substantive contribution to the modernization of the Red Army, his life ended abruptly at the early age of forty-four when he was executed by a firing squad in the NKVD courtyard on June 11, 1937.[15] Although Tukhachevsky's life ended prematurely, his ideas lived on. The tactical and operational theories he helped to develop were utilized in World War II and, as many would argue, ultimately led the Red Army to its defeat over the Wehrmacht. Clearly, it is the longevity of their ideas and not their physical beings that are testimony to the success of these men. The nuclear navy has been in existence for some forty years, and it is unlikely that nuclear propulsion will be rendered obsolete in the near term. In Tukhachevsky's case, the longevity of his ideas lay not only in the application of his concepts of deep operations to World War II battles or the expression of his theories in Soviet military doctrine for decades, but also in the "sovietization" of U.S. military doctrine in the 1980s.[16] The U.S. Army's "AirLand Battle" doctrine and NATO's "Follow on Forces Attack" concept, whereby troops would penetrate enemy territory rapidly in waves or echelons supported by air cover and long-range munitions and using airborne assault and highly mobile tank groups to facilitate breakthroughs and penetrate quickly to the depths of the enemy's defense were concepts suspiciously reminiscent of Tukhachevsky's "deep battle." The technologies, including reconnaissance strike complexes, sensors, and heat-seeking missiles that sharply reduced the time to make decisions in war and enabled operations to be conducted at night or in bad weather were new, but the means of applying them were vintage "Tukhachevsky."[17]

Because Rickover lived forty years longer and in a much more "open" society than Tukhachevsky, there are simply more sources available on Rickover, from official congressional testimony to the intimate revelations of friends, colleagues, and subordinates which offer a clearer picture of the man's personality. Few interviews are available with Tukhachevsky's subordinates that would provide an understanding of what it was like to work for him, what drove him, and how he related to people.

These discrepancies notwithstanding, several of Admiral Rickover's entrepreneurial characteristics—as described by Lewis—were shared by Marshal Tukhachevsky. They included his ability to exploit contradictions inherited from the past, to enhance his autonomy and flexibility, to convince his colleagues and superiors of his preferences in institutions upon which he was dependent, and to reduce dependence on organizations beyond his control.[18] Just as Rickover was able to convince his superiors and ultimately the public that nuclear-propelled submarines were vital to the nation's security, so too was Tukhachevsky able to convince the communist party that the advanced weapons technologies and operational strategies he supported would be indispensable in a future war against hostile Western and Eastern neighbors.

A common characteristic of successful entrepreneurs is not only their unflinching devotion to their work, but also the degree to which their work defines them. As Duncan put it, "Rickover saw Naval Reactors as an extension of himself; there was never any doubt in his mind—nor in the minds of others—who was in charge."[19] Rickover himself, in an article he wrote for *Management Magazine*, stressed "ownership" of one's job and total "responsibility" for it as among the key characteristics of successful managers in large bureaucracies.[20] He believed that unless a manager took responsibility for all the failures and successes of the organization and worked harder than anyone else, it would be impossible to inspire others to commit fully to the projects at hand. While serving in the Bureau of Ships, Rickover earned the respect of Admiral Mills because he "got the work done" and regularly made personal visits to damaged ships to uncover the source of the damage and claim responsibility for it.[21] His tireless work ethic is legendary; many of his subordinates have recalled the many times they cancelled vacations and missed family gatherings on holidays for the benefit of the nuclear program. For Rickover, working around-the-clock was not an unusual occurrence. As he noted in the management article, "Any individual has only so much time to work, with an absolute limit of 24 hours each day."[22]

But the basis of his leadership qualities and political skill—as many biographers and associates of Rickover have noted—was his knowledge.[23] Few could approach Rickover's command of the technical details and procedures related to nuclear reactors and ship and submarine engineering. Captain Beach noted that although iconoclasts typically do not survive in the navy, "Rickover knew the most and that saved him."[24] Like Rickover, Tukhachevsky was extremely knowledgeable in the technical details of the rearmament projects he oversaw and constantly strove to improve his knowledge. This devotion to and knowledge of tasks relates to another characteristic: he "derived sustenance from accomplishment and not 'good behavior' "— that is, he was willing to go out on a limb for something he believed in despite the political risk involved. Both men were passed over for promotions and given unsavory assignments during their careers, but these temporary setbacks did not deter them, and, if anything it, appears that they grew even more determined. By the same token, they were consummate managers with considerable political prowess. Finally and perhaps most fundamentally, they viewed the organization as a means of achieving their goals and not as an end in and of itself.[25]

This chapter focuses on two entrepreneurial characteristics which that were central to Tukhachevsky's success: his ability to articulate a vision of the RKKA and its role and requirements in a future war, and his ability to exploit the contradictions that emerged between the quest for military professionalism and the ideological and rhetorical requirements of the Bolshevik, and especially Stalinist, regimes. Tukhachevsky deftly used the highly politicized environment of the First Five Year Plan period to discredit the military theorists with whom he disagreed. Indeed, it seems almost paradoxical that the chief military innovator would resort to ideological denunciation in order to advance his professional goals.[26] The idea of the military (or any nonparty institution) deriving benefit from the adroit use of ideology is certainly at odds with the political scientist Roman Kolkowicz's understanding of the term. Ideology, in his view, was a means of subjugating and constraining the military, whose power the party was constantly keeping in check with an elaborate array of political controls, including political indoctrination.[27] Ideology, simply put, was synonymous with confinement, not expedience.

Several of Tukhachevsky's accomplishments and substantive contributions to Soviet military art while commanding the Leningrad Military District from 1928 to 1931, and in Moscow again from 1931 to 1935 as chief of armaments, are reviewed in this chapter, including a brief excursus illustrating Tukhachevsky's bureaucratic prowess in promoting the expansion of civil aviation—a goal that very conveniently dovetailed with that of Stalin—by taking charge of the matter and protecting or "buffering" it from influences that could have weakened Tukhachevsky's control or undermined the project altogether.[28]

Finally, I explore the sources of claims that Tukhachevsky had poor personal relations with Stalin and Voroshilov, and I attempt to show that despite these personal tensions—which in my view have been exaggerated—Stalin, Voroshilov, and Tukhachevsky cooperated rather well between 1928 and 1936 because they realized that the success of the Red Army's rearmament programs—and ultimately the security of the

Soviet state—would depend on a favorable modus operandi among them.

Skillfully Exploiting Contradictions

Hyman Rickover was "a man well-suited to his time," according to Lewis.[29] There is an element of truth in this. It is not at all obvious that Rickover would have had the same success today that he enjoyed in the immediate postwar era. His considerable technical expertise and leadership qualities notwithstanding, Rickover carefully exploited an unusual set of circumstances that arose from contradictions then existing between naval conservatism and traditionalism and America's passion for technological progress.

Although the United States had replaced Great Britain as the preeminent naval power in the world by 1945, the U.S. Navy was still clinging to obsolescent traditions—such as the predominance of the surface fleet—even when the importance of submarines and aviation had been demonstrated clearly in both world wars and when the armed forces were grappling with new and powerful platforms and weapons systems, such as long-range aircraft that would render the surface fleet vulnerable to more accurate attack.[30] In addition, the vagaries of postwar demobilization, combined with civilian attempts to reassert control over military activities by creating a department of defense and thereby diminishing the independent cabinet status of the navy, contributed to a sense of malaise within the navy which impeded its efforts to rethink its global mission.[31] Rickover, simply put, was able to combine all these influences and put them to work for him. He initially encountered some opposition from members of the navy hierarchy who, in an effort to challenge the U.S. Air Force monopoly over strategic bombing missions, were more interested in equipping their aircraft carriers with nuclear weapons than their submarines with nuclear engines.[32]

With the help of Rickover's superiors the tremendous advantages inherent in nuclear-propelled submarine's which would be quieter and thus harder to detect and which could dive deeper and remain underwater far longer than diesel submarines soon became self-evident.[33] The implications for national security were enormous. Rickover and his staff were developing the nuclear submarine as the chill of the Cold War was setting in and thus making the military rationale of the hard-to-detect nuclear submarine even more compelling. The Soviets' rapid expansion of their conventional submarine arsenal in the mid-1940s, combined with their testing of the atomic bomb in 1949, made the promise of a quieter and thus less vulnerable U.S. submarine—and potential nuclear deterrent in its own right—very attractive. Nuclear propulsion also promised countless civilian spinoffs, permitting the costs of development to be shared.[34] Indeed, Rickover is also credited with building the first civilian nuclear power station in Shippingsport, Pennsylvania, which served as a model for the construction of light-water reactors in the United States.[35]

Tukhachevsky was also a man well suited to his time who was able to exploit numerous contradictions existing in society generally, and in the military particularly, during the early years of Stalin's rule. Like Rickover, who was operating in the euphoric atmosphere of the postwar United States, Tukhachevsky was serving the Red Army in the heady days of the "great transformation" of a predominantly backward, agricultural society into a modern industrialized state. Stalin was a fervent proponent of technological progress, and he challenged the country to catch up to and overtake the West in this regard. Tukhachevsky, it is very clear, had similar ambitions for the Red Army.

At the same time, there was a contradiction between the rhetorical break with and indeed contempt for tsarist traditions and, with some exceptions, continued reliance on the military professionals who served the tsars, to build and modernize the army. Voroshilov openly promoted the use of "old professor specialists" in the military academies, while Stalin, at least rhetorically, opposed their participation until 1931.[36] In general, the party's efforts to maintain a delicate balance between supporting and promoting military-technical expertise by means of granting some autonomy to commanders and weapons designers while simultaneously ensuring their political reliability were routinely handled by periodic dismissals *(chistki)* of unfit military communists.[37]

In addition, there were the contradictory combat lessons of past wars: the passive, relatively immobile trench warfare of World War I counterpoised with the copious maneuver of the civil war.[38] Throughout the 1920s the lessons from these wars were debated frequently in Soviet military journals. Not only were the tactics and strategies employed in both wars contradictory, but also many argued that a future war would be one of technology and advised Red Army troops to train for operations in defensive and offensive combat environments.[39] Finally, Stalin's highly politicized environment was replete with contradiction between political conformity and technological progress. Tukhachevsky was extremely skillful at maneuvering through and weaving together these contradictions and using them to his advantage, as the following section illustrates.

Stalinist Ideology and the RKKA

Before we turn to a discussion of Tukhachevsky's use of ideology to promote his agenda, a few words should be said about ideology in general and how it evolved (or devolved, as the case may be) during Stalin's tenure as general secretary. David Joravsky addresses the issue of ideology under Stalin most eloquently in his work on the legendary peasant-agronomist, T. D. Lysenko.[40] Upon agreeing to a minimalist definition of ideology as "supposedly rational beliefs shared by a group only because they are members of the group," Joravsky attempts a more precise definition of what makes a belief ideological: "When we call a belief ideological, we are saying at least three things about it: although it is unverified or unverifiable, it is accepted as verified by a particular group, because it performs social functions for that group."[41] The task of the scholar, he notes, is to discover the functions of ideology.

Although Stalin spoke often of the dialectical unity between theory and practice, in reality such references were "decorative flourishes on one of the maddest versions of political realism imaginable," according to Joravsky.[42] Indeed, from late 1929 on, theory was subordinated to practice and the central committee became the official and legal locus of Soviet philosophy until 1950.[43] Joravsky credits Stalin with turning Marxist-Leninist theory into "a treasury of incantations suitable to bless any statement that political bosses wish to make."[44] Reference to these incantations became a litmus test for their acceptance by the party's editorial authorities.

Georgii S. Isserson, a respected theorist of Soviet operational art and a member of the General Staff, cast the years 1926-1930 as the era that witnessed the politicization of Soviet military doctrine and strategy in his periodization of Soviet military thought from the 1917 October Revolution until the outbreak of World War II.[45] Military discussions not only had to have Marxist-Leninist ideological underpinnings, but were also supposed to tout the party's "general line" of enthusiasm for the industrialization and collectivization campaigns.[46] This politicization was spurred in part by the creation of the military section of the Communist Academy,[47] which endeavored to bring ideological "debate" to military discourse in a Marxist-Leninist framework.[48] Over time, it became increasingly incumbent upon military writers to endow their work with the proper political spin. Some authors who failed to comply with this requirement were subject to criticism in the press, although "compliance" was not always applied objectively or systematically.

Perhaps the best example of someone who was unjustly pilloried for abandoning Marxist principles was Alexander Svechin. Although Svechin's work was infused with "materialist" perspectives from Friedrich Engel's thesis on the state's "forces of production," and despite the efforts of some authors to come to his defense precisely on this point,[49] Svechin did not survive these and many other slanderous attacks by his "colleagues" in the long run.

Tukhachevksy proved extremely adept at finding ideological roots in support of the advanced weapons technologies he hoped to procure. Engels, for example, underscored the importance of the country's "forces of production" for constructing an army and fleet and lauded the revolutionary qualities of new weapons such as artillery.[50] A good example of Tukhachevsky's reliance on quotations from Engels can be found in his foreword to the Russian translation of the work of the Prussian military theorist, Hans Delbrück, entitled *Die Geschichte der Kriegskunst im Rahmen der politischen Geschichte.*[51] In his foreword, Tukhachevsky criticized Delbrück's opposition to (or, more likely, disregard of) materialism, calling him a "vehement enemy of materialism," yet maintained that many of Delbrück's historical examples were influenced by Marx and Engels.[52] Upon quoting Delbrück, Tukhachevsky wrote that Delbrück's conclusions could be labeled "Marxist" in their treatment of the importance of economics to social relations and military art.[53] Because Tukhachevsky agreed with some of Delbrück's ideas, he went to great lengths to show that they contained Marxist elements in order to legitimize his admiration for the ideas of an imperialist author. Indeed, Tukhachevsky's success in infusing military writings with Marxist ideology is reflected in histories and biographies of him. According to one author, "Tukhachevsky's name is associated with the formulation and development of Soviet military science based on the principles of Marxism-Leninism."[54]

In addition to coloring one's work with Marxist overtones, adherence to the party's "general line" or, more bluntly, enthusiasm for Stalin's collectivization and industrialization projects, was also an editorial requirement. In contrast to Svechin's relative silence on the state's industrialization goals, Tukhachevsky's outspoken optimism for the five year plan and its implications for widespread rearmament was distinctive.[55] Whereas Svechin generally advised against putting too much emphasis on peacetime defense production in favor of measures that would gradually ensure a healthy economy, Tukhachevsky's innovative ideas about force employment and generation were predicated on the enormous industrial gains and technological improvements in the economy that the plan would bring in the future.[56] These industrial gains, in Tukhachevsky's view, would in large part be translated into improving the defense industries whose weapons production would eventually help close the gap with the well-endowed armies of its Western competitors. In essence, these two military theorists personified the tension between satisfying military requirements in the short run (peacetime procurement) and forsaking such rapid growth in favor of general and proportional industrial development in the long run, which would be called upon in the event of war to shift to defense production. At least until 1931, Stalin's views on this matter coincided with Svechin's.

Because the coloring of one's text with Marxist ideology and optimism for the five year plan appeared to be enforced somewhat arbitrarily by Stalin's editorial authorities, it seems unlikely that "ideological conformity" in and of itself was a strong criterion for the adoption of strategies and tactics or the procurement of new weapons technologies. But it proved a useful weapon to Tukhachevsky in attacking his opponents and one that he utilized quite masterfully on several occasions. A good example of one of Tukhachevsky's simplistic attacks is contained in an article entitled "What do we expect from [the journal] *War and Revolution?*" *(Voina i revoliutsiia)*. Unlike some of the other contributors who wanted to increase the readership and strengthen the scholarship of particular journal articles, Tukhachevsky focused on the need to censor particular authors, such as Alexander Svechin, who were opportunists masking themselves in "pseudo-Marxist methods."[57]

> We clearly see how blatantly opportunistic, right-leaning, and decadent theories are penetrating our military-scientific literature; covering up with various types of noble robes and fig leaves....The successes of Marxist-Leninist enlightenment are forcing all opportunists to mask themselves in "pseudo-Marxist" methods.[58]

Tukhachevsky went on to state that *Voina i revoliutsiia* must reflect the "general line" of the communist party and that its "ammunition must be aimed at opportunists who are impeding the improvement of the country's defense."[59] But Tukhachevsky himself was not beyond reproach. In a review of Tukhachevsky's report on the character of modern war, Tukhachevsky was accused of misusing the label "opportunist."[60] According to the author of this review, who was associated with the Communist Academy, Svechin was guilty of "simple political illiteracy" and not of "opportunism." The author also implied that Tukhachevsky was unusually hard on Svechin because he failed to hold other military theorists—such as Vladimir Triandafillov[61]—to the same ideological standards. However, this criticism of Svechin was rather mild in comparison with the harsh denunciations he would receive the following year from members of the Section for the Study of War in the Communist Academy.[62] It is interesting to note that the academy itself was reprimanded in June 1930 for "lagging behind the tempo of current events" and failing to give enough attention to the industrialization and collectivization campaigns.[63] This may have had something to do with the academy's decision to attack Svechin so virulently the following year.

Tukhachevsky inveighed against Svechin's work most forcefully in the Communist Academy's collaborative work, *Opposing Reactionary Theories on the Military-Scientific Front: Criticism of the Strategic and Military-Historical Views of Professor Svechin,* published in 1931.[64] Svechin's *Strategiia* was the volume most frequently denounced by the academy, even though that work had served as the General Staff Academy's textbook for many years, had won the prestigious Frunze prize for military literature as late as 1928,[65] and had supported some of the ideas presented in Tukhachevsky's *Future War* study published in 1928.

Quoting from *Strategiia,* Tukhachevsky criticized Svechin's unwillingness to distill the features of contemporary war into a "red soviet strategic doctrine."[66] Tukhachevsky, as his own writings reveal, was similarly reluctant to draw up a universal military doctrine and underscored, as did Svechin, that the continuous elaboration of doctrine was imperative. In an article that Tukhachevsky wrote the same year that *Strategiia* was published, he too claimed that it is "incorrect to speak of a universal strategy" because the character of war and social conditions of a given state are constantly changing, and one's strategy is in constant need of revision.[67] Foremost on Tukhachevsky's mind was the need "to cleanse our military thought from Svechinesque digression."[68] He also called Svechin "anti-Soviet" for failing to support the role of political commissars, an "agent" of imperialist intervention sabotaging the technical development of the RKKA, and a "right opportunist."[69] Svechin was taken to task primarily for underestimating the degree to which the fulfillment of the First Five Year Plan would serve the interests of rearmament and thus enable the Red Army to plan for a fast-paced and decisive war of destruction.[70] Their questionable veracity notwithstanding, these charges and labels made the positions of Tukhachevsky and Svechin appear more antithetical than they really were. They discredited Svechin's views and helped Tukhachevsky to advance his own.

Another example of Tukhachevsky's use of Engels to quash his theoretical opponents is found in a stenographic report from an RVS meeting of May 28, 1928, while Tukhachevsky was still serving as chief of staff.[71] In the report, delivered to an audience of thirty-eight RVS members and representatives of the navy, including a leading naval strategist, Mikhail A. Petrov. Tukhachevsky stressed that the geopolitics and military capabilities of the "continental" Soviet state were the complete opposite of those of the insular sea powers of Japan and Great Britain, and that it made little sense to invest heavily in a large shipbuilding program. Naval missions, he argued, should support ground-force operations, and the investment should be in coastal defenses, naval aviation, and weapons of support—not in destroyers (*linkory—lineinyi korabl'*). Tukhachevsky flattered Petrov in his report, calling him an "outstanding strategist," and then cut to the chase, relying on quotes from Engels's "Anti-Dühring" to support his case. He read an excerpt from "Anti-Dühring" underscoring the point that while a surface fleet is the main combat arm of sea powers, it is the rifle troops, artillery, and aircraft that are important to continental states such as the USSR. Because a large naval fleet is not needed, "to spend vast sums of money on it is unnecessary."[72] Despite an equally eloquent response from Petrov in which he provided examples of the important roles played by the Russian navy in the Crimean War and spoke to unproven yet potential resources and capabilities that other powers—especially Germany—would have in the future, Petrov basically challenged Tukhachevsky's view that the sea was merely "an arena for the investment of weapons." Rather, in Petrov's view, it was a "strategic direction." Two years later, Petrov; Nikolai Ignatiev, chairman of the scientific-technical committee of the navy, and Arkady Toshakov; chief of staff of the Baltic fleet, who also attended the RVS meeting, were accused of being "saboteurs" trying to implement "anti-Marxist theories" and were arrested.[73]

This examination of Tukhachevsky's use of ideology to serve his own ends, tainted though it was with its own strokes of hypocrisy and contradiction, nonetheless illustrates that adherence to Stalin's "general line" was, when used skillfully, a simplistic but powerful tool in winning over ideas and eliminating opponents. In this endeavor, Tukhachevsky was a master craftsman. Having looked at the methods with which Tukhachevsky eliminated his opponents, let us now turn to an analysis of the ideas he set in place.

Formulating a Vision of Future War

Tukhachevsky's treatise on future war, published in 1928, spelled out in enormous detail the combat and economic potential of the allegedly hostile states bordering the western Soviet Union, the possible coalitions that could form among them to attack the USSR, and the course that several variants of war with them could take.[74] In providing the military with the most concrete vision of future combat on which to base its defense requirements available in the late 1920s, *Future War* undoubtedly confirmed Tukhachevsky's authority and expertise as an extraordinary and prescient strategic thinker. Tukhachevsky's vision of the RKKA, armed with modern operational concepts and state-of-the-art weaponry, was not unlike Admiral Rickover's vision of the U.S. Navy equipped with nuclear-propelled submarines capable of evading enemy detection. Both men's visions may have been perceived as overly ambitious at first, but over time won the respect of key decisionmakers.

Just as Rickover exploited the contradictions between naval surface-fleet traditions and the competing technological advances that jeopardized those traditions in the aftermath of World War II, Tukhachevsky pulled together a concept of future war from many diverse sources. Indeed, someone was desperately needed to synthesize the disparate combat experiences and lessons of the relatively immobile operations of World War I (i.e., trench warfare and defensive maneuvers) and the civil war (i.e., highly mobile maneuvers and offensive tactics), and to place them in the context of the "new dangers" emanating from "hostile" states on the USSR's western borders. Appreciating the confusion and uncertainty, Tukhachevsky issued Directive no. 20.030 on January 26, 1926 calling for a comprehensive study of a potential conflict in the European theater.[75] Two years and 735 pages later, such a study was produced.

According to the study, the chief mistake in World War I had been the universal underestimation of the ever-changing conditions of war and Germany's overestimation of the military factor in preparation for the war.[76] Because it had been preoccupied with preparing for combat operations in the "First Period of War" during which rapid maneuver and deep penetration of the enemy's territory would occur, the German army failed to plan adequately for a protracted war contingency.[77] This lack of foresight cost it dearly. In attempting to rectify this imbalance,

Future War stressed the importance of political and economic factors in war planning, in addition to military ones, and devoted hundreds of pages to identifying the political and economic capabilities and instabilities of the Soviet Union's potential enemies on its western borders: Romania, Poland, Finland, and the Baltic States.[78]

In keeping with Lenin's conception of modern war, the authors of the study maintained that a future war would be a "class war" launched by the imperialists and thus a clash of socio-economic systems, a struggle pitting world imperialism against the first socialist state.[79] Couching the Leninist boilerplate in a contemporary context, the authors wrote that the imperialists would attempt to bring decay and corruption to the USSR's rear by means of disseminating harmful propaganda in collusion with kulaks, nepmen, bourgeois intelligentsia, and religious clergy.[80] Partly because World War I fostered the breakup of the "Imperialist Front" and partly because of the growth of national revolutionary movements in colonial and semicolonial countries, it was underscored that class contradictions were festering in capitalist countries at the turn of the decade that would eventually manifest themselves in all-out war.[81]

Upon evaluating the sociopolitical status of Poland, Romania, Finland, Latvia, and Estonia, the authors concluded that Poland had the most internal strife and Finland the least, and that all these countries would find their "internal political situations" unfavorable in the event of war against the Soviet Union.[82] Noting that the political and moral decay of the USSR's enemies would not happen quickly, however, the authors were careful not to overestimate the effects of internal turmoil on these states' combat potential.[83]

The Nature of a Coalition War

A major premise on which the study was based was that a future war would be a coalition war.[84] The bourgeois states comprising the enemy coalition would consist of a variety of unsavory characters ranging from conspirators and bankers financing the war to disseminators of anti-Soviet propaganda.[85] The "States of Capitalist Encirclement" were divided into four groups: those openly hostile to the USSR, powerful states that would join the anti-Soviet front, states uninterested in war with the USSR (owing to geographical location, for example), and friendly states. Great Britain was singled out as the most hostile country toward the USSR,[86] and fears of France joining Great Britain to form an anti-Soviet military alliance with the Baltic States,

Poland, and Romania were especially pronounced.[87] How individual countries fit into these four categories is summarized in Table 6.1.

It is interesting to note that Germany, while topping the list of "potential" enemies, was not identified as an inevitable adversary. This reflected the ambivalence toward Germany that emerged in the mid-1920s era of *Locarnopolitik* when Germany was playing off East against West. As one scholar puts it, "In 1925 it had been believed on the Wilhelmstrasse that a balance between Russia and the West, that is, a détente in the West without a military alliance or a renunciation of German ties with Russia, offered the best means of achieving the objectives of German policy both in Eastern Europe and on the Rhine."[88] Indeed, with the 1927 break in Soviet-British diplomatic relations, the option of severing ties with Russia and joining the "anti-Soviet" chorus in London was viewed favorably by some German diplomats.[89] But in the short run, German Foreign Minister Gustav Stresemann declared neutrality and assured Russia of German military assistance in the event of a Polish attack on Russian soil.[90] As Chapter 4 illustrates, Soviet uncertainty and indeed fear of German intentions toward the USSR would taint their relationship.

Imperialist Intentions and Variants of Future War

The imperialist wartime objectives, it was hypothesized, were to liquidate the Soviet system, seize its market and natural resources, and make it fully subordinate to imperialist influence.[91] Although war was inevitable, no guidance was provided as to when it might be launched. Nonetheless, it was seen to be both large in scale and long in duration, lasting from several months to three to four years.[92] Four new factors were introduced as having enormous impact on a future war: the grand size of modern armies, the daunting material demands of war, the role of the civilian worker in the war effort, and the conduct of operations deep in the enemy's rear with air-delivered chemical attacks and other methods aimed at harming the enemies' morale.[93]

Three combat scenarios or "variants" of future war were devised that the authors believed were most likely in the late 1920s.[94] The first variant—an attack on the USSR's western borders by its neighbors who would be supported with material and technical means from England and France and their allies, while Germany remained neutral—was considered the most probable of the three. The second variant envisioned an attack on the USSR's western borders by the armed forces of western contiguous countries, partially supported by the armed

TABLE 6.1 Groupings of States Hostile and Friendly Toward USSR[95]

Status	States
States openly hostile	England, France, Poland, Romania, Finland, Estonia, Latvia, Lithuania, Italy
States liable to join anti-Soviet front	Germany, Czechoslovakia, Hungary, Bulgaria, Yugoslavia, Greece, Belgium, Japan, United States
States and regions uninterested in war with USSR	Sweden, Norway, Denmark, Switzerland, Austria, Albania, Persia, Latin America
Friendly states	Turkey, Afghanistan, China, countries of the Arab east, Africa, Indonesia, British India, Mongolia

forces of England, France, and other large imperialist states. The role of Germany in this variant is not clear. The third variant was one of attack on the USSR's western, southern, and eastern borders by the armed forces of a broad imperialist bloc including Finland, Estonia, Latvia, Lithuania, Poland, Romania, England (via Turkey, Persia, and Afghanistan), Chinese militarists, and Japan.

Threats to the Soviet Union's western borders from Poland and Romania, with and without the participation of the Baltics and Finland, were regarded with the most trepidation. Poland was viewed as a potentially very grave menace, given its comprehensive railroad net.[96] According to the study, the Polish advantages lay in their ability to perform strategic regroupings and especially to concentrate maximum force on key axes for launching powerful counterattacks to which the Red Army would not have the capability to respond quickly or effectively enough. In essence, the Polish rail jeopardized Soviet war plans. In light of these Polish transportation advantages, the study offered the following advice for coping with the Polish-Romanian threat.

> In the first period of war, we will have approximate equality of forces which will eliminate the possibility of rapid destruction of all our western neighbors, with the exception of small states such as Estonia and Latvia, which, given their insignificant power and shallow territorial depth can be quickly annihilated and sovietized (*sovetirizovany*). But with states like Poland and Romania there will

> be no such quick elimination. Their resistance will be broken not with a lightning, destructive, relentless offensive, but with successive operations in stages; successive annihilation of armed forces, attrition of their material and manpower resources, which in its own time, should lead to socio-political shocks within the countries poised against us [emphasis mine].[97]

What is especially interesting about these passages is the discussion of difficulties associated with employing a strategy of destruction under these circumstances. Although Tukhachevsky subsequently went on to condemn Svechin's views of attrition- and destruction-oriented war, the discussion contained in this study could be labeled "Svechinesque."[98] Svechin advised against the peacetime procurement of weapons in the enormous quantities required to conduct a war of destruction, albeit allowing for the possibility of the enemy resorting to such a form of war.[99] The budgetary requirements alone were liable to ruin the economy, in Svechin's view.[100] Like Svechin, Tukhachevsky doubted that the USSR had the economic capacity to prepare for a strategy of destruction because, in order to do so, one side must have a clear superiority in manpower and weapons and neither of these conditions prevailed.[101] Thus, although Tukhachevsky essentially agreed with Svechin that a strategy of destruction could be used only in certain circumstances and that the Soviet economy and level of the RKKA's technical rearmament at that time did not portend the successful employment of this strategy, perhaps the key difference lay in Tukhachevsky's conviction that this situation would soon be remedied. Once the RKKA acquired enough weapons—which the industrialization plans would underwrite—the army would be in a position to plan a strategy of destruction more confidently, based on deep, decisive, and rapid operations conducted jointly by air and ground forces units.

Tukhachevsky examined the sources of the attrition/destruction dichotomy in his foreword to the translation of Hans Delbrück's book on military history and in so doing attempted to show that Svechin had misrepresented the origins and content of these concepts.[102] While a detailed inspection of the historical evolution of attrition and destruction is beyond the scope of this chapter, Tukhachevsky essentially blamed Svechin for three things: casting attrition and destruction—the two faces of war—à la Delbrück as a sharp dialectical contradiction,[103] paying insufficient attention to political objectives in wartime generally and to the importance of class warfare and revolutionary wars specifically, and failing to appreciate the conditions under which a strategy of destroying the enemy should be employed.[104] The tenor of Tukhachevsky's attacks is well represented in the following passage.

> Comrade Svechin proclaims that he is a Delbrück-idealist turned Svechin-Marxist. But this is an enormous claim without foundation. If Delbrück distorted Clausewitz, then comrade Svechin perfected Delbrück's eclecticism and, applying it to the current epoch... rejects the possibility of solving political contradictions with decisive armed force.[105]

It should be noted that this attrition/destruction controversy was widespread and not limited solely to Tukhachevsky and Svechin, although they were conceivably the most prominent military figures to debate the issue.[106] The title of an article written at this time captured the controversy: "The Battle for the Character of a Future War."[107] The evidence suggests that Tukhachevsky worked very hard to make "deep battle" a reality, facing many obstacles along the way. This "battle" was eventually won by Tukhachevsky and his team, however, as an examination of the 1936 Field Regulations (*Polevoi Ustav,* or *"PU"*) of the RKKA reveals.[108] The second principle of the 1936 regulations reads: "Red Army combat operations will always be oriented toward the annihilation of the enemy. Gaining a decisive victory and the total destruction of the enemy are the basic objectives in a war imposed upon the USSR."[109]

Leningrad as Laboratory: The "Deep Battle" Emerges

Upon departing the uninventive, rubber-stamping machinery in Moscow, as he disparagingly described the Red Army staff where he served as chief for three years, Tukhachevsky clearly made the most of his new position as commander of troops of the Leningrad Military District in the spring of 1928, delving into numerous innovative operational and technical projects.[110] Leningrad, it should be mentioned, was a thriving center of military R&D and defense industry and therefore an ideal location in which Tukhachevsky could put his creative energy to work.

According to Alexander Todorskii, one of Tukhachevsky's biographers and himself a civil war hero,[111] "The three years of service in Leningrad were one of the 'brightest periods' in Tukhachevsky's military career."[112] This successful period was facilitated in large part by his close collegial relationships and friendships with I. E. Slavin, I. F.

Fed'ko, and B. M. Feld'man[113] and the fellow military theorists with whom he would work out the "deep battle" tenets and thereupon revise the Red Army's existing field regulations: head of the Operations Directorate of the RKKA staff, Vladimir Triandafillov; head of the RKKA staff, Alexander Yegorev;[114] Chief of Armaments Ieronim P. Uborevich, deputy head of the Directorate of Mechanization and Motorization, Konstantin Kalinovskii, and Chief Inspector of Artillery Alexander I. Sediakin.

One of Tukhachevsky's closest and most valuable colleagues was Vladimir Triandafillov,[115] whose work on "successive operations" laid the groundwork for the further tactical and operational elaboration of the "deep" operational and tactical theories that evolved in the 1930s.[116] According to one Soviet scholar, Triandafillov's *Kharakter operatsii sovremennykh armii,* first published in 1929, was the culmination of numerous working drafts outlining the theory of successive offensive operations in the 1920s.[117] Among the theory's elements that were detailed by Tukhachevsky and others were the following: First, the offensive would consist of three parts: an initial operation (*iskhodnaia operatsiia*), the followup or pursuit operation *(operatsii presledovaniia),* and the decisive operation *(reshitel'naia operatsiia)* which aimed to destroy the enemy totally by preventing it from regrouping its forces.[118] The success of a "decisive offensive" would hinge on the correct choice of axis for the main attack, the proper massing of forces on selected axes, the echelonment of troops, and the employment at the outset of a "strike army" (*udarnaia armiia*) to facilitate breakthroughs.[119] Throughout the 1930s, this theme was elaborated upon and new units such as parachute and airborne assault teams and other high-speed tank and motorized rifle units were designed to carry out these "deeper" combat missions.

According to Isserson, Triandafillov made a further contribution to the evolution of the deep battle with his proposal to employ three echeloned tank groups for the simultaneous destruction of the enemy's entire tactical defense.[120] Two tank groups were designed for closer-in infantry support while the third long- range group would combat enemy artillery in the rear.[121] Isserson called Triandafillov's report on the tank groups a "brilliantly condensed version of Tukhachevsky's ideas."[122] The Field Regulations of 1925 and 1929 and numerous other classified instructions and manuals were the result of their combined work.[123] Ivanov claimed that Tukhachevsky not only managed the commission that drew up the 1929 Field Regulations, but also wrote several chapters himself.[124] According to Ivanov, Tukhachevsky "became the first advocate of the new regulations."[125]

Archival documents, however, convey that Tukhachevsky was not very satisfied with the 1929 version of the Field Regulations and may not necessarily have gotten his full say in their elaboration. In a lengthy letter to Khalepskii written in March 1931, Tukhachevksy seemed especially distraught that the "tank issue" had been viewed so narrowly and urged that a rigorous reexamination of the tank's combat role be conducted.[126] He continued by underscoring that tank support and accompaniment of infantry—the mission that always topped the list of tank priorities (including that in the 1929 Field Manual version)—was only one of several tasks that should be assigned to tank units in a deep and decisive offensive.[127] Tukhachevsky spelled out in great detail the missions of the various tank groups that would penetrate an enemy defense and perform tasks in the rear. He also listed six types of tanks needed for these missions:[128]

- TIA (*tank istrebitelia artillerii*—anti-artillery tank)
- TDP (*tank desantov pekhoty*—infantry assault tank)
- TIP (*tank istrebitelia pulemetov*—anti-machine gun tank)
- TSP (*tank soprovozhdeniia pekhoty*—close infantry support tank)
- TS (*tank spetsial'nogo naznacheniia*—i.e., special-mission tank)
- TP (*tank radioupravleniia*—radio control tank)

The opposition to Tukhachevsky's tank employment ideas was undoubtedly concentrated in the cavalrymen of the civil war, the legendary "First Cavalry Army" whose members included Voroshilov, Dybenko, Yegorov, and other members of the RKKA staff who were unwilling to abandon the reliance on cavalry units to perform the offensive maneuvers required of the modern battlefield. Even Reichswehr General Hermann Geyer, upon visiting three Soviet military districts in the summer of 1929, remarked on the "completely outdated cavalry tactics" of the Red Army.[129] In particular, he believed that psychological and political motives, in addition to memories of the civil war, or *Bürgerskriegerinnerungen,* fed Voroshilov's reluctance to consider alternative methods of force employment.

In spite of the tragic deaths of Triandafillov and Kalinovskii in a plane crash in 1931, Tukhachevsky continued to hammer out a theory of deep battle that would find its fullest expression in the 1936 Field

Regulations with chief of armaments Ieronim Uborevich, who wrote the first "unofficial" deep battle instructions in the early 1930s.[130]

In addition to drafting innovative operational concepts, the most daunting task before Tukhachevsky was to move these operational concepts from paper to the battlefield by creating the units, training the soldiers, and equipping them with the modern weapons needed to fight in the manner he had envisioned. Leningrad proved to be a perfect laboratory in which to test his ideas, and his position as commander of the Leningrad Military District gave him the authority to do so.

Although a complete description of Tukhachevsky's projects and activities in Leningrad is beyond the scope of this chapter, I mention several. For example, Tukhachevsky created the first experimental combined air and motorized assault detachment from the 11th Rifle Division consisting of automobiles, motorcycles, parachutes, tanks, and experimental jet-propelled cannons, and he was the first to conduct a combined airborne assault landing with heavy weapons and combat equipment.[131] Tukhachevsky established the NIID (scientific research institute for dirigible construction) and wrote lengthy reports on the combat possibilities of dirigibles,[132] oversaw tank and armor development,[133] searched for powerful aircraft motors, and became a strong proponent of civil and military aviation.

Perhaps most important was Tukhachevsky's role in developing the Gas Dynamics Lab (GDL) where the groundwork for the Soviet "Katiusha" rockets,[134] in addition to incendiary phosphorus bombs, anti-aircraft bombs, and torpedo-carrying aviation, was laid.[135] The Tikhomirov and Artem'ev lab, established in 1921, was expanded and strengthened under Tukhachevsky's tutelage. Upon his arrival in Leningrad in May 1928, Tukhachevsky immediately set to work on the projects already begun by the Artem'ev and Tikhomirov team. In June the laboratory was renamed the Gas Dynamics Laboratory, falling under the auspices of the military scientific research committee of the RVS SSSR.[136] New talent was recruited for the propulsion projects, and the staff of scientists and engineers grew from ten in 1928 to twenty-three in 1930. During this time the range of projects expanded too and included research not only on jet-propelled rockets, but also on methods for using rockets for launching the speed of aircraft during takeoff and landing, for launching aircraft from ships, and for creating liquid-fueled engines for rockets and aircraft.[137]

The Entrepreneur Ascendant: Tukhachevsky as Chief of Armaments

Tukhachevsky's tenure in Leningrad provides numerous demonstrations of his entrepreneurial prowess in terms of spanning boundaries and reducing uncertainty by penetrating and indeed creating research institutes and traveling back and forth between the design labs and weapons factories.

In June 1931, Tukhachevsky was named deputy chairman of the RVS, deputy war commissar, and chief of armaments of the RKKA, thereby replacing Uborevich. These prestigious promotions seemed to shatter notions that Tukhachevsky had been "exiled" to Leningrad or had permanently done damage to his relationship with Stalin and other military leaders. If there had been questions about Tukhachevsky's judgment or expertise in 1928, these doubts were put to rest in 1931. As one of Tukhachevsky's biographers, V. M. Ivanov, recalled:

> The new assignment granted Tukhachevsky profound authority in executing decisions adopted by the party and government. It opened unprecedented opportunities for applying his multifaceted military knowledge and organizational skills. This period in the life and activities of Mikhail Nikolaevich was undoubtedly his most productive. It was also the period during which his creative power really blossomed.[138]

Tukhachevsky's talents and contributions notwithstanding, there were new and compelling security concerns in 1931 arising from the situation in the Far East, particularly regarding Japan's intentions toward Outer Mongolia and Manchuria. In short, the party and government began to appreciate these new threats, and defense was assumed a higher priority. Now back in Moscow, Tukhachevsky focused primarily on the technical reconstruction of the armed forces and, according to Ivanov, "spent enormous energy on developing new weapons systems and preparing them for mass production."[139]

In a manner very reminiscent of Rickover, and in keeping with the aforementioned entrepreneurial characteristics, Tukhachevsky took personal control of the jet propulsion effort, trying to coordinate the work of all design and scientific institutions dealing with rocket technology, including hydrodynamic laboratories and military-technical academies. When named chief of armaments in August 1931, Tukhachevsky took the bold step of subordinating the Gas Dynamics

Lab to himself through his chief of staff and gave oversight and consultative responsibilities to the chief of the Artillery Directorate and the chief of the Artillery Scientific Research Institute (ANII) simultaneously.[140] In order to strengthen the GDL's rocket propulsion program, Tukhachevsky transferred a group of top engineers from the ANII to the GDL and freed B. Petropavlovskii from his administrative duties as head of the GDL to focus exclusively on scientific research. This reorganization and concentration of effort on jet propulsion projects resulted in the expansion of the GDL to a staff of 120 by December 1932 and to new projects and responsibilities. As Biriukov recounts, numerous self-propelled and finned rocket prototypes were designed and tested, and work on equipping fighter and reconnaissance aircraft with rockets and launchers for them was initiated. Indeed, it was Tukhachevsky's "interference" that assisted the GDL in obtaining a heavy bomber (TB-1) for experimental purposes. While he was working with the GDL and GIRD (jet propulsion study group), he pursued his dream of creating a research institute (RNII) devoted solely to rocket propulsion. In May 1932 he proposed the RNII in a report to the Politburo's Defense Commission and identified areas in which it would differ from or build upon propulsion projects currently under way. His chief objective was to create an entity that would transform the ongoing research into the practical application of self-propelled engines that would be used to launch conventional and chemical weapons from a variety of platforms—an experimental base for the furtherance and elaboration of the work done heretofore at the GDL. He even went so far as to state that the creation of his proposed institute should be a top priority and that its construction should be completed by January 1, 1933.[141] Perhaps this is a good example of Tukhachevskian audacity at its ripest. Tukhachevsky's wishes were not automatically granted; numerous commissions were created to evaluate his proposal. In August, Voroshilov issued a resolution calling for the folding of the GDL and the GIRD into one organization subordinated to the NKTP (Peoples Commissariat of Heavy Industry). In response, in September Tukhachevsky issued his own RVS SSSR order on the creation of the RNII. At the same time, STO was formulating a decree on the creation of the RNII, which was published in October. Although a year was spent on organizing the experimental and production bases, by 1935 the RNII was in full swing.

At this time Tukhachevsky also became more involved in the clandestine military collaboration with the Reichswehr, traveling to Germany on occasion to oversee the Red Army's participation, as he did in 1932, for example, when he observed the Reichswehr's autumn combat maneuvers.[142] Tukhachevsky devoted considerable attention to the joint chemical warfare research and the testing of aircraft motors in Lipetsk in the early thirties as well, as discussed in Chapter 4.

An Entrepreneurial Excursus: Tukhachevsky Gives Substance to Stalin's Vision of Civil Aviation, or "15,000 Tons by 1932?"

As in Tukhachevsky's study of a future war, wherein he managed to "concretize" foreign threats and hypothesize potential combat scenarios, correspondence from the military archives among Stalin, Voroshilov, and Tukhachevsky regarding the expansion of civil aviation in the Soviet Union—for civilian and military purposes—provides very interesting insights into Tukhachevsky's "entrepreneurial prowess" in carrying out one of Stalin's goals: to increase civilian aircraft tonnage to 15,000 tons by 1932.[143] As already mentioned, there are parallels with Rickover's experience and in general with the characteristics of public entrepreneurs during the "mature" stage of their careers, when efforts were made to reduce the uncertainty of their environments by gaining control over key organizations, protecting themselves or "buffering" by limiting the influence of organizations that would oppose them, and finding outside sources of influence that would help them. Rickover, for example, was successful in absorbing an entire division of Westinghouse into his nuclear program, which would deliver drawings and machines for the program directly to him. Moreover, in being "double-hatted" and serving the navy as well as the Atomic Energy Commission, Rickover was able to play one off against the other. According to Admiral Zumwalt, Rickover "was a master at blurring the line, pretty fuzzy to begin with, between the two jobs."[144] The following excursus offers a snapshot of Tukhachevsky's buffering skills.

In response to a letter sent by Stalin and Voroshilov to Sovnarkom Chairman Viacheslav Molotov of the central committee, calling for quicker action on the civil aviation front than the Rudzutak Commission[145] appeared to be taking, Tukhachevsky, who apparently had access to the letter, got down to business immediately.[146] Within weeks he drew up his own proposal for aviation, dirigible, and aircraft motor construction and sent it to Stalin and Voroshilov directly. He worked hard to convince many of the relevant players in the debate of the importance of civil aviation as seen by Stalin, criticized those comrades who thought Stalin's goals were too ambitious, and set about creating a research institute for dirigible construction located in Leningrad and therefore under his supervision. He also recommended against placing the new organ for civil aviation in the hands of VSNKh, which would, in his words, "ruin the matter," and made a politically savvy point of calling for the construction of enough aircraft for the mission of "battling the saboteurs of agriculture and forestry", that is, those who were resisting the collectivization of the countryside, such as the "rich" peasants.[147]

> We should consider the fact that without superiority in civil aviation, as a basis of military aviation, we cannot solve the defense tasks of the country and of its vital centers in general; the defense of Leningrad—which supplies 40-50 percent of the army's [material needs]—in particular. In light of the virtual non-existence of civil aviation in our country and the absolute weakness of our military air force, we believe that it is of tantamount importance to make up for lost time and organize quickly a powerful civil air force as the single basis for developing a military air force. The solution to this problem will require hundreds of millions of rubles ... and we must act courageously.[148]

Stalin also called for building a new defense industrial base east of the Volga especially for the construction of motors, aircraft, and dirigibles, and recommended establishing a "special organ" to coordinate civilian and military aircraft coordination and mobilization.

In response to Stalin's letter, Tukhachevsky reassured him that the Rudzutak commission met the day after his letter was received, and went on to describe the subcommission's civil aviation proposal (including orders for light and heavy aircraft and motors for the remaining years of the First Five Year Plan) in a letter to Stalin and Voroshilov on August 28, 1930.[149] In the conclusion of the letter, Tukhachevsky requested that Stalin and Voroshilov increase budgetary allocations and create a special directorate for civil aviation, preferably a commissariat. He noted that it was necessary to avoid decentralizing the program by dividing it among various councils and commissariats, such as VSNKh, NKPS (Peoples Commissariat of Transportation), and NKPiT (Peoples Commissariat of Postal and Telegraph Services). It was particularly "dangerous" to transfer the factories to VSNKh.[150] Tukhachevsky's aversion to VSNKh seems to have stemmed from his past experience with the council which traditionally delayed or neglected defense concerns in their own drafts of long-term industry plans. A particularly vivid illustration of Tukhachevsky's distaste for VSNKh was revealed in a letter he wrote to Voroshilov one year later concerning the unwarranted intervention by the Mobilization-Planning

Directorate of VSNKh into the affairs of individual defense industries by reducing military orders that had already been accepted by individual defense enterprises, and which also apparently had the backing of Stalin.

> Ninety per cent of my time is absorbed by fighting with VSNKh: Pavlunovskii, Martinovich and Smilga. They always try to reduce our requests, orders and so on. I must constantly refer the matters to Sergo (Ordzhonikidze)—as he is much more objective.[151]

Tukhachevsky reprehended the deputy chief of the main directorate for Civil Aviation, Jan Anvel't,[152] for objecting to the "grand plan" of building approximately 5,000 planes in the course of the 1932/33 annual plan.[153] In light of the vast shortages of qualified cadres and the nascent industrial base, Anvel't conveyed his skepticism that more than 3,000 aircraft could be built within such a short period.[154]

On September 5, 1930, the Politburo issued a decree on accelerating the pace of civil aviation development, which called for the "grand plan" of constructing 5,000 aircraft by the end of the First Five Year Plan.[155] At about the same time, a letter was sent from Stalin to Molotov proposing that Stalin's crony, Lazar Kaganovich, head up the Department of Aviation and Dirigible matters. In the same letter, he requested the creation of a Directorate of the Civilian Air Force under the auspices of Sovnarkom, which would unite the functions of the inspector of Civil Aviation and the Directorate of the Factories dealing with civil aviation and dirigible construction.[156] Anvel't, in a report on accelerating the development of air forces, also endorsed the creation of a Civil Aviation Directorate headed by Kaganovich.[157] Given the tremendous difficulties inherent in manufacturing motors for the aircraft, the practicality of fulfilling the Politburo request of September 5 was raised again in December 1931 in a letter from A.Goltsman to Stalin.[158] Stalin, in turn, passed the document off to Kuibyshev for further study.[159]

This brief excursus into the official documentation reveals that Tukhachevsky not only succeeded in helping Stalin's goal of 5,000 planes become a Politburo decree, but also got his way in terms of institutional arrangements. The civil aviation organ became a separate directorate of the Sovnarkom and therefore did not end up in VSNKh's hands, and the dirigible R&D institute whose formation he advocated was established and located in Leningrad.[160]

Personalities, Politics, and the Public Entrepreneur

> ...at the very beginnings of their careers, [public entrepreneurs] experience dissonance between what they believed they were recruited for and what, in fact, they actually encountered. They tend not to give into the "go along to get along" values and the clubbiness of fraternal association. Instead, they studiously insist on serving the goals for which they entered the organization and they do so as thoroughly as possible.[161]

Admiral Rickover and Mikhail Tukhachevsky were known to be brusque in their dealings with associates and highly intolerant of anyone who impeded the accomplishment of their goals. Indeed, both men possessed a strong sense of purpose and responsibility for the security of their respective nations that transcended concerns for subordinates' feelings, bureaucratic structures, or even their military institutions. As Lewis writes of public entrepreneurs, they "are almost self-destructive in their narrow, near literal devotion to public organizational goals."[162] The typical entrepreneur "enters the organization imbued with a zeal seldom equaled by his peers" but soon turns out to be either "unwilling or unable to internalize the organizational norms that were supposed to lead toward meeting major social goals."[163] In other words, the entrepreneur soon grows frustrated with the standard operating procedures (SOPs) inherent in his bureaucracy that seem to him inefficient at best and counterproductive at worst. He inevitably confronts the individuals who uphold these SOPs, irritating many of them.

In an effort to gain control over the development of a nuclear submarine within the Bureau of Ships, Rickover stepped on the toes of his superior, Admiral Mills, who believed he was making a concession to Rickover in creating a coordinator for nuclear matters. But to Rickover's mind, Admiral Mill's proposed organization was too broad and he told Mills exactly what he thought. Rickover ultimately wanted to wrest control of the nuclear program from the Atomic Energy Commission and to build the reactor with his handpicked staff within the Bureau of Ships. As Lewis aptly phrases it ,"this was Rickoverian audacity at its ripest."[164] Mill's response was to assign Rickover's top men to other offices. This dispersion eventually led Rickover's group to be disbanded and he was temporarily demoted. Undeterred, he continued "working" Admiral Mills and eventually convinced him of the importance of the "true submarine." Admiral Mills created a nuclear power branch of the Bureau of Ships known as Code 390 and chose

Rickover to head it up.[165] Owing to his persistence and audacity, Rickover's ideas were transformed from mere suggestion into the navy's top priority.

Although we may have less information on the attitudes his peers attitudes toward Tukhachevsky than we do of Rickover's, what we do have suggests a similar pattern. Tukhachevsky's biographers have maintained that he deliberately resigned from his position as chief of the RKKA staff in 1928 because of frustrations with the bureaucratic nature of the staff and his colleagues within it, who continually put up roadblocks and thwarted his "audacious" ideas for rearmament, for institutional arrangements, and, in general, for change. Why his colleagues reacted so vehemently is a topic of some debate, although some scholarship suggests that Tukhachevsky did not "fit in" because he had not served, as had many of the other staff members, in the prestigious First Cavalry Army, or *Konarmiia,* in the civil war and did not grant them the kind of respect that they believed they were owed or because Tukhachevsky challenged the role of cavalry in a future war.[166] In 1919, Stalin brought in fellow comrades from Tsaritsyn, Voroshilov, and Shchadenko to serve along with Budennyi on the Konarmiia's revolutionary military council; thus, the ties formed there may have contributed to their dislike of an outsider-turned-leader.[167] A contributing factor to the staff conflicts may have been resentment over Tukhachevsky's "aristocratic" background, which afforded him attendance at prestigious academies such as the First Gymnasium in Penza and the Alexandrovsky Military College in Moscow followed immediately by a commission to the highly regarded Semenovsky Guards Regiment in the Imperial Army in 1914.[168] Voroshilov, in particular, had no professional military training and whether or not he was jealous of Tukhachevsky is a matter of mere speculation.

In any event, the tension that Tukhachevsky encountered in the Red Army staff is well documented in Soviet sources describing the bitter polarization of the RKKA staff in the interwar years.[169] Lennart Samuelson uncovered archival evidence further substantiating reports of conflicts among the staff members and the battle for control over defense planning in the late 1920s.[170] Tukhachevsky, who headed the RKKA staff from 1925 to 1928, regarded it as "an organ uniting the entire preparation of the country for war, as a working organ of the High Command in directing combat actions in the TVD [Theater of Military Operations]."[171] Other staff members, including N. N. Kuzmin, A. M. Postnikov, and M. K. Levandovskii, favored a division of responsibility between the staff and the Main Directorate of the RKKA, fearing that the "concentration of the most important functions related to troop readiness could lead to the undesirable exaggeration of the role of this organ in the system of high command control."[172] In other words, those who wanted two organs, one for operational matters and one for administrative matters, feared that without this division of responsibility, the head of the RKKA staff would become inordinately powerful. According to Samuelson, one of the main conflicts was over the control of mobilization plans. Tukhachevsky requested that the RKKA chief of staff and collegium, which included representatives from mobilization sections of relevant commissariats, take control of the "whole drafting of the industrial mobilization plans," as opposed to only the army's mobilization plans, in a report written to the Military Commission of STO in 1927.[173] As a means of ensuring that Gosplan respond to the army's economic mobilization requests, Tukhachevsky reportedly proposed that a defense sector be established within Gosplan to be directed by Tukhachevsky himself. Although he did not become chairman of the sector, as he apparently wished,[174] its creation secured for the military a voice in Gosplan's budgetary decisionmaking processes. Like Tukhachevsky, Voroshilov harshly criticized the VPU (Defense Industry Directorate) of the VSNKh for failing to link the development of defense industries to the plan for industrial development in general, and thus it seems unlikely that Tukhachevsky's efforts in getting the Defense Sector established within Gosplan to better coordinate the efforts of civilian and military mobilization could have provoked ire on the part of Voroshilov; rather, it was a move that benefitted the professional goals of both men.

It should be remembered that Tukhachevsky's position as chief of staff was multifaceted and all-consuming; mobilization and planning issues were not his only responsibilities. While serving in this position, as we now know well, Tukhachevsky spent an enormous amount of time overseeing the drafting of a 700-page treatise detailing future war scenarios; most of his work at the time was conceptual, not bureaucratic. Tukhachevsky's encounter with the naval supporters of a large surface fleet has also been well documented. As already noted, not only did Tukhachevsky's ideas on the roles and structure of the navy prevail, but also the naval strategists with whom he exchanged views were later arrested for their "anti-Marxist" views.

In keeping with the suggestion of Tukhachevsky's excessive influence, another scholar recently quoted from an unidentified report sent to Voroshilov in 1928 by fellow Red Army officers, S. M. Budennyi, A. I. Yegorev, and P. E. Dybenko, who allegedly joined together to protest the "dangerous centralization of the whole problem of organization, force development and operational thinking in the hands of a single authority—namely, M. N. Tukhachevsky."[175] Indeed, a recent interpretation holds that the personality conflicts between Tukhachevsky and other staff members—Voroshilov, Budennyi, Dybenko and even Yegorev—were keen and that they "constantly complained" about him.[176] Eventually they got together and wrote a letter to Voroshilov demanding that he fire Tukhachevsky. All these interpretations share a common thread: Tukhachevsky's modus operandi conflicted with that of his colleagues, and the frustration he felt led him to resign. Whether it was a personality issue, a substantive issue, or some combination thereof, the source of Tukhachevsky's tension with the other members of the RKKA staff is perhaps less important than the fact that the RKKA staff was simply an organization in which he could not operate; could not "expand boundaries" or "reduce uncertainty." His resignation, therefore, was very appropriate—Leningrad offered him a better environment in which to work.

Other scholars have suggested that Voroshilov criticized Tukhachevsky's "deep battle" concepts at a plenum of the RVS in November 1933.[177] Perhaps the most convincing illustration of an area in which Tukhachevsky and Voroshilov disagreed is discussed in an article by Iovlev. According to documents uncovered in the Ministry of Defense (MOD) Archives, Voroshilov opposed Tukhachevsky's idea of creating motorized rifle and tank corps, favoring only brigade-sized units.[178] Although Tukhachevsky apparently won some of the initial battles on this issue,[179] Voroshilov ultimately prevailed and the mechanized corps were disbanded. According to Ivanov, this was one of the biggest mistakes made on the eve of World War II.[180] A. Ryzhakov, a Russian scholar who also had access to the MOD archives, described the debate over tank organization much differently.[181] The differences in opinion on tank employment, as he reports them, occurred after the Spanish Civil War. In order to resolve some of these tank issues, a commission headed by the deputy chairman of the War Commissariat, G. I. Kulik, and including Shaposhnikov, Budennyi, Shchadenko, Timoshenko, and others, met for three weeks in August 1939. D. G. Pavlov's complaints about corps-sized tank employment in the Spanish Civil War were considered, but the majority of the commission's members voted to preserve the tank corps.

Despite their differences, there are many areas in which Tukhachevsky and Voroshilov cooperated and jointly brought projects to fruition for the benefit of the Red Army. Even while Tukhachevsky was operating in the difficult environment of the RKKA staff, there were occasions when he was called upon to offer his expertise and to assist Voroshilov in numerous conceptual and budgetary debates. A compelling example of this is found in debates over resource allocations to the navy—an area in which Voroshilov and Tukhachevsky agreed that cuts were necessary. At an RVS meeting in May 1928, Voroshilov opened the debate saying that the "staff believes that the republic is spending too much money on naval forces and we need to discuss it."[182] Tukhachevsky was then given the floor and eloquently confronted the proponents of a large shipbuilding program for the navy. He noted that the naval directorate was prone to change its mind and said that now it wanted to spend 18 million rubles modernizing the Frunze and other ships to make them "first rate" and capable of sinking English "super-Dreadnoughts," even though one English Dreadnought could easily sink the Soviet fleet in ten minutes. He went on to say that a large surface ship program was totally out of sync with the country's war plans and only in sync with the naval patriotism of the sailors. Not only did Tukhachevsky's recommendations for reduced expenditures on the naval program and missions confined mostly to defensive and auxillary roles prevail, but also the men with whom he disagreed were later arrested for their views as "saboteurs."

Documents from the German archives detailing the secret collaboration between the Red Army and the Reichswehr also illustrate the cooperation between Tukhachevsky and Voroshilov quite well. The chemical weapons testing taking place on Russian soil by the Germans—an area of particular interest to the Red Army given the threat of air-delivered chemical weapons in a future war—was overseen jointly by Tukhachevsky and Voroshilov.[183] Numerous documents attest to the persistence with which they approached the Germans and pressed for more "hands-on" experience and greater access to the chemical weapons research for their scientists than the Germans were willing to grant.

There are also examples whereby Voroshilov was not only rather tolerant of and open to Tukhachevsky's suggestions and ideas, but also willing to carry them out. In a letter to Voroshilov in May 1930, Tukhachevsky requested that the chemical directorate be outfitted with smokescreens launched from aircraft, which he happened to read about in a recent issue of the *US Naval Institute Proceedings*. While Voroshilov's response to this request is unknown, it suggests that at the very least, Tukhachevsky was not bashful about asking his boss to purchase new technologies.[184]

Most biographies also mention the interpersonal tension which existed between Tukhachevsky and Stalin.[185] Tukhachevsky's intelligence and alleged popularity are often cited as the source of Stalin's envy, which led, ultimately, to Stalin's decision in 1937 to murder his nemesis.[186] According to Isserson, "Tukhachevsky never stood on solid ground and was very vulnerable. ... His relationship with Stalin... was fraught with unpleasantness...The sword of Damocles hung above him for a very long time."[187] Yet Tukhachevsky had his own modus operandi for relating to Stalin, that apparently worked well throughout most of the interwar period. Tukhachevsky resorted to political maneuvers if he felt that such maneuvers would help him reach his goals; one colleague of Tukhachevsky's recalled, for example, that Stalin was sometimes more receptive to Triandafillov's proposals than to Tukhachevsky's. Thus, Tukhachevsky would ask Triandafillov to present the ideas to Stalin as a means of ensuring their acceptance.[188] Stalin, then, "seized upon" Triandafillov's ideas and even claimed "coauthorship" with Triandafillov.[189]

As discussed in Chapter 2, several scholars have maintained that the rearmament proposal drawn up by Tukhachevsky in 1930 earned him Stalin's wrath. But this "wrath" was rather short-lived. A few years later, when the threat from Japan developed, Stalin was required (*vynuzhden byl*)[190] to reexamine the Tukhachevsky report that he had previously called "rubbish."[191] Perhaps it is not coincidental that in the same year, Tukhachevsky was named deputy defense minister and chief of armaments.

Indeed, Stalin and Tukhachevsky coexisted rather well for many years and depended upon one another for the modernization of the Red Army; Stalin had the bucks and Tukhachevsky had the brains. As late as 1935, it should be remembered, Tukhachevsky was awarded the highest military honor in the country when he was named Marshal of the Soviet Union. Even after having Tukhachevsky executed, Stalin is reported to have mentioned how much Tukhachevsky contributed to the advancement of military science.

Few relationships are conflict-free. Given the high-pressure environment in which these three men worked, it is hardly surprising that differences would occasionally emerge among them. Moreover, Stalin and Voroshilov had their own "special relationship." According to Stalin's foreign minister, Maxim Litvinov, the two were known to shout insults at each other and were especially at loggerheads over the course of military action to take in the Far East in 1929 and over the role of the Red Army in the collectivization drive.[192] Nikita Khrushchev revealed during his secret de-Stalinization speech in 1956 that relations between Voroshilov and Stalin were marked by considerable strain.[193] Over the years, according to Khrushchev, Voroshilov was often excluded from Politburo meetings and denied access to party documents.[194] Khrushchev also noted in his speech that Voroshilov was required to call in advance of the meetings to find out whether he would be granted permission to attend them. His permission to do so, when granted by Stalin, was given grudgingly.[195] It seems that Voroshilov, who has been made out as an obsequious and timid associate of Stalin's is better described as an assertive bureaucrat who was willing to speak his mind to Stalin and others without fear of negative repercussions.

In a similar manner, Rickover lacked the "go along to get along" personality traits of his superiors and associates, and this undoubtedly contributed to his being routinely passed over for promotions and excluded from events celebrating his accomplishments. As Theodore Rockwell recounts, when the first nuclear-propelled submarine, the Nautilus, sailed submerged from Pearl Harbor to Portland, England, in August 1958, Rickover was not even included among the guests of the White House invited to celebrate the achievement.[196] He was also passed over for promotion to Rear Admiral several years in a row and it was only with the help—and indeed outrage—of key congressmen that the promotion came through in 1953.[197]

Conclusions

Mikhail Nikolaevich Tukhachevsky was indisputably the major facilitator of and contributor to innovation in the Red Army during the First Five Year Plan period. Drawing on his innate talent, intelligence, foresight, and formidable political prowess, Tukhachevsky was capable of exploiting to his full advantage, and to the advantage of the Red Army and the Soviet state, the sharp contradictions inherent in the highly politicized environment of the early years of Stalinist industrialization and his own training and experience as a professional soldier.

In spite of his "aristocratic" upbringing, Tukhachevsky joined the Bolshevik cause and temporarily became a fervent proponent of revolutionary wars. Although he served in the civil war, commanding several fronts at the age of twenty-six, he subsequently became one of that war's biggest critics and cautioned against drawing lessons from a war based on improvisation and Bolshevik spirit. Both he and Voroshilov frequently invoked the "Great War" as the model of wars to come, ones in which countries' manufacturing capabilities would determine the outcomes and not mere uniformity and intensity of combat spirit.

Tukhachevsky's theoretical writings, at least until 1928, echoed many of the prevailing ideas of the time; especially those of Alexander Svechin. As the comparison of their writings from mid-1920s reveals, they were of one mind on many issues, even regarding the nature of a future war. But Tukhachevsky's reverence for his superior ended in 1929, when he began to vehemently attack Svechin's work—the very work that he relied upon to make some of his points in his enormously successful and prescient treatise, *Future War.* This harsh and slanderous attack was especially evident in the Communist Academy's compendium denouncing Svechin in 1931, and its vehemence may have had something to do with the party's general crackdown on organizations that failed to give due regard to the party's general line.

The main issue on which the two seemed to disagree was the strength of the state economy to support rearmament and peacetime defense procurement. While Svechin was less confident that the Soviet economy could support substantial peacetime procurement, Tukhachevsky was convinced that Stalin's industrialization plans would enable the kind of rearmament that he envisioned and that was necessary for the realization of his innovative force employment concepts. These diverse views of the economy formed the basis of the divergent types of wars for which they believed the USSR should prepare: Svechin's "attrition model" versus Tukhachevsky's "decisive offensive" or "destruction" model.

Tukhachevsky's success was due partly to his ability to meld the interests of the RKKA with those of the state and particularly Stalin. In the interests of technological progress and economic and military security, Tukhachevsky's vision of a modern Red Army was the same as Stalin's vision of the Soviet state. While their respective methods of achieving this goal may have differed on occasion, by mid-1931, with the Japanese invasion of Manchuria and the threats to the Soviet Union engendered by the invasion, defense became a top priority. From the time that Tukhachevsky assumed the post of chief of armaments in 1931 until he was named marshal of the USSR in 1935, Tukhachevsky's entrepreneurship was in its ascendancy and the Red Army was reconfigured according to his vision, with relatively little interference from civilian sources.

Notes

1. Barry Posen is among the most fervent advocates of this view. See his *The Sources of Military Doctrine: France, Britain, and Germany Between the Wars* (Ithaca: Cornell University Press, 1984), pp. 54-55. See also Morris Janowitz, *The Professional Soldier* (Glencoe: Free Press, 1960), pp. 22-26.

2. Kimberly Marten Zisk, *Engaging the Enemy: Organization Theory and Soviet Military Innovation* (Princeton: Princeton University Press), pp. 47-81.

3. Eugene Lewis, *Public Entrepreneurship: Toward a Theory of Bureaucratic Political Power, The Organizational Lives of Hyman Rickover, J. Edgar Hoover, and Robert Moses* (Bloomingon: Indiana University Press, 1980).

4. The biographies upon which I have relied are: V. M. Ivanov, *Marshal M.N. Tukhachevskii* (Moscow: Voenizdat, 1985); Lev Nikulin, *Tukhachevskii* (Moscow: Voenizdat, 1963); Alexander I. Todorskii, *Marshal Tukhachevskii* (Moscow: Izdatel'stvo politicheskoi literatury, 1963) and *Vospominaniia druzei i soratnikov* (Moscow: Voenizdat, 1986); G. Isserson, "Zapiski sovremennika o M.N. Tukhachevskom, *Voenno-istoricheskii zhurnal,* no. 4, 1963; and, to a lesser extent, Thomas Butson, *The Tsar's Lieutenant: The Soviet Marshal* (New York: Praeger, 1984), and Shimon Naveh, "Tukhachevsky" in Harold Shukman, ed., *Stalin's Generals* (New York: Grove Press, 1993), pp. 255-273. Others have focused on the events immediately preceding his arrest and death, including Victor Alexandrov, *The Tukhachevsky Affair* (London: MacDonald, 1963); Lidiia Nord, *Marshal M.N. Tukhachevskii* (Lev: Paris, 1978); and Rudolf Strobinger, *Stalin enthauptet die Rote Armee: der Fall Tuchatschewskij* (Stuttgart: Deutsche Verlags-Anstalt, 1990). See also Kurt Agricola, *Der rote Marschall: Tuchatschewskis Aufstieg und Fall* (Berlin: Verlag "Die Wehrmacht," 1939).

5. As contained in *M.N. Tukhachevskii: Izbrannye proizvedeniia,* vols. I and II (Moscow: Voenizdat, 1964).

6. See, in particular, Tukhachevsky's personal inventory, Fond 37605.

7. Kimberly Marten Zisk, *Engaging the Enemy,* pp. 8-9. See also, V. G. Kulikov ed., *Akademiia General'nogo shtaba* (Moscow: Voenizdat, 1976) and Morris Janowitz, *The Professional Soldier,* pp. 350-354.

8. Lewis, *Public Entrepreneurship,* p. 52. Rickover's success in getting funding for his projects is well documented in Francis Duncan, *Rickover and the Nuclear Navy: The Discipline of Technology* (Annapolis: Naval Institute Press, 1990).

9. My attempt at ferreting through some of the budgetary information on the defense five year plan was discussed in chapter 2.

10. Norman Polmar and Thomas Allen, *Rickover* (New York: Simon and Schuster), p. 245. For Secretary Lehman's experience in trying to retire Rickover,

see the introduction to *Command of the Seas: Building the 600 Ship Navy* (New York: Scribner, 1988), pp. 1-8.

11. Polmar and Allen, *Rickover,* p. 245.

12. Duncan, *Rickover and Nuclear Navy,* p. 16.

13. Ibid., pp. 233-234.

14. Norman Polmar and Thomas Allen, "The Plot to Get Rickover," *Washingtonian Magazine,* vol. 17, April 1982.

15. The details and interpretations of Tukhachevsky's arrest, trial, and murder will be examined below.

16. Zisk, *Engaging the Enemy,* chapter 2.

17. Donald Starry, "Extending the Battlefield," *Military Review,* no. 61, March 1981, and Bernard Rogers, "Follow-on Forces Attack: Myths and Realities," *NATO Review,* no. 32, December 1984.

18. Lewis, *Public Entrepreneurship,* p. 9.

19. Duncan, *Rickover and the Nuclear Navy,* p. 281.

20. Hyman Rickover, "Management in Government," in *Management Magazine,* vol. 1, no. 1 (September 1979), pp. 16-17.

21. Polmar and Allen, *Rickover,* pp. 99-105.

22. Rickover, "Management in Government," p. 18.

23. Ibid, p. 288. See also Jonathan Miller, "The Ancient Submariner," *New Republic,* vol. 177, November 1977, p. 17.

24. Duncan, *Rickover and the Nuclear Navy,* foreword.

25. Lewis, *Public Entrepreneurship,* pp. 231-236.

26. Jacob Kipp goes a step further and states that Tukhachevsky was partly responsible for ending professional debate in the Red Army with his political statements. As I see it, he merely took advantage of the situation and slandered his opponents in order to achieve his professional objectives. The professional debate continued well into the 1930s, albeit "cloaked in Stalinist dress." See Jacob Kipp, "General-Major Svechin and Modern Warfare: Military History and Military Theory," in *Strategiia* (Minneapolis: East View Publications, 1992), p. 49.

27. Roman Kolkowicz, *Political Controls in the Red Army: Professional Autonomy versus Political Integration* (Santa Monica: RAND, 1966), pp. 19-24.

28. Lewis borrows this term, "buffering," from James D. Thompson who used it "to indicate the extent to which the basic action of the organization is protected from disruption by outside sources of contingency." See Lewis, *Public Entrepreneurship,* p. 10.

29. Ibid., p. 93.

30. Ibid., pp. 29 and 40.

31. Ibid., pp. 39-40.

32. Duncan, *Rickover and the Nuclear Navy,* foreword.

33. Ibid., p. 43. See also Captain Edward Beach's foreword in Duncan's book, *Rickover and the Nuclear Navy.* Beach was a self-proclaimed "Rickover boy" and enthusiast of the nuclear program in the navy.

34. Lewis, *Public Entrepreneurship,* p. 91.

35. Jonathan Miller, "Ancient Submariner," p. 17. See also Richard Hewlett and Francis Duncan, *Nuclear Navy, 1946-1962* (Chicago: University of Chicago Press, 1974), chapter 8.

36. Writing in 1929, Voroshilov called for the retention and utilization of "old professor-specialists" in the military academies for at least ten more years. RTsKhIDNI, Speech at the Frunze Academy, I October 1929, Voroshilov Fond 74, op. 1, d. 154, l. 16.

37. The tension that existed between civilian roles and professional roles of the Red Army's soldiers was also a topic of debate. Some military leaders were alarmed that 50-80 percent of the command staff spent evenings attending civilian institutes. See St. Ivanovich (Talin), *Krasnaia armiia* (Paris: Sovremennye zapiski, 1931), p. 55.

38. Tukhachevsky would go on to point out that the maneuver periods of World War I, albeit few and far between, were more relevant for future war preparations than those of the civil war. See Tukhachevsky et al., *Budushchaia voina,* Chast' VI (Operational and Organizational Issues), RGVA, F. 33988, op. 2, d. 688, l. 92.

39. The Soviet political-military weekly, *Voennyi Vestnik* contained numerous articles throughout the 1920s debating the role of offensive and defensive maneuvers in a future war. See author's *Historical Roots of Contemporary Debates on Soviet Military Doctrine and Defense,* Note 3348-AF/ A (Santa Monica: RAND, 1991).

40. David Joravsky, *The Lysenko Affair* (Cambridge: Harvard University Press, 1970).

41. Ibid., p. 2. Joravksy points out that often the beliefs with the most emotional appeal are the least verifiable and thus, "the social consequence of the ambiguity of ideological slogans is that efforts to translate them into specific beliefs and policies are unavoidably arbitrary and fiercely disputed" p. 6.

42. Ibid., p. 9.

43. Ibid., p. 234

44. Ibid., p. 228.

45. RGVA, "K istorii razvitiia sovetskoi voenno-teoricheskoi mysli do Velikoi Otechestvennoi voiny," found in Isserson's personal papers, F. 40871, op. 1, d. 34, l. 11-12. In this draft, Isserson divided up military thought from 1917 to 1940 into five stages.

46. The party's "general line" varied with its programmatic agenda. See Arch Getty, *The Origins of the Great Purges: The Soviet Communist Party Reconsidered* (Cambridge: Cambridge University Press, 1985), p. 11.

47. The Communist Academy (Komakademiia), according to Joel Shapiro, evolved into a "major Marxist theoretical and methodological center" that served as a counterweight to the non-Marxist Academy of Sciences. At its June plenum of 1930, the academy was asked to move away from theory and to attend to more "practical" matters like supporting the industrialization campaign. See Shapiro, "A History of the Communist Academy, 1918-1936" (Ph.D. diss., Columbia University, 1976), especially chapter 3.

48. Isserson, "K istorii", p. 12. According to Isserson, "The First Congress of the VNO (*Voenno-nauchnoe obshchestvo*) and the military section of the Communist Academy revived military-scientific work. From the Congress' platform Marxist-Leninist thinking was expressed....All ideological positions on the military-scientific front were won over by young party-minded military-scientific cadres."

49. See the collective review of Svechin's book, *Evoliutsiia voennogo iskusstva,* vol. II, in "Voennoe iskusstvo i klassovaia bor'ba," *Voina i revoliutsiia,* book 8, 1928, p. 148. According to the authors of this review, whose identities were withheld, "This work is indisputably a materialist work. The influence of the forces of production on military art is underscored throughout the book in clear and concrete forms....One may quarrel with the author's basic conclusion-his forceful argumentation is aimed at proving his old theory of attrition....But no one may dismiss the materialist basis of his position."

50. M.N. Tukhachevsky, "Voina kak problema," 1928, in *Izbrannye proizvedeniia,* vol. II (Moscow: Voenizdat, 1964), p. 3.

51. M. N. Tukhachevsky, "Predislovie k knige G. Del'briuka: "Istoriia voennogo iskusstva v ramkakh politicheskoi istorii," 1930, *Izbrannye proizvedeniia,* pp. 116-146.

52. Ibid., "Anti-Dühring" and "Die Möglichkeiten und Voraussetzungen eines Krieges der Heiligen Allianz gegen Frankreich im Jahre 1852."

53. Ibid., p. 120.

54. Iu. Biriukov, "Rol' M.N. Tukhachevskogo v razvitii sovetskoi aviatsii i raketnoi tekhniki," in *Iz Istorii Aviatsii i Kosmonavtiki,* no. 25, 1975, p. 3.

55. See this discussion in Chapter 2. Svechin's works also predated the First Five Year Plan furor, with editions of *Strategiia* published in 1926 and 1927 whose research was undoubtedly conducted earlier. It is unlikely, however, that Svechin would have gone out of his way to applaud Stalin's efforts because doing so was hardly the job of a professional soldier, in his view. A. A. Svechin, *Strategiia* (Moscow: Voenizdat, 1926 and 1927).

56. See *Strategiia,* especially pp. 72-90 in chapter "Ekonomicheskii plan voiny." According to Andrei Kokoshin, "Much of what A.A. Svechin wrote, noting the weakness of the technical equipment of the Red Army in a future war, proved to be valid, despite the fact that the scale of industrialization was much more significant than he had assumed." See Kokoshin and Lobov, "Foresight (General Svechin on the Evolution of the Art of War)," *Znamia,* no. 2, 1990, in Joint Publications Research Service, 13 April 1990, p. 20.

57. "Chto my ozhidaem ot '*Voiny i Revoliutsii*'," book 12, 1929, pp. 4-6. It was pretty clear that the journal would be infused with ideology and would indeed seek to censor authors who failed to use the Marxist-Leninist framework. In another article concerning the future of the journal, the author concluded: "The [editorial board of *Voina i revoliutsiia]* should consist not only of official representatives from the military's central apparatus and the military academy, but also theoretical Marxists working in the Communist Academy on historical materialism. ...The journal, in actuality, should become a Marxist

organ of military-scientific thought." See "Marksizm i teoreticheskii organ voennoi mysli," *Krasnaia zvezda,* 28 December 1929, p. 2.

58. Tukhachevsky, "Chto my ozhidaem," p. 6.

59. Ibid.

60. See the book review by A. Golubev of *Kommunisticheskaia akademiia. Sektsiia po izucheniiu problem voin. Zapiski. Tom 1,* 1930, contained in *Voina i revoliutsiia,* book 10, 1930, pp. 107-108.

61. Vladimir Triandafillov was the author of *Kharakter operatsii sovremennykh armii,* 1929, and is credited with formulating the idea of "successive" operations, the forerunner of "deep operations."

62. Jacob Kipp, "Gen-Major Svechin and Modern Warfare," p. 49.

63. Shapiro, *A History of the Communist Academy,* p. 240.

64. Kommunisticheskaia akademiia pri TsIK SSSR, Leningradskoe otdelenie, *Protiv reaktsionnykh teorii na voenno-nauchnom fronte: Kritika strategicheskikh i voenno-istoricheskikh vzgliadov professora Svechina* (Moscow: Voenizdat, 1931). It should be noted that Tukhachevsky was one of several contributors (including K. Bocharev, I. Slutskin, A. Sediakin, P. Suslov, I. Duplitskii, I. Fendel', V. Dunaevskii, and I. Gasukin) to this piece, attempting to discredit Svechin.

65. RGVA, 23 November 1928, F. 33987, op. 1, d. 674, l. 50.

66. *Protiv,* p. 6.

67. Tukhachevsky, "Voprosy sovremennoi strategii," Moscow, 1926, p. 4.

68. Ibid., p. 16.

69. *Protiv,* pp. 5-8.

70. Kipp, "Maj-Gen. Svechin and Modern Warfare,"p. 49.

71. RGVA, F. 4, op. 1, d. 501, l. 11, as cited in N. Iu. Berezovskii, "Na bor'bu s 'limitrofami'," *Voenno-istoricheskii zhurnal,* no. 4, 1993, pp. 53-62.

72. Ibid., p. 56

73. Ibid., p. 54.

74. Eighty copies of this classified document were prepared between 1926 and 1928 by the Fourth Directorate of the Red Army staff and almost all of them were destroyed in the 1930s. One remaining copy is housed at RGVA, Fond 33988, op. 2, dela 679-688. Other contributors to the study were Ian. M. Zhigur, head of the Army Staff's Intelligence Directorate; Ian K. Berzin (Berzin was a pseudonym for Kiuzis Peteris)—member and later director of the RKKA's Intelligence Directorate; and A. N. Nikonov.

75. *Future War,* Chast' I, l. 7-8.

76. Ibid., l. 3-4.

77. Ibid., p. 4. Svechin had also criticized the Germans' preoccupation with the Schlieffen Plan, which paid scant attention to secondary axes of attack. See *Strategiia,* pp. 255-256.

78. See sections II-V of *Future War* which scrutinize the manpower capabilities, economic and combat potential, and political characteristics of the USSR's hostile neighbors. Svechin's *Strategiia,* it should be noted, was also mindful of political and economic influences, yet Tukhachevsky would go on to

attack Svechin a few years later on the grounds that his work was insufficiently focused on political issues. See Kokoshin, "Alexander Svechin: War and Politics," *International Affairs*, 1988.

79. Milovidov ed., *Filosofskoe nasledie V.I. Lenina i problemy sovremennoi voiny*, Moscow, Voenizdat, 1972, chapters 1 and 2.

80. *Future War*, Chast' I, l. 23.

81. Ibid, Chast' V, l. 3.

82. The internal strife was due to these countries' varying degrees of agricultural and nationality problems, class warfare, and ripe-for-revolution proletariats. *Future War*, Chast' V.

83. *Future War*, Chast' V, l. 57.

84. Tukhachevsky stressed even before the *Future War* study was written that each member of the adversaries' coalitions must be studied in great detail. "The existence of a coalition does not mean that resources are allocated equally to each member of the coalition. Some have bread, some have heavy industry and still others have oil....A war plan must not envision destroying the entire coalition at once, but piecemeal.... If these pieces of war are put together properly, then even the weakest countries may obtain an advantageous correlation of forces." See "Voprosy sovremennoi strategii", 1926, p. 15.

85. *Future War*, Chast' I, l. 20-23.

86. Ibid., l. 25.

87. Ibid.

88. J. Jacobson, *Locarno Diplomacy: Germany and the West, 1925-1929* (Princeton: Princeton University Press, 1972), p. 130, and Manfred Zeidler, *Reichswehr und Rote Armee: Wege und Stationen einer ungewöhnlichen Zusammenarbeit, 1920-1933* (München: Oldenbourg, 1993), pp. 129-134.

89. Ibid.

90. Ibid., p. 131.

91. *Future War*, Chast' I, l. 19-20.

92. Ibid., Chast' VI, l. 92.

93. Ibid., Chast' V, l. 3.

94. Ibid., Chast' I, l. 36-56.

95. Ibid., l. 35-36.

96. *Future War*, Chast' VI, l. 21-22. Bruce Menning has written extensively on the mismatch between Soviet war plans and the capacity of the Soviet rail net to underwrite them. See his paper, "Soviet Railroads and War Planning, 1927-1939," presented at the AAASS Convention, Boston, 1996.

97. Ibid., l. 22-23.

98. According to Svechin, "With respect to the political aims of war, we have come to the conclusion that the responsibility to orient the activities of the front in the form either of attrition or destruction lies with the political leadership after lengthy consultation with the strategist. The contradiction between these forms is much deeper, important, and filled with more ... consequences than the contradiction between defense and offense." *Strategiia*, p. 252. Tukhachevsky later censured Svechin's views on attrition and

destruction in at least two publications: *Protiv,* and more "academically" in "Predislovie k knige G. Del'briuka "Istoriia voennogo iskusstva v ramkakh politicheskoi istorii," vol. 4, *Novoe vremia* (Moscow: Gosizdat, 1930).

99. Svechin, *Strategiia,* p. 259.

100. Ibid., p. 58.

101. *Future War,* l. 18.

102. Tukhachevsky, *Predislovie.*

103. Note the irony of Tukhachevsky's criticism of Svechin for overplaying the dialectic.

104. With the exception of Svechin's lack of enthusiasm for "revolutionary wars," the rest of these accusations were without foundation. Drawing on Clausewitz and Delbrück's writings, Tukhachevsky again tried to discredit Svechin, albeit in a more "highbrow" manner.

105. Tukhachevsky, *Predislovie,* p. 134.

106. For a cogent summary and discussion of some of the other theorists who debated the attrition vs. destruction strategy, see Kipp, "General-Major Svechin," pp. 40-47.

107. Viktor Novitskii, "Bor'ba za kharakter budushchei voiny," *Voina i revoliutsiia,* book 3, 1929.

108. According to Biriuzov, the "deep battle" was officially legitimized and reflected for the first time in the 1936 Field Regulations. See Biriuzov, "Voenno-teoreticheskoe nasledstvo," p. 44, and the Field Regulations themselves, *Vremennyi polevoi ustav RKKA 1936,* Moscow, 1937, translated by JPRS-UMA-86-031 and contained in USSR Report, *Military Affairs,* 12 June 1986.

109. Ibid., p. 2.

110. The various interpretations of Tukhachevsky's resignation from the RKKA staff are examined below. See also Lev Nikulin, *Tukhachevskii,* p. 167.

111. A. I. Todorskii was a model Bolshevik, commander, and civil war hero who also "skillfully directed the central bureau of party cells dealing with the Academy's most pressing issues." See the description of Todorskii contained in A. I. Radzievskii, ed., *Akademiia imeni M.V. Frunze* (Moscow: Voenizdat, 1973), pp. 80-81.

112. Todorskii, *Marshal Tukhachevskii,* p. 83.

113. Isserson also includes among Tukhachevsky's friends Efimov, Kork, Mezheninov, and Uritskii. See Isserson Fond 40871, op. 1, d. 16, l. 17.

114. The available biographical information is vague on Egorev's position between 1928 and 1931. In the early 1920s he apparently headed the Ukrainian and Byelorussian Military Districts and in 1931 became head of the Red Army staff. See entry for Yegorev in *Voennyi entsiklopedicheskii slovar'* (Moscow: Voenizdat, 1983), pp. 250-251.

115. In a memo to Triandafillov in April 1931, Tukhachevsky had two comments about a draft of the air force regulations that he had recently read: "[its] authors do not use the Russian language grammatically and they formulate their ideas extremely poorly." Such frank observations are usually

confined to one's closest colleagues, suggesting that Triandafillov was indeed one of Tukhachevsky's. RGVA, F. 33988, op. 2, d. 693, l. 189.

116. *Akademiia imeni Frunze,* pp. 92-93.

117. P. Savushkin, "K voprosu o zarozhdenii teorii posledovatel'nykh nastupatel'nykh operatsii (1921-1929)," *Voenno-istoricheskii zhurnal,* no. 5, 1985, p. 80.

118. Ibid. According to Savushkin, "The goal and main contents of the decisive operation were the complete destruction of the enemy's forces on a given axis without permitting him to regroup and reinforce himself with reserves."

119. Ibid., p. 82.

120. Isserson, *Zapiski sovremennika,* p. 69.

121. The tanks groups were divided into PP (*podderzhka pekhoty*—infantry support) and DD (*dal'nego deistviia*—long-range action).

122. Isserson, *Zapiski sovremennika,* p. 69.

123. Ibid.

124. Ivanov, *Marshal M.N. Tukhachevskii,* p. 269.

125. Ibid.

126. RGVA, Tukhachevskii to Khalepskii (Tukhachevsky's personal inventory), 3 March 1931, F. 37605, op. 2, d. 1, l. 2. In addition to the reception of his operational ideas, Tukhachevsky may also have been disappointed by Voroshilov's decision to request far fewer tanks than Tukhachevsky recommended in 1930. See Samuelson, "Soviet Defence Industry Planning," p. 131.

127. F. 37605, op. 2, d. 1, l. 2.

128. Ibid., l. 3.

129. BA-MA, N221/10, S. 15, Ruslandreise Gruppe Geyer, 14 October 1929.

130. Isserson Fond, l. 22.

131. Ivanov, *Marshal Tukhachevskii,* pp. 274-275. Boris Feld'man, chief of staff of the LVO, wrote a report about the combined air and motorized assault in the fall of 1930. See RGVA, "Otchet o provedenii avia-moto-desanta 3.9.30 g. na okruzhnykh manevrakh LVO," F. 33988, op. 2, d. 699, l. 44.

132. RGVA, October 1930, F. 33987, op. 2, d. 346, l. 25-31.

133. RGVA, F. 33987, op. 2, d. 344, l. 5. Several documents contained in this inventory regarding tank development and testing in Leningrad were authored by Tukhachevsky.

134. Ibid., p. 276. See also, Tsypkin, "Origins of the Soviet Military R&D System."

135. Ivanov, *Marshal Tukhachevskii,* p. 277.

136. Biriukov, "Rol' Tukhachevskogo," p. 6.

137. Ibid.

138. Ivanov, *Marshal Tukhachevskii,* p. 281.

139. Ibid., p. 283.

140. Biriukov, "Rol' Tukhachevskogo," p. 7.

141. Ibid., p. 12.

142. BA-MA, RH 2/2217. See also John Erickson, *The Soviet High Command,* pp. 341-343.

143. In my view, Tukhachevsky followed Stalin's lead in the development of civil aviation and therefore was not in a position of having to *convince* Stalin of its importance, as Samuelson suggests. See Samuelson, "Soviet Defence Industry Planning," pp. 131-132.

144. Polmar and Allen, *Rickover,* p. 215.

145. Before a separate directorate or commissariat for civil aviation was created, the commission dealing with civil aviation was led by comrade Jan E. Rudzutak. Janis Rudzutakis was a prominent Latvian communist and Politburo member who, among other things, oversaw the chemicalization drive and the Central Control Commission in the 1930s.

146. RGVA, TsK VKP(b)—Stalin and Voroshilov (in Sochi) to Molotov (in Moscow), 16 August 1930, F. 33987, op. 2, d. 346, l. 5.

147. RGVA, To Members of the Rudzutak Commission from Tukhachevsky, "K voprosu o razvitii grazhdanskogo vozdushnogo flota," July 1930, F. 33987, op. 2, d. 346, l. 43. Although Tukhachevsky was intimately involved with the commission's work and acted as an advisor to it, it is not clear whether he was actually a member of the commission.

148. RGVA, F. 33987, op. 2, d. 346, l. 5.

149. RGVA, Letter from Tukhachevsky to Stalin and Voroshilov, 28 August 1930, F. 33987, op. 2, d. 346, l. 52.

150. Ibid.

151. Tukhachevsky, Zapiska Voroshilovu, 23.7.31, RGVA, F. 33987, op. 3, d. 155, l. 159, cited in Samuelson, "Soviet Defense Industry Planning," p. 159.

152. Anvel't was an active communist from Estonia who, before assuming his position as deputy chief and later chief of the Main Directorate of Civilian Air Forces (Glavnoe upravlenie grazhdanskogo voennogo flota), was associated with the Zhukovsky Air Force Academy.

153. RGVA, F. 33987, op. 2, d. 346, l. 52.

154. RGVA, Letter to Tukhachevsky from Anvel't, 4 August 1930, l. 33.

155. RGVA, Postanovlenie, ibid., l. 34.

156. RGVA, Stalin to Molotov, undated, ibid., l. 54-58.

157. RGVA, Anvel't Report, 20 August 1930, l. 54 and 62-67. According to the *Bolshaia Sovetskaia Entsiklopediia,* Anvel't himself occupied that position from 1929 to 1935.

158. RTsKhIDNI,1 December 1930, F. 558, op. 1, d. 2937, l. 1-3.

159. Ibid.

160. The institute was called NIID (Nauchno-issledovatel'skii institut po dirizhablestroeniiu). See RGVA, 22 October 1930, F. 33987, op. 2, d. 346, l. 16 and October 1930, l. 31.

161. Lewis, *Public Entrepreneurship,* p. 15.

162. Ibid., p. 17.

163. Ibid., p. 14.

164. Lewis, *Public Entrepreneurship*, p. 44.

165. Ibid., p. 52.

166. Zen'kovich, *Zagovor Marshala*, p. 4.

167. Stephen Brown, "Communists and the Red Cavalry: The Political Education of the Konarmiia in the Russian Civil War, 1918-1920," *Slavonic and East European Review*, vol. 73, no. 1 (January 1995), p. 92.

168. Shimon Naveh, "Tukhachevsky," in Harold Shukman, ed., *Stalin's Generals* (New York: Grove Press, 1995), p. 259.

169. V. Danilov, "Ot shtaba RKKA k general'nomu shtabu raboche-krestinskoi krasnoi armii, 1924-1935," *Voenno-istoricheskii zhurnal*, No. 8, 1978, pp. 101-106.

170. Samuelson, *Soviet Defense Industry Planning*, chapter 2. See also Nikolai Zen'kovich, "Zagovor Marshalov," *Novosti razvedki i kontrrazvedki* (7:64), 1996, p. 4.

171. Danilov, "Ot Shtaba..., p. 103.

172. Ibid., p. 104.

173. Samuelson, "Soviet Defense Industry Planning," p. 69.

174. Ibid., pp. 78-80.

175. Shimon Naveh, "Tukhachevsky," p. 265.

176. N. Zen'kovich, "Zagovor Marshala," p. 4.

177. S. Biriuzov, "Voenno-teoreticheskoe nasledstvo M.N. Tukhachevskogo," *Voenno-istoricheskii zhurnal*, no. 2, 1964, p. 44.

178. A. Iovlev relied on documents from the Ministry of Defense Archives to support this view. See "Tekhnicheskoe perevooruzhenie krasnoi armii", *Voenno-istoricheskii zhurnal*, no. 12, 1964, p. 11.

179. Ivanov, *Marshal Tukhachevskii*, p. 274.

180. Ibid.

181. A. Ryzhakov, p. 109.

182. Berezovskii, "Bor'ba s limitrofami," p. 54.

183. BA-MA, RH12/4, r. 54, S. 63-72.

184. RGVA, Tukhachevsky to Voroshilov, 25 May 1930, F. 33988, op. 2, d. 693, l. 120.

185. The differences between Tukhachevsky and Voroshilov concerned force employment (tank brigades and cavalry) more than weapons production, etc. See Iovlev, pp. 10-11.

186. See, especially, Shimon Naveh, entire chapter.

187. RGVA, F. 40871, op. 1, d. 16, l. 16.

188. Todorskii, *Vospominaniia druzei i soratnikov*, pp. 132-133. It should be remembered that this was hearsay and not hard evidence.

189. Ibid., p. 133.

190. Note, once again, the use of the impersonal verb form rendering unclear exactly *who* forced Stalin to reread the report.

191. Ibid., p. 169.

192. Maxim Litvinov, *Notes for a Journal* (New York: William Morrow, 1955), pp. 126-127.

193. "Rech' Khrushcheva na zakrytom zasedanii XX s"ezda KPSS," München, 1956, p. 53.

194. Ibid.

195. Ibid.

196. Theodore Rockwell, *The Rickover Effect* (Annapolis: Naval Institute Press, 1992).

197. Duncan, *Rickover and the Nuclear Navy*, p. 13.

7

Postscript: *Yezhovshchina* and the End of Innovation

By the mid-1930s, the favorable military culture in which innovation had flourished for most of the interwar period was quickly disintegrating as Stalin and his NKVD informers infiltrated, disrupted, and indeed damaged the lives of thousands of Soviet citizens. Although his power appeared secured and his leadership confirmed and duly symbolized by the celebratory Seventeenth Party "Congress of Victors" in 1934, to his mind the battles were just beginning. Suspicions about the motives of his colleagues grew into unrivaled fears of sabotage and plots against his personal livelihood. These fears then found expression in the widespread physical elimination not only of his "fellow" revolutionary Bolsheviks such as Nikolai Bukharin, but also of prominent Red Army officers. On May 26, 1937, Marshal Tukhachevsky and seven other high-ranking officers were arrested as "traitors" for their alleged contact with fascist military circles, they were tortured into confessing their "crimes" and shot before a firing squad. This marked the beginning of a "cleansing" of the military establishment writ large and the numerous arrests and dismissals of officers.

The "Great Terror" or *Yezhovshchina,* named after Nikolai Yezhov who headed the People's Commissariat of Internal Affairs (NKVD), is well documented in numerous studies of the Stalin era. This bloody "purge" of the officer corps is commonly viewed as having devastated the leadership of the RKKA, which in turn led to the poor performance of the Red Army in the initial battles of World War II. New scholarship, however, suggests that the elimination of the officer corps was not as extensive as previously believed and that the shortage of officers was only part of the problem. The purges at the top occurred simultaneously with a rapid expansion of the army at the bottom, which brought chaos to the manning and organization of the RKKA and contributed to the disaster of June 1941.[1] Thus, while its ultimate harm to the performance of the Red Army in Operation Barbarossa is generally agreed upon, it is also clear that the *Yezhovshchina* and its accompanying chaos harmed innovation in three ways. First, it destroyed the culture conducive to military innovation and the top RKKA strategist, Marshal Tukhachevsky, whose future war scenarios and 1935 war games warned and prepared the army for the Wehrmacht's onslaught. I would agree wholeheartedly with Williamson Murray's observation that "most military innovation ceased," at this point.[2] Certainly, some of the sources of innovation already discussed had died natural deaths by the mid-1930s. In 1933 the German-Soviet collaboration came to an end when German military "equality" was reinstated at the Geneva Disarmament Conference. From then on, the Germans saw little sense in spending millions of Deutschmarks on military training in Russia—it was time to bring these operations home.[3] Second, memoirs written by Soviet weapons designers attest to the increasingly disruptive role played by Stalin in the weapons design process. Fortunately, however, by the mid-1930s many of the artillery and tank prototypes were beyond the point of cancellation, and although Stalin's presence at weapons designers' meetings was feared by those in attendance, in reality there was little he could do to affect the procurement process. Third, the Japanese threat was subdued at this point and resources were poured into building an infrastructure in the Far East. At least in the mid-1930s, all was quiet on the eastern front. While all these activities and threats changed from their former "shrillness" to a "lull," it was Tukhachevsky's execution that truly symbolized a sudden halt to military innovation when the state lost its premier military theorist and strategist.

Tukhachevsky's Demise

Tukhachevsky's rapid ascent in 1931 was accompanied by an equally rapid descent between 1936 and 1937. His star peaked in November 1935 when he was promoted to the rank of marshal of the Soviet Union along with Kliment Voroshilov, Semyon Budennyi, Vasilii Bliukher, and Alexander Yegorev. He continued to write profusely about military threats from the West—indeed, German propaganda at the time was clear about its attitude toward the Russians and was rife with anticommunist sentiment and references to Slavic *Untermenschen*. Tukhachevsky, who indeed was knowledgeable about the strength and intention of the Wehrmacht, having dealt extensively with the *Truppenamt* via the clandestine collaboration, tried in vain to publicize military threats to the USSR and drew up a war game for the RKKA's response, which he presented to the General Staff in 1935. Marshal Yegorev apparently disapproved of Tukhachevsky's scenario, in which the Germans would launch a surprise attack, and introduced one in which the Red Army mobilized first and absorbed the first blows.[4] Isserson joined Yegorev and others who disputed Tukhachevsky's vision, but he pursued them nonetheless. Despite numerous rebukes, in fact, Tukhachevsky was still publicizing the need for fortifications on the Soviet Union's western borders and making presentations to the General Staff Academy on the probability of a German attack through Poland as late as the winter of 1937—even after the former chief of mechanization and motorization, Innokenty Khalepskii, replaced him as chief of armaments in April 1936.

Who Framed Marshal Tukhachevsky?

Precisely who orchestrated the arrest, who framed Marshal Tukhachevsky—Stalin, the NKVD, the Gestapo, or some combination thereof—is still not completely understood. What we do know is that Tukhachevsky and Commissar of Foreign Affairs Maxim Litvinov traveled to London together in early 1936 to attend the funeral of King George V of England. During that trip, Tukhachevsky apparently stopped off in Germany and France and met with several military and political figures there, unwittingly providing his enemies with more "evidence" of unsavory contacts with German officers to be used against him later.[5] He also apparently attended a reunion in Paris of his French comrades with whom he had been imprisoned in Ingolstadt, Bavaria, during World War I and was accompanied, according to French General Gamelin, by a bevy of NKVD agents watching his every move.

When he returned, however, he was asked to hand over his chief of armaments portfolio to the former head of the motorization and mechanization directorate of the army, Innokenty Khalepskii. Although he was apparently still scheduled to attend the coronation of King George VI the following year, it was announced in May 1937 that Tukhachevsky would not be allowed to attend the coronation after all because of the discovery of a "plot" by a German-Polish group to commit a terrorist act against him. Five days after his trip cancellation, he was reassigned to the command of the Volga Military District in Kuibyshev, and on May 26 was arrested there. He confessed under torture by NKVD Chief Yezhov that he had collaborated with the Nazis to overthrow the Soviet leadership, and these "confessions" apparently are marked by his blood.[6] The secret court proceedings lasted less than four hours on June 11 and were conducted by Tukhachevsky's "comrades": V. V. Ulrikh, Semyon Budennyi, Vasilii Bliukher, Boris Shaposhnikov, and others.[7] Tukhachevsky and his fellow accused (Iona Yakir, Ieronim Uborevich, August Kork, Vitovt Putna, Vitalyi Primakov, Boris Feld'man, and Robert Eideman) were swiftly sentenced to execution by firing squad the next day, with Bliukher assigned to command the execution. The agents allegedly revved up their truck engines in the courtyard of the NKVD building at 11 Dzerzhinskii Street to mask the sound of gunfire.[8] Exactly six months later, Marshal Yegorev would hail the party's elimination of the "Trotskyite-Bukharinist wreckers, spies, and murderers who crept into the ranks of the party, government and Red Army—and who tried to weaken the strength of the army and destroy the defensive capabilities of our great motherland."[9]

The earliest and still least understood point in the historiography of Marshal Tukhachevsky's demise is the murky international episode, the "Tukhachevsky Affair," publicized by Victor Alexandrov in his work by the same name in 1963.[10] The crux of this "affair," set in the pre-World War II era of espionage and counterintelligence, was the production of counterfeit documents showing that Marshal Tukhachevsky was in league with the Nazis in a plot to overthrow the Soviet leadership. The documents were reportedly prepared over the course of several days in April 1937 by agents of Gestapo leader Reinhardt Heydrich; forgeries were easy to manufacture based on Tukhachevsky's correspondence with Reichswehr officers during the period of collaboration. The existence of these documents was then "leaked" to Czechoslovak President Eduard Benes, who in turn passed the information to Stalin and his French allies. Soviet agents then purchased the documents from the Nazis for the equivalent of 200,000 Deutschmarks.

Although journalists and historians earlier believed that such a "plot" against Stalin was plausible, this theory has been discredited by virtually all subsequent research.[11] There is less unanimity, however, over the question of the motives and origins of the forged documents implicating Tukhachevsky in crimes against the state. Some believe that the central figure in the creation and transmission of the documents was the White emigré General Skoblin, who was living in Paris at this time. Skoblin was associated with The Russian General Military Union, an emigré organization, and was an alleged agent for both the Germans and the Soviets.[12] Skoblin is believed to have been the recipient of an NKVD fabrication suggesting that Tukhachevsky was plotting a coup against Stalin. Skoblin, then, relayed the message to Berlin where his contact, Heydrich, acted upon it even though it was an NKVD plant. General Volkogonov, in an interview with the journal *Okriabr* in 1988, reported that the information against Tukhachevsky had indeed originated with General Skoblin, who passed it on to Yezhov, who in turn sent it to Stalin.[13] On the other hand, the director of the secret archives in the Ministry of Foreign Affairs claimed, upon opening the Tukhachevsky file, that there was no evidence that Stalin had ever received the material.

While we may never know exactly who ordered the fabrications or who processed them, we know full well that Tukhachevsky was high on Stalin's hit list, and numerous scholars over the decades since his murder have asked why. Much of the scholarship has focused on the relationship between Stalin and Tukhachevsky formed in the crucible of the civil war. In particular, the responsibility for the Red Army's defeat in the Battle of Warsaw in 1920 is commonly regarded as the main point of contention between the two and one of lasting significance, at least for Stalin. During the Polish campaign, Tukhachevsky, who earned distinction for successfully routing General Denikin in earlier battles, commanded the main offensive of Red Army forces advancing north of Warsaw. Meanwhile, Stalin was the main political commissar assigned to the forces of the Southwestern Front under the command of Yegorev, whose units included the now infamous First Cavalry Army, or Konarmiia, led by Semyon Budennyi, which was attacking near Lwow. The Southwestern Front failed to quickly execute the orders received from Moscow to move north from Lwow to Warsaw. Stalin, as chief political commissar, refused to cosign with Yegorev's Moscow order to move north and join Tukhachevsky's Western Group and was recalled for his insubordination.[14] The army was turned back at Warsaw and dreams of fomenting revolution to the west were crushed. Tukhachevsky, in a fateful move, assigned the blame for the defeat to the failures of Stalin's Southwestern Front and went on to analyze those failures in his lectures at the Military Academy.[15] What made matters worse, perhaps, is that even Vladimir Lenin agreed with Tukhachevsky's assessment, asking, "Who on earth would want to get to Warsaw by going through Lwow?"[16] Some twenty years later, Stalin apparently placed the blame for the failed campaign squarely on Tukhachevsky's shoulders, charging him for his "criminal delay."[17]

As this study has illustrated, there is some evidence of disagreement between Stalin and Tukhachevsky after the civil war. In particular, a rearmament proposal submitted by Tukhachevsky in 1930 was received unfavorably by Stalin and Voroshilov because it smacked of "red militarism." The seriousness of this rift is diluted significantly, however, by Stalin's apology to Tukhachevsky for his "harsh reaction" to the proposal, which was later adopted. Tukhachevsky's promotion to marshal of the Soviet Union in 1935 also raises questions about Stalin's enduring enmity against Tukhachevsky.

That Stalin believed Tukhachevsky was conspiring with Germans in a plot against him—based either on his work with *Truppenamt* officers during the period of military collaboration or on his associations with fellow prisoners in Ingolstadt during World War I—also rings hollow in light of Stalin's persistent diplomatic and economic overtures to the Germans right up until the Wehrmacht's Operation Barbarossa was launched against the Soviet Union in 1941.[18]

Thus, even the most intimate access to archival holdings is unlikely to clear the air and answer the "why" question satisfactorily. Alec Nove summed this up best: "There seemed to be pathological excesses in the Stalin terror which defy all logical explanation."[19]

Notes

1. Roger Reese, *Stalin's Reluctant Soldiers: A Social History of the Red Army, 1925-1941*, chapter 5.

2. Williamson Murray and Allan Millett, *Military Innovation in the Interwar Years* (Cambridge: Cambridge University Press, 1996), p. 325.

3. Manfred Zeidler, *Reichswehr und Rote Armee: Wege und Stationen einer ungewöhnlichen Zusammenarbeit* (München: Oldenbourg, 1993), p. 284.

4. John Erickson, *The Road to Stalingrad: Stalin's War with Germany,* vol. 1 (New York: Harper and Row, 1975), introduction.

5. Alexandrov, *The Tukhachevsky Affair,* p. 72.

6. "Pokazaniia Marshala Tukhachevskogo," *Voenno-istoricheskii zhurnal,* no. 8, 1989, p. 44.

7. Dmitri Volkogonov, *Stalin: Triumph and Tragedy* (New York: Grove Weidenfeld, 1988), p. 321.

8. Robert Conquest, *The Great Terror: A Reassessment* (New York: Oxford University Press, 1990).

9. Alexandr Egorov, Speech at a meeting of Viazma voters, *Pravda,* 11 December 1937, p. 4.

10. Victor Alexandrov, *The Tukhachevsky Affair* (London: MacDonald, 1963).

11. Among those who believed in the probability of a plot to overthrow Stalin were Walter Duranty, Isaac Deutscher, Sir Bernard Pares, Sir John Maynard, and even Bukharin's widow, Anna Larina. See Alexandrov, *The Tukhachevsky Affair,* pp. 182-183; Conquest, *The Great Terror,* p. 470; and Anna Larina, *This I Cannot Forget: The Memoirs of Nikolai Bukharin's Widow* (New York: W.W. Norton, 1993), p. 59.

12. Conquest, *The Great Terror,* p. 198.

13. Walter Lacquer, *Stalin: The Glasnost' Revelations* (New York: Scribner, 1990), p. 347.

14. Evan Mawdsley, *The Russian Civil War* (Boston: Allen and Unwin, 1987), p. 258.

15. Robert Tucker, *Stalin as Revolutionary, 1879-1929* (New York: W. W. Norton, 1973), p. 205.

16. Conquest, *The Great Terror,* p. 184.

17. Volkogonov, *Stalin: Triumph and Tragedy,* p. 47.

18. Bernd Wegner, ed., *Peace to War: Germany, Soviet Russia and the World, 1939-1941* (Oxford: Bergharn Books, 1997).

19. Alec Nove, "Filling in a Barbarous Blank," in a review of *Let History Judge: The Origins and Consequences of Stalinism,* Roy Medvedev ed., *Times Literary Supplement,* 17 November 1989, p. 1258.

8

Concluding Remarks

The tumultuous First Five Year Plan period (1928-1933) was a time of tremendous innovation in the Soviet Workers' and Peasants' Red Army. Stalin's mandate of technological progress for the Soviet state as a whole gave the RKKA considerable latitude to experiment with new combat theories, design and borrow new weapons technologies, and create new defense industries—in essence, to forge a new and modern army. A constellation of unusual environmental conditions prevailing at this time enabled talented military theorist, commander, and "entrepreneur" Mikhail Nikolaevich Tukhachevsky to rise rapidly through the ranks and take a leading role in the transformation of the RKKA. Tukhachevsky's keen ability to articulate a vision of the Red Army and to define its role in a future war against hostile neighbors was compelling to his colleagues and provided a template for the army's technical and tactical modernization.

Despite the daily dissemination of anticapitalist propaganda by the central committee, in reality access to foreign markets and technical expertise was ready and abundant; opportunities for study abroad were encouraged and thousands of foreign technicians came to the Soviet Union to lend a hand in the construction of socialism. By borrowing technical processes and methods both clandestinely, via collaboration with the Reichswehr, and openly from the other countries where many of these processes were already well established, the Red Army was able to skip several R&D stages and thereby expedite its weapons-procurement programs. The clandestine ties with the Reichswehr proved especially beneficial in the area of chemical weapons research, and the purchase of tanks in Great Britain and the United States helped to jump-start Soviet tank R&D programs. Simultaneously, indigenous R&D programs got off to a good start, leading eventually to the production of a range of high-quality weapons in large quantities that would support the Red Army in World War II, such as the "Katiusha" rocket, Degtiarev automatic rifle, and T-34 tank.

Conflicts in the Far East gave teeth to the profuse rhetoric about impending military threats and the prospect of war in distant combat theaters. The seizure of the Chinese Eastern Railway (CER) by the Kuomindang in 1929, which resulted in the deployment of RKKA troops to the region to engage the Chinese, provided an opportunity to employ new operational theories and test new weapons prototypes. Assault-landing maneuvers and encirclement operations, which had existed until this time only on paper, were employed in real combat in Manchuria. Although the CER conflict resulted in an array of "extraordinary expenditures" that had not been previously budgeted for combat equipment and personnel, there is little evidence that these requirements resulted in an immediate infusion of resources from other sectors by party and government authorities. In fact, some documents suggest that naval R&D projects were curtailed or cut back substantially in response. The Soviet citizenry at large were asked to make personal contributions to the ODVA by rendering a portion of their salary to the war effort or sending gifts to the troops. However, with the Japanese invasion of northern China in 1931 and the subsequent transformation of Manchuria into the Japanese puppet state of Manchukuo, rearmament became a higher priority of the communist party. R. W. Davies's economic analysis of the Soviet defense budget suggests that defense industries received a larger share of capital investment after 1931. The stenographic reports of the Seventeenth CPSU Party Conference and Congress also illustrate persuasively that concern for the Far East threat had grown considerably in the minds of the party elite. It is undoubtedly "no accident" that a more comprehensive three-year defense plan was introduced in 1931 as well. From this time forward, defense continued to claim increasing shares of capital investment from the state budget.

In identifying and examining several factors that facilitated theoretical and technical innovations in theory and weapons design during this period, I have argued that the Red Army was a separate institution with its own agenda to advance, its own political battles to fight, and budgets to bolster. Stalin certainly had input in military affairs, but there is little evidence that he managed the military singlehandedly or intervened to the point of significant disruption and delay before 1935. In light of these findings, the totalitarian model is of questionable validity in explaining the modernization of the RKKA between 1928 and 1933. This study joins the ranks of others that have either identified discontinuities in policymaking during Stalin's tenure or have made distinctions between early and "mature" Stalinism in the areas of culture, education, science, technology, and economics. It shifts the totalitarian image of "full-blown Stalinism" from 1929 to the mid-1930s.

Before 1931, there is little evidence that Stalin focused on military threats to Soviet soil in any context but a purely political one by which he could insist on party unity and accuse his opponents of being dangerous dissenters who were fragmenting the party. In fact, it was up to the military professionals to convince Stalin and the communist party that rearmament was important, so removed were they, initially, from this issue. As demonstrated in Chapter 2, the Red Army used the 1927 war scare and Marxist-Leninist writings on the inevitability of war to bolster their requests for resource allocations. An annual "Defense Week" was established and numerous paramilitary organizations were created to propagandize military threats and prepare the populace for a future war.

Unlike its fellow armies in other countries, the RKKA had missions of a civilian as well as a military nature, and these missions sometimes clashed. The Red Army's political commissars or "watchdogs" were undoubtedly irritants to professionally minded soldiers. Likewise, the recruitment of *Krasnoarmeetsy*, to assist in the collectivization campaign resulted in numerous desertions and disruptions by soldiers and ultimately was vehemently opposed by the war commissar himself. But civilian initiatives and measures to ensure ideological conformity were not all bad. Marshal Tukhachevsky was capable of using ideology and exploiting enthusiasm for the First Five Year Plan in order to advance his own ideas and overturn those of his theoretical opponents. It is somewhat ironic that the very man who embodied and advanced military professionalism was the same man who resorted to simplistic political and ideological denunciation of former colleagues in order to advance his innovative concepts of operational art and weapons design.

World War I offered lessons about the importance of a state's industrial base and war-making capacity, the complexities of coalition warfare, and the need to consider alternative methods of force employment depending on the combat scenario at hand. But neither the defeat in World War I nor the intervention of Stalin and the communist party was the primary motivation for innovation in the Red Army. Rather, the Red Army possessed some of the elements identified by Rosen and Zisk as contributing to military innovation: reform-minded individuals, intelligence on the strength and weapons developments of other potentially hostile states, and the capacity to change or "reconceptualize" current Soviet military practices in response to the military developments and practices of those states.

This work also raises questions about equating heavy industry with defense, especially during the First Five Year Plan. The evidence has become even more compelling in recent years, with the opening of the military archives and the general interest in reexamining the interwar years, that a tension between peacetime military procurement in the short run, and gradual, heavy industrial development that would be convertible to wartime production in a crisis in the long run, was debated by military, economic, party, and governmental figures throughout the interwar period.

Kliment Voroshilov played more than a perfunctory role as war commissar. His oversight of the tank R&D program, his extensive efforts to improve the technical qualifications of defense industrialists, his willingness to oppose Stalin on issues of troop commitment to the Far East and the use of soldiers in the collectivization campaign, his role in defining combat missions, and his participation in the German-Soviet collaboration demonstrate that Voroshilov possessed a range of bureaucratic and technical skills as well as an independent mind. This analysis, therefore, challenges the common portrayal of Voroshilov as Stalin's "tool and toady" whose only aim was to please and flatter the *Velikii Vozhd*.

Given the complexities and contradictions present at this time in Soviet history, the story of the Red Army's innovation is astounding. The Red Army pulled itself up by its bootstraps and successfully exploited the opportunities at hand while overcoming numerous obstacles that could have slowed its journey down the path of modernization and innovation. Tukhachevsky's extraordinary bureaucratic talent or "entrepreneurship" and his knowledge of technical matters ranging from the intricacies of aircraft motor construction to the optimal size of an artillery battalion are impressive indeed. Tukhachevsky's entrepreneurial prowess is evident in his ability to exploit many of the unusual features of the Stalinist environment: Stalin's industrialization mandates, Russia's technological backwardness, the importance of Bolshevik spirit and the salient role of Marxist-Leninist ideology, and the use of foreign expertise and designs. Mikhail Nikolaevich Tukhachevsky transformed the RKKA from an emasculated militia-style army into a modern and formidable military power. His innovative tactical and technical contributions to Soviet military science and weapons design were not only crucial to the army's ability to defeat the Wehrmacht in World War II but also had lasting influence on the elaboration and refinement of Soviet military doctrine throughout the Cold War.

Acronyms

ANII	Artillery Scientific Research Institute
ARCOS	Anglo-Russian Cooperative Society
CER	Chinese Eastern Railroad
CPSU	Communist Party of the Soviet Union
DT	Degtiarev Tank
GDL	Gas Dynamics Lab
GIRD	Jet Propulsion Study Group
GVPU	Main Directorate of the Defense Industry
IKKI	Executive Committee of the Comintern
IMEMO	Institute of World Economic and International Relations
KPD	German Communist Party
MOD	Ministry of Defense
NAMI	Central Scientific-Research Automotive and Motor Institute
NIID	Scientific Research Institute for Dirigible Construction
NKPiT	People's Commissariat of Postal and Telegraph Services
NKPS	People's Commissariat of Transportation
NKTP	People's Commissariat of Heavy Industry
NKVD	People's Commissariat of Internal Affairs
NKVM	People's Commissariat of Military and Naval Affairs
ODVA	Special Far East Army
OGPU	Soviet Secret Police
OKK	Special Agricultural Corps
PU	Field Regulations
PURKKA	The Political Directorate of the Red Army
RKKA	The Workers' and Peasants' Red Army
RNII	Research Institute Devoted to Rocket Propulsion
RVS	Revolutionary Military Council
STO	Council of Labor and Defense
VNO	Military Scientific Society
VSNKh	Supreme Economic Council

Selected Bibliography

Primary Sources

*D'iakov, Iu. L., and Bushueva, T. S. *Fashistskii mech kovalsia v SSSR: Krasnaia Armiia i Reikhsver. Tainoe sotrudnichestvo, 1922—1933.* Moscow: Sovetskaia Rossiia, 1992.

Guderian, Heinz *Errinerungen eines Soldaten.* Heidelberg: Kurt Vowinkel, 1951.

Hilger, Gustav and Meyer, Alfred *The Incompatible Allies: A Memoir History of German-Soviet Relations, 1918-1941.* New York: Macmillan, 1953.

Ipatieff, V. N. *Zhizn' odnogo khimika: The Life of a Chemist. Oxford:* Oxford University Press, 1946.

Kommunisticheskaia akademiia pri TsIK SSSR, Leningradskoe otdelenie *Protiv reaktsionnykh teorii na voenno-nauchnom fronte: Kritikastrategicheskikh i voenno-istoricheskikh vzgliadov professora Svechina.* Moscow: Voenizdat, 1931.

Krivosheev, G. F., ed. *Grif sekretnosti sniat: poteri vooruzhennykh sil SSSR v voinakh, boevykh deistviiakh i voennykh konfliktakh.* Moscow: Voenizdat, 1993.

Larina, Anna *This I Cannot Forget: The Memoirs of Nikolai Bukharin's Widow.* Gary Kern, trans. New York: Norton, 1993.

Litvinov, Maxim *Notes for a Journal.* New York: William Morrow, 1955.

Polevoi Ustav RKKA: 1929. Moscow: Gosizdat, 1929.

Vremennyi polevoi ustav RKKA 1936. Moscow, 1937 Translated by JPRS-UMA-86-031 and contained in USSR Report, Military Affairs, 12 June 1986.

Vremennyi polevoi ustav RKKA, Chast' II. Moscow: Voennyi vestnik, 1926.

Zhukov, Georgii K. *Vospominaniia i razmyshleniia,* vol. 1. Moscow: Novosti Press, 1983.

Bundesarchiv-Militärarchiv (BA-MA), Freiburg, Germany

Bestandsgruppe	Aktenbände
RH 1	14
RH 2	66, 1140, 2213-19, 2227, 2285, 2289-99, 2300-2305, 2417-18, 2452, 2736, 2746, 2755, 2762
RH 8	467, 894, 924, 961, 3621-25
RH 12-1	35, 40, 56-64, 85-88, 114
RH 12-4	54
Msg 2/782	Ludwig von Sicherer, "Tomka. Ein deutsches

Geheimunternehmen hinter dem eisernen Vorhang in den Steppen des Wolga-Gebietes bei Wolsk."

Nachlässe (Personal Papers)

Hans Delbrück NL17
Hermann Geyer N221
Ernst Köstring N123
Werner von Blomberg N52
Oskar von Niedermeyer N122
Kurt von Schleicher N42
Hans von Seeckt N247
Joachim von Stülpnagel N5

Russian State Military Archive

Rossiiskii gosudarstvennyi voennyi arkhiv (RGVA)
Moscow, Russian Federation

Fond	Opis'	Dela
51	2	52, 68, 96, 101, 102, 144, 151, 167, 169, 270, 328, 333, 348, 388, 329, 348, 388, 405, 406, 407, 409
31811	1	1, 14, 31, 82, 99, 109, 140, 141, 266, 305, 331, 340, 344, 425, 455
33879	1	1, 8, 510, 668
33987	1	634, 657, 658, 660, 661, 662, 663, 664, 665, 674, 676, 677, 678 680, 681
33987	2	340, 344, 346, 349, 351, 352-54
33988	1	611, 615, 616, 622, 624, 627, 630 633, 634, 636, 637, 639, 638, 677
33988	2	670, 679-682-689, 693, 694, 695, 699, 700, 701, 702
33988	2	679-688
33989	1	22, 25, 38, 57, 63, 67, 69, 76, 82, 85, 97

Key to Inventories (Fondy)

51	Finansovoe upravlenie krasnoi armii
33879	Upravlenie dal'nevostochnogo krasnoznamennogo fronta
33988	Sekretariat 1-go zamestitelia predsedatelia RVSR-RVS SSSR
31811	Glavnoe avtobronetankovoe upravlenie krasnoi armii
33987	Sekretariat predsedatelia RVSR-RVS SSSR
33989	Sekretariat 2-go zamestitelia predsedatelia RVSR-RVS SSSR

Personal Inventories (Lichnye Fondy)

37605	Tukhachevsky, Mikhail Nikolaevich
40871	Isserson, Georgii Samoilovich

The Russian Center for the Preservation and Study of Documents of Recent History

Rossiiskii Tsentr khraneniia i izucheniia dokumentov noveishei istorii (RTsKhIDNI), Moscow, Russian Federation

Fond	Opis'	Dela
558 (Stalin)	1	2852, 2853, 2856, 2880, 2891, 2894, 2901, 2905, 2906, 2910, 2912, 2937, 2957, 2973, 2987, 3000, 3001, 5050
74 (Voroshilov)	1	145, 154, 159, 343, 367

Stenographic Reports, Collected Works, Articles, and Speeches

Bliukher, V. K. *Stat'i i rechi.* Moscow: Voenizdat, 1963.

Stalin, I. V. *Sobranie sochineniia.* vols. 1-13 Moscow: OGIZ, 1952.

Tukhachevskii, M. N. *Izbrannye proizvedeniia.* vols. I and II Moscow: Voenizdat, 1964.

Voroshilov, K. E. *Stat'i i rechi.* Moscow: Partizdat TsK VKP(b), 1936.

XVI konferentsiia vsesoiuznoi kommunisticheskoi partii (b): stenograficheskii otchet. Moscow, 1929.

XVI s"ezd vsesoiuznoi kommunisticheskoi partii (b): stenograficheskii otchet. Moscow, 1930.

XVII konferentsiia vsesoiuznoi kommunisticheskoi partii (b): stenograficheskii otchet. Moscow, 1932.

XVII s"ezd vsesoiuznoi kommunisticheskoi partii (b): stenograficheskii otchet. Moscow, 1934.

Periodicals: Journals and Newspapers

English

Europe-Asia Studies
Foreign Affairs
Journal of Slavic Military Studies
Slavic Review
Slavonic and East European Review

German

Militärgeschichtliche Mitteilungen
Vierteljahrshefte für Zeitgeschichte
Zeitschrift für Geschichtswissenschaft

Russian

Izvestiia
Krasnaia zvezda
Pravda

Torgovo-promyshlennaia gazeta
Voennaia mysl'
Voennaia nauka i revoliutsiia
Voenno-istoricheskii zhurnal
Voennyi vestnik
Voina i revoliutsiia
Voprosy istorii

Secondary Sources

Books

Alexander, Arthur *Armor Development in the Soviet Union and the United States.* Santa Monica: RAND, 1976.

Alexandrov, Victor *The Tukhachevsky Affair.* London: MacDonald, 1963.

Amann, Robert, and Cooper, Julian, eds. *Industrial Innovation in the Soviet Union.* New Haven: Yale University Press, 1982.

Arendt, Hannah *The Origins of Totalitarianism.* New York: Meridian Books, 1951.

Armstrong, John *The Politics of Totalitarianism: The Communist Party of the Soviet Union from 1934 to the Present.* New York: Random House, 1961.

Bailes, Kendall *Technology and Society under Lenin and Stalin: Origins of the Soviet Technical Intelligentsia, 1917-1941.* Princeton: Princeton University Press, 1978.

Bialer, Seweryn, ed. *The Domestic Sources of Soviet Foreign Policy.* Boulder: Westview Press, 1981.

Bullock, Alan *Hitler and Stalin: Parallel Lives.* New York: Knopf, 1992.

Conquest, Robert *The Great Terror: A Reassessment.* New York: Oxford University Press, 1990.

Cooper, Julian "Defence Production and the Soviet Economy, 1929-1941" Centre for Russian and East European Studies (CREES) Discussion Paper, SIPS no. 3. University of Birmingham, 1976.

Dallin, David *The Rise of Russia in Asia.* New Haven: Yale University Press, 1949.

Davies, Robert W. *The Economic Transformation of the Soviet Union 1913-1945.* Cambridge: Cambridge University Press, 1994.

____. *The Soviet Economy in Turmoil, 1929-1930.* Cambridge: Harvard University Press, 1989.

____. *Soviet Defense Industries during the First Five-year Plan.* Centre for Russian and East European Studies, Discussion Paper No. 27 University of Birmingham, August 1987.

Douhet, Guilio, (German translation). *Luftherrschaft.* Berlin: Drei Masten Verlag, 1935.

Duncan, Francis *Rickover and the Nuclear Navy: The Discipline of Technology.* Annapolis: US Naval Institute Press, 1990.

Dvoinykh, L. V. et al, eds. *Tsentral'nyi gosudarstvennyi arkhiv Sovetskoi armii. Putevoditel' v dvukh tomakh, Tom 1.* Minneapolis: East View Publications, 1991.

Erickson, John *The Road to Stalingrad: Stalin's War with Germany* vol. 1. New York: Harper and Row, 1975.

_____. *The Soviet High Command: A Military Political History, 1918-1941.* London: St. Martin's Press, 1962.

Fainsod, Merle, *How Russia Is Ruled.* Cambridge: Harvard University Press, 1963.

Fedotoff-White, Dmitri *The Growth of the Red Army.* Princeton: Princeton University Press, 1944.

Fishman, Ia. M. *Voenno-khimicheskoe delo: posobie dlia nachal'stvuiushchego sostava RKKA.* Moscow: Gosizdat, 1929.

Fitzpatrick, Sheila, ed. *Cultural Revolution in Russia, 1928-1931.* Bloomington: Indiana University Press, 1978.

Friedrich, C. J. and Brzezinski, Z. K. *Totalitarian Dictatorship and Autocracy,* 2d ed. Cambridge: Harvard University Press, 1965.

Getty, J. Arch, *Origins of the Great Purges: The Soviet Communist Party Reconsidered, 1933-1938.* Cambridge: Cambridge University Press, 1985.

Glantz, David, and House, Jonathan *When Titans Clashed: How the Red Army Stopped Hitler.* Lawrence, University Press of Kansas, 1995.

Halperin, Morton *Bureaucratic Politics and Foreign Policy.* Washington, DC: Brookings Institution, 1974.

Haslam, Jonathan *Soviet Foreign Policy 1930-1933: The Impact of the Depression.* New York: St. Martin's Press, 1983.

Hilger Gustav, *The Incompatible Allies.* New York: Macmillan, 1953.

Hohn, R., and Harahan, J., eds. *The Command of the Air* USAF, Warrior Studies Washington, DC: Office of Air Force History, 1983.

Ianguzov, Z. Sh. *OKDVA na strazhe mira i bezopasnosti SSSR.* Khabarovsk: Khabarovskoe knizhnoe iz-vo, 1970.

Ivanov, V. M. *Marshal M. N. Tukhachevskii.* Moscow: Voenizdat, 1985.

Ivanovich, St. (V. I. Talin') *Krasnaia armiia.* Paris: Sovremennye zapiski, 1931.

Jacobson, J. *Locarno Diplomacy: Germany and the West, 1925-1929.* Princeton: Princeton University Press, 1972.

Janowitz, Morris, *The Professional Soldier: A Social and Political Portrait.* Glencoe: Free Press, 1960.

Joravsky, David, *The Lysenko Affair.* Cambridge: Harvard University Press, 1970.

Kavtaradze, A. G., *Voennye spetsialisty na sluzhbe Respubliki Sovetov 1917-1920.* Moscow: Nauka, 1988.

Kolkowicz, Roman *Political Controls in the Red Army: Professional Autonomy Versus Political Integration.* Santa Monica: RAND, 1966.

_____. *Soviet Party-Military Relations: Contained Conflict.* Paper no. 3371 Santa Monica: RAND, May 1966.

_____. *The Soviet Army and the Communist Party: Institutions in Conflict.* Report no. 446-PR Santa Monica: RAND, 1966.

Kuzmin, N. F. *Na strazhe mirnogo truda (1921-1940).* Moscow: Voenizdat, 1959.

Laqueur, Walter *Stalin: The Glasnost Revelations.* New York: Scribner, 1990.

Lehman, John *Command of the Seas: Building the 600 Ship Navy.* New York: Scribners, 1988.

Lewis, Eugene *Public Entrepreneurship: Toward a Theory of Bureaucratic Political Power, The Organizational Lives of Hyman Rickover, J. Edgar Hoover, and Robert Moses.* Bloomington: University of Indiana Press, 1980.

Lih, Lars, ed. *Stalin's Letters to Molotov, 1925-1936.* New Haven: Yale University Press, 1995.

Mawdsley, Evan *The Russian Civil War.* Boston: Allen and Unwin, 1987.

Medvedev, Roy *Let History Judge: The Origins and Consequences of Stalinism.* New York: Columbia University Press, 1989.

Milsom, John *Russian Tanks.* London: Arms and Armour Press, 1970.

Mostovenko, V. D. *Tanki.* Moscow: Voenizdat, 1956.

Murray, Williamson and Millett, Allan *Military Innovation in the Interwar Years.* Cambridge: Cambridge University Press, 1996.

Nikulin, Lev *Tukhachevskii: Biograficheskii ocherk.* Moscow: Voenizdat, 1963.

Ogorkiewicz, Richard *Technology of Tanks* vols. I and II. Surrey: Janes Information Group, 1991.

Parrott, Bruce *Politics and Technology in the Soviet Union.* Cambridge: MIT Press, 1983.

Pietrow, Bianka *Stalinismus Sicherheit Offensive: Das "Dritte Reich" in der Konzeption der Sowjetischen Außenpolitik.* Melsungen: Schwartz Verlag, 1983.

Polmar, Norman, and Allen, Richard *Rickover.* New York: Simon and Schuster, 1982.

Posen, Barry R. *The Sources of Military Doctrine: France, Britain, and Germany between the Wars.* Ithaca: Cornell University Press, 1984.

Reese, Roger *Stalin's Reluctant Soldiers: A Social History of the Red Army, 1918-1941.* Lawrence: University Press of Kansas, 1996.

Rosecrance, Richard, and Stein, Arthur *The Domestic Bases of Grand Strategy.* Ithaca: Cornell University Press, 1993.

Rosen, Stephen Peter *Winning the Next War: Innovation and the Modern Military.* Ithaca: Cornell University Press, 1991.

Rotmistrov, P. A., *Istoriia voennogo iskusstva.* Moscow: Voenizdat, 1963.

____. *Vremia i tanki.* Moscow: Voenizdat, 1972.

Schapiro, Leonard *Totalitarianism.* London: Pall Mall Press, 1972.

Seaton, Albert and Joan *The Soviet Army: 1918 to the Present.* New York: NAL Books, 1986.

Shukman, Harold, ed. *Stalin's Generals.* New York: Grove Press, 1993.

Stoecker, Sally *Historical Roots of Contemporary Debates on Soviet Military Doctrine and Defense.* Santa Monica: RAND, 1991.

Sutton, Anthony *Der leise Selbstmord: Amerikas Militärhilfe an Moskau.* Bern: Verlag SOI, 1976.

____. *National Suicide: Military Aid to the Soviet Union.* New Rochelle: Arlington House, 1973.

____. *Western Technology and Soviet Economic Development, 1917-1930.* Palo Alto: Stanford University Press, 1971.

Svechin, Alexander *Strategiia.* Kent Lee, ed. and trans. Minneapolis: East View Publications, 1992.

____. *Strategiia.* Moscow: Voenizdat, 1926.

Todorskii, A. I. *Marshal Tukhachevskii.* Moscow: Gospolitizdat, 1963.

____. *Vospominaniia druzei i soratnikov.* Moscow: Voenizdat, 1986.

Triandafillov, Vladimir K. *Kharakter operatsii sovremennykh armii.* Moscow, 1929.

Tucker, Robert C. *Stalin as Revolutionary 1879-1929.* New York: Norton, 1973.

____. *Stalinism: Essays in Historical Interpretation.* New York: W. W. Norton, 1977.

____. *The Soviet Political Mind: Studies in Stalinism and Post-Stalin Change.* New York: Praeger, 1963.

Ventsov, S. *Narodnoe khoziaistvo i oborona SSSR.* Moscow: Molodaia gvardiia, 1931.

Volkogonov, Dmitri *Stalin: Triumph and Tragedy.* New York: Grove Weidenfeld, 1988.

Von Boetticher, Manfred *Industrialisierungspolitik und Verteidigungskonzeptionen der UdSSR 1926-1930: Herausbildung des Stalinismus und 'äusere Bedrohung.'* Düsseldorf: Droste Verlag, 1979.

Von Hagen, Mark *Soldiers in the Proletarian Dictatorship: The Red Army and the Soviet Socialist State, 1917-1930.* Ithaca: Cornell University Press, 1990.

Wilson, James Q. *Bureaucracy: What Government Agencies Do and Why They Do It.* New York: Basic Books, 1989.

Zaleski, Eugene *Planning for Economic Growth in the Soviet Union: 1918-1932.* Chapel Hill: University of North Carolina Press, 1971.

Zeidler, Manfred *Reichswehr und Rote Armee: Wege und Stationen einer ungewöhnlichen Zusammenarbeit, 1920-1933.* München: Oldenbourg, 1993.

Zisk, Kimberly Marten *Engaging the Enemy: Organization Theory and Soviet Military Innovation, 1955-1991.* Princeton: Princeton University Press, 1993.

Doctoral Dissertations

Bone, Jonathan "Socialism in a Far Country: Development and Socioeconomic Change in the Soviet Far East, 1922-1939" University of Chicago, forthcoming.

Hulse, Melvin A. "Soviet Military Doctrine, 'Militarization' of Industry, and the First Two Five-Year Plans: Developing the Military-Economic Mobilization Potential of the Soviet Union for Total War" Georgetown University, 1990.

Samuelson, Lennart "Soviet Defence Industry Planning: Tukhachevskii and Military-Industrial Mobilization, 1927-1937" Stockholm School of Economics, Sweden, 1996.

Shapiro, Joel "A History of the Communist Academy, 1918-1936" Columbia University, 1976.

Tsypkin, Mikhail "Origins of the Soviet Military Research and Development System" Harvard University, 1985.

Index